# Vibrant Collaboration

How more honesty and intimacy in teams leads to better collaboration.

by Heinz Robert

with contributions from
Sascha Hümbeli, Kaouthar Darmoni,
Hilary Bradbury & Lara Catone,
Nilima Bhat, Jeff Hearn, ...

Edited by Kirk Marshall

# Table of Contents

© 2021 Heinz Robert

Vers. 1.0

ISBN 978-3-347-38784-3 (Hardcover)

ISBN 978-3-347-38785-0 (e-Book)

**Cover design:** Heinz Robert
**Editing:** Kirk Marshall, Interview Kaouthar Darmoni by Ashley Curtis
**Editor:** Heinz Robert
**Printer and Publisher:** tredition GmbH, Halenreie 40-44, 22359 Hamburg

# Prologue

....................................

*Some day, after we have mastered the winds, the waves, the tides and gravity, we shall harness...the energies of love. Then, for the second time in the history of the world, man will have discovered fire.*
- Pierre Teilhard de Chardin

Have you ever felt love at work? Love for the job you do, love for the working environment, love for a colleague, or even your boss? I assume you said Yes to at least one of these questions. And even if you said No to all of them, how did *that* influence the way you did your work, or the relationships to your coworkers?

During collaboration within teams and organizations, sometimes dynamics appear between the co-workers that lead to various conditions that influence how they relate with each other. Conditions which include but are not limited to stagnation, tension, stability, harmony or flow. Particularly, the dynamics between feminine and masculine forces seem to amplify these dynamics. With feminine and masculine, I don't mean women and men, but the essential principles which can be active in different

8

flavors in all genders. Many of these dynamics are generated by feelings and emotions, and even sexual attraction, or its opposite, feelings which often go unnoticed by the people involved but which can have consequences.

In this book I want to explore how such emotions, as well as our life force and our honest and intimate relations in the workplace, are influencing our collaboration in teams and organizations.

One of the essential factors might be our Eros, the sexual energy and basic vital force. Philosophers, theologians and scientists have explored and studied this life energy for centuries. Our life-force energy which has been given various names in different cultures (Eros, Libido, Élan vital, Chi, Kundalini, Tummo, Orgon, etc.), is alive within us in different levels of intensity, and it can be increased, transformed and moved with practice, and used consciously for a more effective and constructive collaboration and co-creation, through sublimation or transmutation. Applied honesty, authenticity and a more consciously lived intimacy can support the transmutation of this life-force. And, in turn, this can lead to better conditions in the workplace, more inspiration, productivity, etc.

Many books and research papers that I've read since I started to work on this book focus on the subject of sexism, sexual violence, harassment and power games in the workplace. This was almost exclusively the case with publications from the '80s or '90s that dealt with sexuality in the workplace. Even now, though things are slowly shifting, not many look at Eros from a more positive perspective, one in which it could be used in a constructive way. Only recently have there been a few publications with a more positive view. Not many authors have addressed this topic because, as if it was a glowing coal, they have been afraid to burn their fingers. But I believe it is a timely and needed issue, and people are becoming more developed and open to new approaches to leadership and collaboration. Current articles on business websites show that leaders are getting more sensitive to intimacy and emotions during work.

A description for Eros I like a lot comes from the book *Eros/ Power* by Hilary Bradbury and William Torbert. They say:

> *Eros can be seen as Life's energy unbound, life surging to live and co-create; life connecting with 'others,' that which lies at the boundary of me and not me, known and unknown, playing in the shadows about to come to light. Eros draws the soul upward/forward in co-creativity. It's a spiritual (but not ascetic) work-play. Eros brings our attention inward into the intersubjective field, because it lives in the space between I and Thou. When fully expressed in connection, it has the potential of co-creating something of true value.*

This work-play of exploring boundaries and the space between us is what brings the creative spark into daily encounters and enriches them with high energy, allowing for self-actualization, so that many aspects of our being can come to the surface – including both the bright and the dark.

## When Ideas Have Sex

I believe in the power of Love. We need love for the work we do, and we need a loving, intimate environment, where all the feelings and emotions of the various individuals involved are welcome, in order to birth new ideas and visions for this broken economy and devastated world. When Eros is alive in us, creativity is following close behind. Many men and women in the past have experienced the power of Eros flowing while they painted marvelous paintings, wrote glorious poetry, or inventing advanced technologies.

Great artists and inventors have often been inspired by their spouses, assistants, or other muses. An erotic stimulation can empower one to think faster or need less sleep, and it can provoke a longing to penetrate the arising questions in life even deeper. I imagine inspired minds and hearts coming together in a team where the erotic energy can flow freely (without exploiting it), to empower individual creativity, supporting the co-creation of innovative developments.

Futurist Barbara Marx-Hubbard speaks about Vocational Arousal, the awakening of the attraction of geniuses to each other, in a passage that's highly relevant to what I say in the paragraphs above:

> *Vocational Arousal is the next step after sexual arousal. It's about specific people. One person attracts you so much more than somebody else. When you are with somebody that attracts you so much that you feel with that person you are more likely to give more of what you want to give, than with anybody else. And that other person feels more*

*likely to give what they want to give by joining with you.*

*Vocational arousal at the next stage of sexual arousal is really enormous significant. That vocation as you feel it unless you find someone or what, that through giving it, they get to give more of what who they are by doing it with you, they are not just helping you. You are not dominating the other, or the other is submitting to you, there is no domination or control. So vocational arousal is an awakening of that attraction, that actually requires you to begin to cultivate all this prophecies that begin to emerge. If you are attracted to somebody to give and that person is attracted to you, and your egoic reactions pop up—I want to dominate it, I want to control it, I want it like this and so on—unless you are able to shift from your egoic response to your essential self, you will not be able to join the geniuses. Nature has put a code in there.*[1]

I have experienced this vocational arousal many times in my life, to the point where I have realized what I can do with it if I don't neglect it, or if I don't try to immediately jump in bed with the person who awakens this energy in me. In some of these work relationships I might have given more than I received. But as I liked being in love with this person, be it an attractive female colleague or a boss who supported me in my career, I did not expect much back in return. Even when the "love" was in some cases not mutual, I still got a lot out of it.

---

1  Barbara Marx-Hubbard, *Evolutionary Women Retreat*, 2008, https://www.youtube.com/watch?v=dwJaocdIYA4 (accessed April 1, 2019).

Fortunately, we see more and more workplaces emerging where people want not only a creative office space and collaboration on an "eye level" but also to see their own intrinsic need for more authentic expression and deeper connection fulfilled within the workplace. Valuing our feelings and emotions as much as our intelligence and physical strength – this should be part of what we do at work, too. Brilliant ideas come not just from hard thinking but appear also from intuition and sensing into a space, to perceive what is actually needed.

We have seen new methods of collaborations and new kinds of organizational structures popping up in the past few years which are informed by a need and longing for more community and collective responsibility. Organizations become more fluid and departments become circles which are interlinked in a big co-creative meshwork. Even individuals who are self-employed come together in co-working spaces and hubs all around the world to entangle their brilliant minds and restless hearts, co-creating in order to bring out projects for a better world. Corporations learn from these social entrepreneurs, as they are the new generation in the workforce and a powerful source of innovations, new ideas and techniques which might otherwise be lost, if the companies don't catch up with this fast development.

## Reinventing Collaboration

The reader might remember all the hype around "Teal organizations" which started around the end of 2015 with the publication of Fredric Laloux's book *Reinventing Organizations*. Now, as a result, many people who had never heard about developmental stages before are coming to understand what this concept of

"Teal" means. Teal is simply the name of a relatively high stage in new and very comprehensive developmental psychology called the Wilber-Combs Matrix, which uses colors to describe the various states. The Teal stage stands for authenticity, systemic thinking (and-and, rather than and/or), building up skills to become an instrument for the greater whole, with access to a free (holistic) consciousness. (You can find a short overview of these stages in Chapter Two of this book, "Understanding Self and Others for More Wholeness in Teams.")

I see some potential obstacles in the unfolding of Teal in the business setting, especially given that many people who have just discovered it come from a different part of this developmental structure, the rational and success-driven business mindset (Orange is the color for this stage in the models I explain later), and therefore they cannot truly embody the Teal ideals they nevertheless see some of the benefits of. These people are sometimes burned out or discouraged by the working environments they have been in for many years, environments which are still traditional, and they are thus in some ways genuinely ready for the new approach that Teal organizations can offer. However, I often hear people speaking about Teal as if it were just a new way of motivating employees, to make them be more productive and effective, to make the workflow more efficient, so the company can make more revenue. In other words, this perspective on Teal is characteristic of the result-driven and strategic approach, not of Teal itself, which is much broader and not just concerned with the bottom line. Yes, this might and will happen, but it shouldn't be — in fact can't be, if the health of the organization is important — the main motivation for trying to become a Teal organization. Bringing in awareness of Eros as the primary life force that drives evolution, raising the dialogue about it, and bringing in practices to the workplaces to embody this force in us, can lead to more wholeness, which is one of the three foundational "break-throughs" common to Teal organizations, apart from Self-management and evolutionary purpose.

Many new approaches towards organizational structures, such as Holacracy, often do leave out the human aspect of collaboration. Holacracy, for example, promotes roles over people and decisions in meetings are made more from an objective, rational justification, based on facts rather than subjective preferences. That might be a good approach to get rid of egoistic thinking and behavior, but it dumps out the baby with the bathwater. As long work is done by humans, we have to value the feelings and emotions which come up in response to events, situations, or statements made by other people. And we have to appreciate the power of our sexual energy, which might influence our moods and consequently the decisions we make. Sometimes we are not very aware of such dynamics, or we even let them play out in unconscious power games. This leads to confusion and tensions that get in the way of the cooperation we need, which does not lead to the desired outcomes of the projects we are working on. We need to understand and harness this powerful erotic force that is there, whether we acknowledge and consciously use it or not.

## A New Field to Explore Together

While doing research for this book I started dialogues on the topic with many people from diverse fields. I wanted to know how they deal with intimacy and the various emotions of the team members at their workplace, and how they support a joyful, creative and intuitive approach to collaboration, one in which individuals can grow in their potential and contribute this growth to the organization and the common good. Most of the conversations I had regarding the topic confirmed how much people need this kind of an approach. Even people in management positions said that, while it might be a hot topic to bring into the corporate world, they themselves see in their daily work many situations in which the dynamics of attraction between colleagues, subtle gender-based power games and various manifestations of erotic energy, are all influencing the way people interact.

Of course, this is a very complex issue, and that's why I'm interested in diverse perspectives on it and why I want to look at it from an Integral perspective. Some people contributed their perspectives for this book as essays or in interviews, and some of my writing is influenced by conversations over the last year. Those I have spoken to are doubtless just a small minority among the many people who continue on this kind of a journey while I write.

Here are some of the questions which I brought into these conversations:

- How can one recognize his or her own feelings and emotions, and find more effective ways to manage, express and include these in a working situation? How can one recognize feelings and emotions in others, deal with them and support others to manage them better, themselves?
- What are the possibilities to express attraction or reluctance to other people, so that they are not hurt in their feelings, and so that a further constructive collaboration is created, maintained, or promoted?
- How can we provide a safe working environment

where intimacy between co-workers is fostered
without exaggeration, over-exploitation, and
suppression of the driving forces?

- How might teams be put together so the diversity of
genders and emerging energetic polarities can be
used for co-creation?
- How can we make the dynamics between people
visible, to help us to make conscious rather than
unconscious choices, and take actions that serve
every stakeholder of the organization, and have a
positive impact on future innovations and
generations?
- How can we live aligned with our personal life
purposes, bringing our whole being into the
workplace, collaborating in a joyful way and still
achieving the most effective performance possible?

These are the kinds of questions I am interested in. And as
you read the following chapters of this book I am just as interested and curious about your views and stories as well; I am sure
you have had experience of this kind of thing before. In fact, I believe it is a fairly universal experience in the business world, so it's
just a matter of how honestly and openly we can bring this topic
into our daily conversations and into public dialogue. Indeed,
what I'm talking about in this book is happening all around us, but
without us talking about it much. My goal here is to start up a dialogue about this essential aspect of business life, so we might
benefit from a conscious understanding of the forces involved,
which up to now have been happening mostly below the surface
of things.

Chapter 1

# Research Findings

*Why should I write a book about such a hot topic, which is taboo to speak about for many people? Where could find literature for my research and who will read that?*

I started doing research for this book in February 2016, after I published my first book, which is part autobiography (a look at my own psycho-sexual development) and part self-help book for men. The autobiographical part charted how I went from engaging in what you might call hypersexual behavior to an understanding that I could transform my libido, with "supra-sex," in a much more fulfilling way. I came across the term *supra-sex* for the first time at a conference in California, when I heard Barbara Marx-Hubbard, by then an 84-year-old futurist, speaking about it as *"a force as great as sex to liberate the vast, dormant potential of humanity."* Sexuality itself can be seen simply as a natural impulse to reproduce our species, but now, since we have too many people on this planet, it is our duty to dive deeper in the meaning of our existence, to develop our consciousness and to engage in relationships based on co-creation. Marx-Hubbard also speaks about vocational arousal, when one is truly passionate about his or her calling for a higher truth, an idea, or the prospect of co-creating something together with others.

18

The concept of Supra-Sex is closely related to that of transmutation, otherwise known as sublimation. Sigmund Freud believed that sublimation was a sign of maturity, and he defined it as the process of deflecting sexual instincts into acts of higher social valuation, being *"an especially conspicuous feature of cultural development; it is what makes it possible for higher psychical activities, scientific, artistic or ideological, to play such an important part in civilized life."* C. G. Jung, however, believed sublimation to be mystical in nature, thus differing fundamentally from Freud's view of the concept. For Freud, sublimation helped explain the plasticity of the sexual instincts (and their convertibility to non-sexual ends). The concept also underpinned his psychoanalytical theories which showed the human psyche at the mercy of conflicting impulses (such as the super-ego and the id).[2]

Sexual sublimation or transmutation, then, is the attempt, especially among members of many religious traditions, to transform sexual impulses or "sexual energy" into a more general kind of creative energy. It is based on the idea that sexual energy can be used to create a spiritual nature, which in turn can create more sensual works, instead of one's sexuality being unleashed in its "raw" state. But psychologists and spiritual schools aren't alone in using the concept of sexual transmutation in their writings. In his 1937 book *Think and Grow Rich*, Napoleon Hill writes about transmutation as the *"switching of the mind from thoughts of physical expression, to thoughts of some other nature."* He dedicates a whole chapter to the transmutation of the sexual energy in this book about the laws of success – something he learned from Andrew Carnegie, the industrialist, often identified as one of the richest people ever. Hill says, for example, that

---

2   *Sublimation (psychology), Wikipedia, https://en.m.wikipedia.org/wiki/Sublimation_(psychology).*

*[t]he transmutation of sex energy calls for the exercise of will-power, to be sure, but the reward is worth the effort. The desire for sexual expression is inborn and natural. The desire cannot, and should not be submerged or eliminated. But it should be given an outlet through forms of expression which enrich the body, mind, and spirit of man. If not given this form of outlet, through transmutation, it will seek outlets through purely physical channels.*

The difference between transformation, as a change of form, and transmutation, as change in substance, can be described in terms of the image of a lump of clay, which can be formed into a statue or a vessel. I can transform the lump into a vase or jug, let it dry, and then it can serve as an object of decoration or even container for water. However, if it is exposed to water long enough it slowly might resolve into mud again. To be able to hold the water for much longer time it has to be fired. In that process the clay will become ceramic or pottery, which removes all the water from the clay, and induces reactions that lead to permanent changes, including increasing their strength as well as hardening and setting their shape. The original material is clay, but the transformed material is something else, ceramic, which has qualities not found in the clay it was transformed from.

## More Recent Literature

The topic of this current book is very complex, and so the range of research I did in the half year before starting to write was very broad. It included books about sexual harassment, studies around sex and intimacy at work, and articles which focus on the management of emotions or intersubjective dynamics within teams. Sexual harassment was a big topic when the Feminist movement started to grow in Europe and the US. Many of the books I found were written by women and focused on this destructive behavior in men. But I was looking for other approaches to the general topic of sexuality in the workplace, a slightly different focus than just when things go wrong (abuse, harassment), important as these topics are.

One book in particular, *Sex at Work*, by Jeff Hearn and Wendy Parker (1987), attracted my attention, as it discusses sexuality in organizations, and how sexuality as an aspect of gender relations is defined through power, language and imagery. Hearn and Parker tried to redefine what is considered private and invisible in the workplace, to analyze what is *"known and obscure,"* *"seen but unnoticed,"* and to reveal sexuality in the workplace as both public and visible. One of the strengths of the book is its attempt to demonstrate how the existing accounts of organizations and of sexuality are dominated by a *"male sexual narrative."* By unmasking this narrative, the authors provide a major indictment of the dominance of male power in hierarchical organizations, whether or not it leads to actual, tangible abuses.[3]

In a later work, Hearn provides a kind of synopsis of this groundbreaking work:

> In 'Sex' at 'Work' and The Sexuality of Organization, the concepts of the sexual (or non-sexual) goals of organizations and sexual work were elaborated. Building on Bland et al., the concept of sexual work, in referring to work done in relation to sexuality, is distinct from that of 'sex work', re-

---

3   Hearn J. and Parkin W., 'Sex' at 'Work'. The Power and Paradox of Organizational Sexuality, Wheatsheaf Books, Brighton, 1987.

21

*ferring to the selling of sex. In particular, the con-
cept of organization sexuality was articulated. Organization sexuality entails the simultaneous,
paradoxical and powerful co-occurrence of organizational dynamics/practices and sexual dynamic-
s/practices: sexuality constructs organization and
organization constructs sexuality. This simultane-
ity distinguishes it from organizational sexuality,
as the latter suggests a particular kind of sexuality
in organization(s). In its original formulation the
following features of organization sexuality were
emphasized: movement and proximity, feelings and
emotions, ideology and consciousness, language
and imagery.[4]*

In this work, Hearn clearly points to the fact that this is
about how sexuality is at play in the workplace, even when abuse
of power isn't taking place. It's an important topic and requires
the attention of people in leadership roles in business.

## Ruled by Hormones, Suppressed
## by False Morality

One of the things which stood out for me in many books is
the assumption that the over-sexualized behavior of men might
be responsible for most of the regulations that have led to a general corporate culture with sometimes very dry and serious
working relations. Sociologists and psychologists in the last few
years have found such sterile ways of relating to each other to be
less than optimal for productive collaboration, and even unhealthy in general.

---

4   Jeff Hearn, *Sexualities, Organizations and Organization Sexualities: Future scenarios and the impact of
socio-technologies (a transnational perspective from the global 'north')*, SAGE Publications, *Organization*
2014, Vol. 21(3) 400–420.

At the same time, researchers are increasingly documenting the beneficial physiological and biochemical effects of positive and supportive touch. This includes a decrease in blood pressure, heart rate, and the stress hormone cortisol, as well as increase of the love hormone oxytocin, a stimulation of the reward regions in the brain, and a reduced activation in stress-related regions. Oxytocin is released in some amount during any social contact and promotes feelings of devotion, trust and bonding.

And it bears repeating that, clearly, the "rules" for physical contact in the workplace change according to what country you are in, so they are not something that is in any way universal. In the U.S., for example, a woman could report "unnecessary touching" to the police if her supervisor gives her a grateful or appreciative soft touch on the back or shoulder, when she has done good work. In some countries people don't shake hands at all, while in others it's totally normal to hug each other when colleagues meet in the morning or say goodbye after work.

Of course, when it comes to certain destructive and obviously unwanted behaviors, like women being touched in a sexual way by a colleague, lawmakers have done their job well to prevent them. But, at the same time, it's a shame that our society has turned away from the positive effects of physical proximity.[5] We have become emotionally distant in many working environments, particularly in bigger companies, or at least in some sectors like banking and insurance, where numbers count more than people. In such working environments, emotional detachment has become symbolic of strong leadership and power. By the same token, many Human Resources departments have degenerated into payroll departments, and only a few are willing to offer

5   Stuart Taylor Jr., "Sex Harassment On Job is Illegal," The New York Times, June 20, 1986, http://www.nytimes.com/1986/06/20/us/sex-harassment-on-job-is-illegal.html (accessed April 1, 2019).

23

workshops supporting relational practices or their employees' intrinsic motivations for their work. Human needs like intimacy have for long time not been in the focus of HR and organizational development.

What's more, even research into organization psychology has often overlooked this aspect of business life:

> *Although intimacy has been recognized as a central concept in understanding human existence, it has been overlooked in the study of organizations and the workplace. This is even more evident when we refer to the relationships between leaders and followers, since leadership and management have been perceived as one of the mechanisms to assure the maintenance of the logic of separation, and a means of reinforcing employees' loyalty and commitment to the organizational sphere and its aims, often at the expense of other spheres.* [6]

In other words, the logic of separation often dominates, and even researchers in the field often accept this as a given and look for ways to promote loyalty in a very top-down way, where all the power resides at the top. Relations between employees at all levels don't seem to count.

I find it interesting, too, that for years masculine-oriented organizations have suppressed erotic emotions, like the Catholic Church has done for centuries. It seems to me that many men have tried hard to emphasize the value of chastity because they don't trust each other, or themselves, to be able to handle the power of the sexual urge. While, obviously, it's best to use our

---

6   Ronit Kark, *Workplace intimacy in leader-follower relationships. Oxford handbook of positive organizational scholarship, 32, 423-438, 2011.*

working time for productive business outcomes and not for mating rituals, to leave out some of our basic human emotions from such a major part of our daily life cannot be healthy for our society as a whole, and for business itself.

As author Peter Fleming points out,

> *A significant avenue of research concludes that organizations have generally suppressed sexuality because it interferes with the axioms of modern work. The proposition here is that capitalist organizations have historically privileged instrumental rationality as a dominant discourse. With the creation of a spatial and symbolic boundary between work and home, labour and leisure, and the public and private in industrialized economies, sex was increasingly marginalized as an inappropriate activity. It still obviously persisted in the form of flirtation, humour, affairs, harassment and games, but from management's point of view sex is treated as a serious misuse of company time.*
>
> *Burrell's (1984) excellent article on sexuality extended this line of argument in organization studies and raised the problem of resistance. For Burrell, sexuality is not just genital pleasure or orgasm. It encompasses the full gamut of libidinal excitations, including sensuality and erotic play (Burrell 1984, 1992). Through a colourful array of historical examples including the church, factory and public institutions, Burrell demonstrates how*

> *legal—rational authority has attempted to eradicate sex at work. It is maintained, 'human feelings including sexuality have gradually been repulsed from bureaucratic structures and have been relocated in the non-organizational sphere—the world of civil society' (Burrell 1984: 99). A number of historical forces have driven this purge: the 'civilizing process' (Elias 1978), the development of religious morality, the spread of calculative rationality and the increased demand to control time and the body. Each of these interrelated forces led to a steady desexualization of organizations.[7]*

In other words, the sexual behavior is there in the workplace, but since it doesn't accord with the models for what workplace behavior is supposed to be (rational, dry), it is relegated to the dung heap, it is simply something that is wrong, not permitted. It goes on nevertheless, but rather than being something potentially useful, it is simply that which is at best a distraction and at worst a problem. According to someone with such a view, nothing good could possibly come of it. This tremendous energy that is everywhere in the workplace is disregarded or suppressed rather than harnessed.

## Higher Power, Less Collaboration

When it comes to teamwork, we can often easily see some discrepancy between the power the person holds in her/his position and his or her engagement in participatory decision-making processes. As Hildreth et al point out, more often than not, collaboration isn't a strength of people at the top of organizational hierarchies:

---

7 Peter Fleming; *Sexuality, Power and Resistance in the Workplace*, 2007, *Organization Studies* 28(02):239–256.

*In multiple studies we found that high-power indi-
viduals, when working together in groups, performed worse than did other groups: individuals
randomly assigned power in an initial task were
less creative when they then worked together in
groups on a subsequent task. Individuals with
higher power who worked together in groups were
also less likely to reach agreement on a difficult ne-
gotiation task, whether these groups comprised actual executives from an extant organization or
participants randomly assigned power in the labo-
ratory. Mediation analyses suggest that groups of
high-power individuals performed worse because
they fought over their relative status in the group,
were less focused on the task, and shared information with each other less effectively. However, high
power individuals were more effective when working on tasks that required less coordination: they
were more creative and persisted longer on a difficult task than other groups. Therefore, group processes are the key problem for groups of high-power
individuals when they work together.*[8]

It's interesting that jockeying for position within the group
becomes so much more important the more powerful the individuals within the group are or perceive themselves to be. Equally
interesting is the observation that they are less willing to share
information than those with less power. Both of these suggest
that the individuals being studied here find it difficult to collaborate – which makes a lot of sense, if they are used to working in

---

8   John Angus D. Hildreth and Cameron Anderson, *Failure at the Top: How Power Undermines
Collaborative Performance*, University of California, Berkeley, Journal of Personality and Social
Psychology 2016, Vol. 110, No. 2, 261 286.

situations where they simply dictate what happens and then leave the rest to those below them. There is no need for collaboration in such situations.

Moreover, when leaders, for whatever reason, don't exclusively use the top-down approach favored by many higher executives, there's room for collaboration. Indeed, a recent study suggests that if a supervisor lacks charisma and therefore comes off as less powerful, then more intimate relationships with employees substitute for power, and all the people seem to perform better within this team.

> *Intimacy is not a construct we often associate with work. Yet, in the current study we found that the extent to which an employee perceives their relationship with their manager as intimate is related to performance. The more employees feel they have a close and exclusive relationship with their managers (i.e., a relationship which enables employees to disclose their inner self, to have the freedom to say what one thinks and feels and to sense one is listened to) the more likely they are to perform better.*[9]

So there seems to be a positive effect if people work together on the so-called eye level rather than when one of them insists on his/her superior position.

Meeting in a space of personal and emotional generosity opens doors to another realm of cooperation and individual happiness.

9   Coller School of Management, Tel Aviv University, *There Is Still Hope For The Non-charismatic: The Role Of Leader-follower Intimacy In Employee's Performance*, Paper for the 3rd Israel Organizational Behavior Conference (IOBC 2016), https://en-coller.m.tau.ac.il/sites/nihul_en.tau.ac.il/files/media_server/IOBC%202016/069.docx (accessed April 1, 2019).

28

> *Close intimate relationships can shape people by influencing the ways they think, how they think (Agnew, Van Lange, Rusbult, & Langston, 1998), and the ways in which they behave (Berscheid et al., 1989). This implies that workplace intimacy in leader–follower relationships can have perceptual, motivational, behavioral, and health consequences, and can result in a wide range of outcomes at the personal and group or organizational level.*[10]

All of these studies strongly suggest that moving away from the old style of top-down leadership allows for a more creative kind of workspace, one where collaboration allows many voices with different ideas to be heard.

## Leader-follower Relations in Transition

This brings us to the topic of what, exactly, good leadership really is, and how we can redefine it in terms of the emerging Teal organizational structures and in terms of what we are beginning to learn about the power of Eros as a positive force in the workplace.

To begin with, we know that effective leadership has to do with the ability of the leader to create positive relationships within the organization. Leadership is sometimes defined as a relational and ethical process, one that involves guiding people who have entered a venture together towards accomplishing change or making a difference, often to benefit the common good.

---

10  Ronit Kark. *Workplace intimacy in leader-follower relationships*, Oxford handbook of positive organizational scholarship, 32, 423-438, 2011.

*Leaders enhance the learning of others, helping them to develop their own initiative, strengthening them in the use of their own judgment, and enabling them to grow and to become better contributors to the organization. These leaders, by virtue of their learning, then become leaders and mentors to others.*[11]

*Leading others to lead themselves is the key to tapping the intelligence, the spirit, the creativity, the commitment, and most of all, the tremendous, unique potential of each individual.*[12]

Each individual in an organization is important, as they concurrently represent and influence the whole. The purpose, vision, and values of the whole come to life as each member of the team describes and applies them. The goal is to build a shared purpose, and to allow the variations and differences among participants to generate creativity and energy, to better fulfill this purpose. We can only imagine what kind of collective potential lies within a group, when every individual is willing and able to bring his or her full power and capacity to the table, in full collaboration.

A very intriguing leadership approach that is somewhat along these lines has been around for a very long time, and perhaps it's worthwhile to look into this approach.

This is the Relational Leadership model, which builds on the work of Mary Parker Follett (1868–1933), a visionary in the field of human relations, democratic organization, and management. She recognized the holistic nature of community and advanced the idea of "reciprocal relationships" in understanding the dy-

---

11 McGill, M. E. and Slocum, J. W. 1993. *Unlearning the organization. Organizational Dynamics* 22(2), pp. 67-79.
12 Charles C. Manz, Henry P. Sims Jr., *SuperLeadership: Beyond the Myth of Heroic Leadership*, p. 34, 1991.

namic aspects of the individual in relationship to others. Follett advocated the principle of what she termed "integration," or non-coercive power-sharing, based on her concept of "power with" rather than "power over."[13] Contemporary author Ronit Kark sums up such models succinctly in the following passage:

> *First, leadership is shared and distributed and is not enacted by a single person. Second, leadership is a social process, in which human interactions are keys. Third, relational leadership results in outcomes of learning, growth, and well-being for the organization, as well as the people involved.*

Kark sums up the whole situation by suggesting we need more of a focus on how intimacy shows up in the workplace. As he puts it:

> *Despite the increasing acceptance of relational leadership, works that focus on the close and intense form of leader-follower workplace intimacy are sparse.*[14]

Although such eye-level leadership styles may be scarse, as Fletcher suggests, this just means that we need to make an effort to understand these models and implement them, because the promise of such models, clearly, is very great.

## Good Relationships keep us happier and healthier

For almost 80 years now, Harvard University researchers have studied a group of 724 men over the course of their whole lives, in order to determine their levels of satisfaction and happi-

---

13  https://en.wikipedia.org/wiki/Mary_Parker_Follett
14  Ronit Kark, 2011.

ness. Around 60 of these men are still alive, and their development has been well documented and tracked, and they are surveyed every two years concerning the details about their physical and emotional health, their employment, their families and their friendships.

The data of the study clearly shows that having people to rely upon, and having fulfilling and authentic relationships, helps our nervous systems to relax and our brains to stay healthy. Furthermore, the same study shows that such relationships reduce emotional pain. Those in the study group who felt lonely were more likely to see their physical health decline and to die younger.[15] *"It's not just the number of friends you have, and it's not whether or not you're in a committed relationship, it's the quality of your close relationships that matters."* says Robert Waldinger, the current and fourth director of this ongoing study.[16]

## More Data Wanted

I have also made my own online survey, which I have based on a questionnaire from one of the books I found, and I added some questions which seemed important for my work.[17] It turned out that this survey was not well-received by its original audience: I only got 75 responses, when I expected 150, and only 23 answered all the questions. Most stopped answering once they got to the very intimate questions about their sexual experiences with supervisors and colleagues in their past and current workplaces. This is a shame, as those were the most valuable

---

15  Robert Waldinger, *What makes a good life? Lessons from the longest study on happiness*, TED Talk, Jan 25, 2016, https://youtu.be/8KkKuTCFvzI (accessed April 1, 2019).
16  Colby Itkowitz, *For 79 Years, this groundbreaking Harvard study has search for the key to happiness. Should it keep going?*, April 17, 2017, https://www.washingtonpost.com/news/inspired-life/wp/2017/04/17/this-harvard-study-found-the-one-thing-we-need-for-happier-healthier-lives-but-researchers-say-theres-more-to-learn/ (accessed April 1, 2019).
17  Barbara A. Gutek, *Sex and the Workplace: The Impact of Sexual Behavior and Harassment on Women, Men, and Organizations*, 1985.

questions, for my purposes. As I wasn't able to collect enough data from this survey, I haven't used it for further investigation.

If you are willing to support my work you still access the survey and fill in your own answers:

https://vibrantcollaboration.com/survey/

Fully aware that only one perspective on this complex topic cannot be enough, I invited other authors, consultants, managers and other people who I thought might have something to contribute. Some of these diverse perspectives you will find in this book, in the form of interviews about experiences having to do with Eros in collaboration that people have had in their work-related life.

By Hilary Bradbury & Lara Catone

# Eros at Work: Transforming Power

*The erotic functions for me in several ways, and the first is in providing the power which comes from sharing deeply any pursuit with another person. The sharing of joy, whether physical, emotional, psychic, or intellectual, forms a bridge between the sharers which can be the basis for understanding much of what is not shared between them, and lessens the threat of their difference.*

*- Audre Lorde (1978)*

Hilary Bradbury and Lara Catone have collaborated on an extended article on Eros and the impact on organizations. From their experience in Action Research and arts they draw some wonderful insights liberating relational joy and vitality at work.

**Hilary Bradbury, Ph.D.,** is founder & curator at AR+ Foundation. She is a scholar-practitioner focused on the human and organizational dimensions of creating healthy communities.

Having been a Professor of Organizational Development for over twenty years, she now supports educators of all types as well as educational institutions in transforming their response to the social-ecological crisis of our times. For this she emphasizes the integration of research and practice, as "Action Research for Transformations" (ART).

Hilary enjoys writing and has authored dozens of journal articles and chapters, starting with a best dissertation award (Academy of Management), then shepherding the bestselling series Handbooks of Action Research (Sage), and the more accessible volumes of the multilingual AR+ Cookbooks (Bradbury and AR+ Associates, 2017, 2019). She relishes working at the edge of self and community development, e.g., uncovering a collaborative response to #MeToo in Eros/Power: Love in the Spirit of Inquiry (Integral Publishers, 2016, with Bill Torbert). actionresearchplus.com

**Lara Catone** is a yoga teacher and somatic sexologist with more than a decade's experience in both fields. She founded The Artemis School for Women's Sexual Wellness, the first and only educational institution to interweave sex education with embodiment-based traditions. Learn more at laracatone.com.

***

The heart of the inquiry that follows concerns how we bring ourselves to collaborations that are generative and empowering for all, including the larger ecology. We pose this inquiry at this time of climate challenge in the hope that we might liberate joy and vitality in our collective pursuits. Key questions are how to work with new possibilities in the combination of gender, power and eros? What is the new story that can transform personal and collective development? And how to practice with this inquiry in a way that accesses creative, embodied, intuitive ways of knowing, including and transcending the rational models we have inherited as they combine in our workplaces.

Our aspiration is that individually and together we may learn new and more vibrant ways to work. This means, we believe, embracing work as a personal and social developmental opportunity, one that moves us from vestigial "power-over" to a new practice of mutuality, of "power-with." The chapter therefore starts by situating our efforts in an historical context. It proceeds with a framework that offers a handful of elements in a life well lived. It then introduces a developmental map by which relational human anxieties, related to money, eros and power, can be transmuted into co-creativity. From procreation to co-creation!

We start however with an invitation to the reader to articulate their own creative, developmental intentions at work. We confess, up front, that some of what we are suggesting for work contexts takes a different tack from the conventional and may even appear to carry elements of the taboo, and paradoxically, the Polyanna-ish, as we suggest that work can be a place of self and other transformation. Important to note, especially for the reader ready to jump in, is that we are not alone. Fredric Laloux (2014) sees organizational design as the development of consciousness in organizational form, similar to the same stages of development we see in individuals (Torbert, 2004) and societies (Freinacht, 2019). Having the workplace be deliberately developmental (Rooke & Torbert, 2005; Kegan and Lahey, 2016) is catching on. We share with these constructivist developmentalists the understanding that our whole selves, including our work-selves, are part of social evolution.

## Where the personal meets the organizational

It is helpful to anchor the abstract in the personal. Taking a moment to reflect, ask yourself, what are your intentions in your workspace? Does the lived culture of your institution reflect its ideals and yours? This checking in with espoused versus enacted intention allows us to begin to see a gap. This gap, far from being something to cover up, can initiate a new dynamic. Assuming we wish to narrow the gap, by working to uncover the beliefs and fears that motivate our current behaviors, a gap is an invitation to match our values to our practice.

Complete the following sentences quickly with the thought that first pops into your mind.

In my work I most want to be recognized for ____

The emotions I consider to be negative at work are ____
The emotions I am least comfortable expressing at work are ____

What I am most afraid for my colleagues/leadership to think about me is____
The interpersonal dynamic I most try to avoid, or fear, at work is ____

My professional relations with people of my own gender are easiest when ____
My professional relations with people of my own gender are most difficult when ____

My professional relations with different genders are easiest when ____
My professional relations with different genders are most difficult when ____

As you review your answers, note:

- The emotional responses. Identify a sentence that activates a lot of energy (not labeling anything a good sensation or a bad sensation – just recognizing the aliveness).
- The surprise. What do you learn about yourself?
- Any mismatch with your core values?
- The matter that holds the most potential creative power.

## Our historical context

We live in a yawning gap between late modernity, with its machine-like rigidities and fixed identities, and a regenerative society that beckons us towards ways of organizing that are more worthy of human aspirations. In the modernist world and according to the dominant worldview, inquiries concerning "energy and aliveness" would be met with silence or confusion, because only the material, the empirical, mattered.

This gap is referred to variously as the Great Transition or Great Turning and is associated with writers as various as Joanna Macy, Kenneth Boulding. Reports on Global Climate Change (IPCC)[18] and increasing social inequality (Stiglitz, 2012)[19] insist that we cross this gap. The former reports give us 10 years on the current path before catastrophic environmental breakdown becomes a shared reality. The latter reports show worrying data on

---

18  https://www.ipcc.ch/
19  https://en.wikipedia.org/wiki/The_Price_of_Inequality

38

economic inequality (albeit at a time of increasing prosperity for all) that portends a mix of violence and/or populist authoritarianism. We need not waste a good crisis.

This chapter invites inquiry into how we may learn new and more vibrant ways to work as part of a new social imagination for what's becoming possible as more minds attend to reimagining the future (Naomi Klein, 2019)[20]. If the entire system needs to be reimagined, and if human creativity is indeed the mechanism of social advancement, we may treat our work as an opportunity to look more closely at why and how we organize together. For those who wish to look closely, we invite a focus on power (privilege) and relational wholeness (eros), so rarely mentioned, yet so keenly felt, when it comes to looking at how we organize, relate and work together. To do this, we should have some historical context concerning working relations, which will help us understand how much of a gap we must cross as we leave behind the Modernist mindsets which we all have been socialized to.

# Broad-brush understanding of the historical shaping of work

Complex, modern society, built by and for the industrial revolution, has always entertained low expectations for how an individual might experience his or her work. Historically, work may be easily confused with slavery. Perhaps this is because the Judeo-Christian tradition had deemed work - or labor - a kind of punishment, a dismissal from an original paradise in which abundance required no work. Perhaps, for most of human civilization, Feudal arrangements held the majority as serfs to serve the few above them in a patriarchal pyramid. The world over, and for the

20  https://naomiklein.org/on-fire/

vast majority, work is readily experienced as a form of penitence. However, while peoples' miserable work lives had originally been short, now they have doubled or even tripled in length. And while creativity, in the past, was the domain of the rare genius, kept in check by a rich patron, now creativity is demanded of even the more average types of workers. "Knowledge workers" everywhere, especially those with a college degree, may earn twice as much as those without, but the connotation that work is servitude, made acceptable by a salary, allows for a direct connection to literal slavery.

Similarities between wage labor and slavery were noted as early as Cicero in Ancient Rome, and this similarity has been noted many times since. With the advent of the Industrial Revolution, Communist thinkers elaborated the comparison between wage labor and slavery (Marx), while Luddites emphasized the dehumanization brought about by machines. This connects America's particularly vicious form of capitalism – called Low Road Capitalism – to its foundations on Slave Plantations. We hear echoes of each of these issues in contemporary political debates, from how much welfare a state should grant the individual citizen (e.g., Universal Basic Income) to the societal dangers of Artificial Intelligence (Robots who make many unemployed).

While progress and prosperity have afforded a rising Middle Class safer and cleaner work environments, only recently have some workplaces begun to address the issue of fostering creativity. The scientific management (Taylorism) that followed the First World War had specifically diminished creativity with admonishments such as "Do not think!" This militaristic emphasis on following the rules of command, no doubt in an effort to reduce human error, mirrored the socialization in the Military that many of the (male) employees accepted. Since the 1970's, however, a far larger and diverse population has been entering the workforce. These women, minorities and younger men are less socialized to, and less tolerant of, Feudalistic, militaristic pyramids. At the same time, the social need for knowledge workers has increased. And so, a tension is now at work between the need for creativity and the need to follow orders from above.

People's material needs have been met, and seeking to create a good life, there is room for more creative work. Not that there is a straightforward link between good paid work and broader urges of creativity. For example, the "greedy occupations," such as law and finance associated with client services, are creative in limited ways, but at the same time they are increasingly demanding more and more of their employees' time, with firms often asking employees in their 30s and 40s to work 60+ hours a week. Meanwhile, among this work-engaged social elite, gender pay gaps and general unhappiness is rising. Moreover, a large majority of people surveyed annually by Gallup answer that they are unengaged with their work, with around 5-10% actively sabotaging their workplace.

It is in this context that we ask you, the reader, whether you could reimagine work as a space of creativity rather than drudgery. We also ask if your work – including the great Work of co-creating a regenerative society – rested on the closing of any gap you may have seen in the answers to the questions at the beginning of this chapter. To answer such questions, we suggest that you first envision your own work as a key ingredient in how you imagine a good life as a whole. And in that context, we can use such a vision to help close the gap in our own developmental inquiry. This might allow work to take its place as an element in a life well-lived.

## Work as part of a good life

We invite our readers to consider that we are more likely to succeed in cooking up a good life for ourselves, with others, when we are able to generate and alchemically blend the following primary "goods" in the right proportions at the right times (Bradbury & Torbert, 2016):

1) good money (resources enough not to have to worry about basic survival all the time);

2) good work (bringing in the necessary resources, through work that exercises us well, makes us good friends, and calls forth our purpose, commitment, contribution, creativity, power, and sense of fulfillment);

3) good friends (that is, people who voluntarily, mutually, and non-possessively love one another enough to face our most daunting questions together [and such friends can, of course, potentially include members of our family]); and

4) good questions (the realm of inquiry in the midst of our daily life, from our most intimate encounters to our broadest civic roles, whereby we may learn over decades how to make good money, do good work, cultivate good friends, and become fully incarnated and wonderful in each waking moment).

Of course, we acknowledge that each of these primary goods is difficult to attain and more difficult to sustain. Billions of people do not have enough of any of them, and billions more may just have enough of one of them, like money, but neither good work, nor more than one or two good friends, nor good, life-transforming questions. Still, this type of framing feels necessary to place creativity and money in their proper places, from early on. The rest of this chapter, then, concerns the interplay among these factors, because in fact work – when truly creative – becomes indistinguishable from play.

As we imply, by the way we have just defined these goods, we propose that they are properly ranked in the reverse order from which they are listed above. Good questions (inquiry, conversation) among friends are the primary keys to the good life in this view, and good money and good work are the more derivative of the four primary goods, necessary for agency to shape our work, but not our primary goal. We now proceed to consider the implications of these ideas for work & creativity. We address organizing then as a nexus of money, purpose, people and inquiry. In this, power & inquiry will be key. Let us explain.

Work, considered as a key to a life well-lived, is not as a matter of "out there," something we do for others or for money. Rather, we tackle it by having it be work "in here." Engaging in work (and play for that matter) is conceived of an exercise in mutual creativity, an inquiry without end, an inquiry that is informing all parts of our life. This inquiry follows from an original impulse. This impulse, which we call life-force, or eros, is the soul's surging forth to become more fully embodied through knowing oneself in relationship. It is the energy that gives life to plants, which in turn furnish animals with oxygen. It is the vibrancy of life itself – which can empower the Great Work.

# Relational Creativity – or Eros
## – our social life-force

Greek mythology describes Eros as emerging from chaos, the formless void. Out of the deep, dark night, the fire of eros erupted, out of the formless came form. Through this initial distinction, suddenly there was the other – and knowing oneself through relationship with the other.

Today, systems scientists, quantum physicists and cosmologists speak of both an inherent evolutionary impulse in the universe and the interrelatedness of all life. What we understand as life comprises complex ecologies within ecologies within ecologies, from the earth nested within the solar system to the 8.7 million living species[21] cohabiting earth to the 30+ million microbes[22] inhabiting the human body. The composting of one life begets the birth of another. In *Matter and Desire: An Erotic Ecology*, biologist Andreas Weber writes:

> *This world is not populated by singular, autonomous, sovereign beings. It comprises a constantly oscillating network of dynamic interactions in which one thing changes through the change of another… This exchange, which draws upon the contradictory forces of various bodies and leaves nothing as it was before, is the basis for the principles of an erotic ecology (pp. 22, 2017).*

---

21  *https://allyouneedisbiology.wordpress.com/2018/05/20/biodiversity-species/*
22  *http://www.microbiomeinstitute.org/blog/2016/1/20/how-many-bacterial-vs-human-cells-are-in-the-body*

Eros imbues our core nature with the impetus to create, re-late and transform. Thus the emphasis on organizing is inherently relational.

From this wider perspective, the personal and the profes-sional become less clearly defined. Because of this, it may serve to take a closer look at the distinctions we have historically made between personal and professional.

What we think of as the personal side of our lives stirs senti-ments in the areas of emotion, expression, intimacy and vulnera-bility. Severing these capacities from the professional realm cuts us off from the essential ways of knowing that are connected to feeling, such as gut instinct. If we are able to get to the energetic space in our professional contexts, there may not be a space to voice the vulnerabilities that we discover there. Most obvious is what is not (supposed) to be allowed in the professional context, namely the intrigue, the attraction, the excitement, the desire – the surging forth of eros. (However, haven't we learned that eros seems to find its way in through the side door?) And how do we even make that something we can discuss openly?

In the end, might the differentiation between personal and professional be a false dichotomy? And where did this false di-chotomy come from in the first place? How did we come to favor the mechanistic and rational at the expense of our feeling, sens-ing selves. Are we truncating the emotional spectrum so as to contain the creativity of our wild joy or repress the anger that aids in defining boundaries? And, finally, what is required when we draw this line between personal and professional? What is lost? What is hindered?

Historically, through the influence of Hellenistic and Protestant Christianity, the erotic was made an object of control and then rendered invisible and taboo (the term was literally erased from the New Testament, where love is described as community-minded *agape*). This likely helped produce first a feudal and then industrial society in which workers were not supposed to be creative or curious but, rather, unquestioning servants to the elites. However, the global socio-economic-environmental complexity that we face as a species today cannot be met without visionary, collaborative creativity, at the heart of which lies the need to be able to lean into the unknown, with big questions. Here, eros rebounds from the shadows to which it was cast.

One major deviation from the primarily repressive approach came in the form of inquiry built into Freud's groundbreaking "talking cure," which became the basis for modern clinical psychology (now augmented by an understanding of hormones and biology which were unavailable to him). Freud had approached the erotic as an object of scientific inquiry, much like any other topic might be approached. Noting how difficult it is to deal scientifically with an object of study that is immaterial, he had to innovate, all the while seeking to remain within the tradition of empirical science. His analyses suggested that the erotic unconscious, equally dominated by aggression (Thanatos/Morbido) and creativity (Eros/Libido), is a life-force streaming though the human mind. This force has the power to take individuals "for a ride." Freud re-purposed the metaphor of an uncontrollable erotic horse, first introduced by Plato, and developed his innovative "talk therapy" to help his patients become aware of and then manage its impulses. The official Freudian stance (derided by the more radical Leftists in Freud's original circle) was that civilization requires a controlled "repression" of erotic instincts, as well as related, violent ones. Departing from Freud's prophetic masterpiece *Civilisation and its Discontents*, futurologist Alexander Bard extends the insights into the internet age to prophesize an ever-growing "consumariat," passively entertained by the digital elites (Bard, 2018)[23].

It is interesting to note that, in a much earlier time and place, Gautama the Buddha had also taught about the uncontrollable unconscious. He had used the local metaphor of a runaway elephant to describe the impulse of the unconscious, and he prescribed meditation as a form of inquiry into and quieting of the unstable human mind. A century after Freud, Western clinical psychology has greeted mindfulness practices with open arms, thus merging these two approaches. Generally speaking, there is the sense that becoming more aware of unbidden thoughts and feelings (through mindfulness-infused talk therapy) allows us to become more enlivened and less under the heel of uncontrollable impulses. Yet we should beware! Eros should always be acknowledged as something bigger than the individual, whose mammalian brain stem, which evolved on the Savannah, remains awash in unconscious anxiety and fear. For this reason, we should be careful about inviting the forces of Eros to play inside civilized contexts. And yet, as the recent 50th anniversary of Gay Liberation (the Stonewall riots in 1969), along with worldwide Gay parades, demonstrate, there is a new opening for this kind of thing and with it a developmental opportunity, in large swaths of the civilized, developed world. We might at least proceed with caution.

Caution would have us understand that the relational erotic realm remains a space full of some of our keenest anxieties *and*

---

23  https://www.storytel.com/se/sv/books/674419-Digital-libido-sex-power-and-violence-in-the-network-society

aspirations. Psychoanalysts explain that this will likely always be the case, as sexual feelings are part of the infant's context, well before a rational ego has developed to process the experiences. These anxieties are often unacknowledged, even in adult life, and even when they are faced, they often remain untransformed in our own experiences with family, school and work-life.

The following elaboration of a developmental approach to relational power moves beyond the default understanding of unilateral power – which can force, extract or violate in the name of control – to one of relational power, infused by eros, to provide a map toward liberation through mutual curiosity and co-creative action. The inspiration for these approaches come from organizational learning, constructivist adult developmental learning (e.g., Rooke and Torbert, 2005), and its application by Bradbury and Torbert (2016), to working through the territory of #MeToo.

# Eros in Developing Future Organizing

*"Mind is a dangerous place, it is best not to go there alone."*

- Annie Lemott

## Power transforming to mutuality: A developmental journey

Our thesis is that Eros may fuel a new way of organizing, grounded in development of self with others in service to the Great Turning toward a regenerative civilization. However, we are convinced that it can only do so if power and eros can combine through inquiry. We also believe a developmental theory about how we humans can transform during a lifetime can aid our inquiry.

The basic proposition of constructivist adult developmental theory (elaborated by scholars such as Michael Commons, Susanne Cook-Greuter, Robert Kegan, Jane Loevinger, Jean Piaget, William R. Torbert and Ken Wilber) is that there is an invariant sequence through which humans experience the different developmental stages. In these stages one "action-logic" provides a center of gravity for sense making and action, and at early stages this center of gravity tends to be self-protective whereas at later stages it becomes quite inclusive and multi perspectival (Torbert, 2004). Each subsequent action-logic is gradually discovered (if at all) through a process of seeing through and thus invalidating the taken-for-granted assumptions of the stage or action-logic it arises from and partially (but not totally) leaves behind. Thus, each later action-logic includes, but is not limited to, the entire domain of the previous action-logics. The transformational process between action-logics does not occur by logic or conversation alone, but rather as each person faces conundrums in everyday life that his or her current approach cannot resolve, and as that person receives some kind of inspiration and support to try new ways of interweaving thought, feeling, and action that he or she never imagined before.

As Torbert explains, the human development process involves gradually coming to recognize how one participates in the play among "four territories of experience." These four "territories" include: 1) the outside world; 2) one's own experience of one's own behavior; 3) one's thinking; and 4) one's post-cognitive, embodied awareness of the interplay among all four territories in the present.

Correspondingly, the types of power and ways of relating that we experience during the early childhood territories of experience compel us, rather than liberate us. Then, in the later adult action-logics, the qualities of power we use become increasingly mutual in nature, and we become increasingly able to inquire beyond our own ego-limits, and thus to be able to exercise power on behalf of values that extend beyond our own self-interest. If one studies power closely, in one's actual practice with others, gradually one begins to realize that mutual power is far more powerful than unilateral power. Unilateral power can sometimes make others conform, but only the exercise of mutual power invites both oneself and others to transform. With regards to power, then, the fundamental move is from unilateral win/lose power to mutual win/win power. Or from hard power to soft power. In Table 1, we simplify and present three stages as examples of this. The first is unilateral, a situation in which relationship is really self-focused; the Independent middle stages allow a kind of parallel rather than intersecting relationality (though some remain in the unilateral mode). The later and rarer stages allow for a transcending of both prior stages in a space of authentic creativity and mutual benefit.

| Unilateral | Personal Eros ("it's all about me") |
|---|---|
| Independent | Relational Eros ("how do we help mutually exploit each other"?) |
| Inter-Independent | Collaborative Eros (how do we manifest something truly creative together?) |

Table 1: Developmental Levels of Expressing Power and Eros

Working with these broad-brush outlines about developmental moves in power and eros, we can start by locating our own tendencies and developmental levels with regard to the erotic (and accompanying decisive) tendencies in ourselves. For this, we turn the camera around on ourselves, as autobiographical beings. As noted by luminaries such as Freud and Buddha, one best be care-full in this inquiry. The extent of the gap between what is and what we intend must be equal to the dynamism available to traverse it.

## 1. Personal Eros. A time of unilateral power and sexuality.

We contact personal eros through noticing what stirs us. Eros might be imagined as wanting us to live more of the good life, steering us there through desire. This desire, however, might be felt as insistent, and it may be accompanied by negative feelings, as relational psychoanalysts (Klein) point out, in the form of envy or violence (or its opposite, depression). The ability to even acknowledge, much less follow, desire is a fairly new phenomenon in human history.

Indeed, we cannot help but count our gender-inclusive workspaces as counterintuitive – they are places from which the erotic is banished, in keeping with the West's long history of treating work as servitude, of putting relational creativity in service to Capital. Yet we are erotic beings. Our yearning is often left to run amok in a shadow state (perhaps fed into the trillion-dollar porn and human trafficking industries). Yet Eros is insistent, and it moves toward wholeness.

By the same token, sometimes, in order to be rid of the seemingly unmanageable feelings that accompany desire, we might project what we want onto someone outside of us, someone who in turn might be a good psychological match, for counter-projection. (Ah, the games of life!) For example, feeling that someone else has the qualities, the job, the money, the power or even the life that we want may lead us to idolize that person and/or feel jealous. We can feel both strong attraction toward and also a need to criticize those we have projected our desires onto. And when we are strongly repelled by someone, we might be projecting qualities that we do not want to face in ourselves. Either way, we are not seeing this other person clearly, and our relationship with this person is distorted by these projections. What's more, within the dance of projection and counter-projection are millennia of culturally-sanctioned gender norms. Finally, as we suggested above, during the early developmental states the ego is self-protective, so this also enters into the situation. Research suggests that women's socialized self-protection is expressed more often as silence (see Belenky et al, 1997)[24], while men's is expressed as aggression. We can carry these means of self-protection forward with us as we move into higher stages of development.

Can you think of an early instance of deep attraction? What underlying power dynamics can you remember or imagine in this scenario?

We began this chapter with a series of sentence stems to reveal underlying beliefs and motivations. Shadow work, illuminating what lives in the unconscious, allows our motivations – that which drives our desires – to become an object of inquiry for us.

---

24 https://en.wikipedia.org/wiki/Women's_Ways_of_Knowing

52

When we make erotic feelings such an object, we create enough space to see, and get perspective on, whatever was previously directing our behavior from the unconscious. When we cannot only sense desire, but also feel and then clearly understand it, we can begin to harness the wildness of eros and bring it into relationship with our more rational, discerning selves. Here we reclaim some of our power. And we may feel quite enlivened by this. We may also – at least at first – feel great shame and possibly anger at how we have been treated by others, or about how we ourselves have treated others.

> *Lara: On my personal journey I have seen that there are ways in which gender plays into particular power dynamics. In the examples below, I share two stories that have arisen in my own self-inquiry, as keys to my learning.*

> *With women that I admire I project eros in the forms of embodied confidence and intelligence. While evoking a feeling of admiration, this particular projection can create feelings of competition and distrust, while activating shame. I will contrast an early example with a later one to indicate how this has played out at different times along my developmental journey.*

> *At the start of my professional life in my mid-twenties, I had a female colleague that I both loved and respected and yet also felt triggered by. I perceived that when we were facilitating together she tried to outshine me and did not give me as much opportunity to contribute. In response, I would enter a space of silent frustration, either shrinking away into the background or making efforts to assert myself that felt untimely and inauthentic. Aware enough of what I was*

*struggling with, I suggested that we find a way to have a regular debrief together, as I knew that I needed a structure to be able to address and unpack what had come up in our class. However, my colleague never seemed to remember this agreement and, feeling defeated, I never reminded her, much less insisted. Even though I did not think any of this was necessarily conscious on the part of my colleague, I started to build up resentment. I never overtly addressed the feelings that I was having and it fed into a diminished sense of self. While this dynamic did not present obvious rifts in our relationship, I believe that it affected our synergy on a subtle level and eventually our work together waned. We drifted apart.*

*I continued to inquire into this dynamic - also present with other colleagues. I saw that one of my primary shame triggers is being perceived as unintelligent, or as if I do not have anything of value to offer. (Isn't life interesting – I have been, in the role of educator, easily exposed to this trigger. We teach what we need to learn!)*

*Fast forward 10 years, and I find myself co-facilitating with another female colleague and this time working with a group of professional educators, all of whom I had a great respect for. At one point one of the student educators voiced a feeling of not being comfortable with some of the group dynamics at a time when I was the lead facilitator. While on an intellectual level I was grateful for this student's feedback, my shame trigger got activated. I was aware of many layers of shame and of being triggered, and my inner dialogue went something like this: "Wow, she just revealed something very important about our container. I see other students re-sponding/reacting to this. I feel heat rising from my solar plexus—shame is here. I feel concern for this student. I have an impulse to try to fix something but also an awareness that things are unfolding in an essential way that does not need to be interrupted. We are a group that can tolerate the heat of discomfort and even benefit from it." Aware of many contributing factors and being kind to myself (after all, what educator has not had negative feedback?), I still felt the dis-comfort of shame and questioned what I could have done better.*

*When my co-facilitator found the opportunity to de-brief with me, she listened compassionately, mirroring me and sharing her own (more positive) experience of what had happened. Talking through it and sharing the insecurity and shame I was feeling helped me to digest the strong emo-tional aspects. From here we moved forward in our planning and facilitation from a clear and integrated place. My vul-nerability had created more trust and strength in our collab-oration. We drifted together rather than apart.*

**Developmental Reflection:** In the first example, Lara was ex-ercising unilateral power, but in the guise of silent self-protection (which is an inverted form of power at the earliest stage of devel-opment). It is unilateral in that neither Lara nor her colleague could dialogue, much less share power. Lara has since realized she had an either/or orientation: If her colleague was shining, she was not. Her strategy was to avoid conflict which prevented learning. As is natural when younger – and a key obstacle to growth if we remain immersed in early action-logics – Lara did not have enough perspective to see her projection. She was subconsciously comparing herself with her colleague, projecting discomfort outward making it mostly about her colleague's behavior.

In the second example, Lara has gained more reflexivity, the ability to see herself in action. This is a key developmental move. It brings the capacity to engage with others as human beings (rather than as fantasy objects who are better or worse than the fantasy of the isolated me). Lara was aware that she felt shame yet was not entirely shut down by the experience. Instead, she was able to have perspective on the somatic sensations of shame and the way that thoughts can "spin" themselves. This capacity – something that is helped by meditation and self-inquiry practices – allowed Lara to remain rooted in her center. Lara moved from repressing what was upsetting her to creating conditions for co-creativity. Shame may be one of the greatest teachers of all, if we can turn to it for its wisdom.

## 2. Interpersonal Eros.

Interpersonal eros is the ability to know ourselves in and through relationship. As we have suggested, the relational aspects of life and in work can induce profound anxiety. Our conditioning as primates – deeply needing to be part of the troupe – is to automatically "save face." At work this can look like having the answers, withholding authentic emotions and armoring our vulnerabilities. From a gendered perspective, we might say the workspace is male coded. For fear of "upsetting the horses" we tolerate work-cultures in which the elephants – or is it horses? – in the room go unnamed, despite causing havoc.

*Lara:* I was meeting with a male investor and potential mentor to discuss a new business possibility. He was at least 20 years older than me. I saw him as having money and business experience, and as a potential bridge to additional investors. In other words, he had the power. When we met via video he made comments about my beauty and my smile. I felt a tad uneasy. I wondered about this and thought: "If I were a man, would he be complimenting my physical appearance? Well, maybe he is being nice?" But maybe he was also degrading himself, and men in general, by placing me, and women, on a pedestal. We might say, in Jungian terms, that he was disowning his own anima, projecting it outside of himself, while being blind to, or at least distracted from, his own privilege, further perpetuating a situation of unilateral power. I began to lean more toward my negative interpretations when this man pestered me to meet in person – outside of normal business hours – even though we were still very much in the exploratory phase of our collaboration and an in-person meeting was not quite warranted.

Can you locate the unchecked eros and projections in this example? Have you ever found yourself on either end of this dynamic?

Unfortunately, this became a missed opportunity for both of us. I tried to be polite while also avoiding him. My creativity and enthusiasm for the project receded. He tried a few more times to get me to meet with him until, I presume, he grew tired or found something more interesting to pursue.

The interpersonal realm, and specifically nonsexual relationships between men and women, provide a very rich, and largely unexplored opportunity for learning and transforming. What if I had been able to more explicitly address the gender and power dynamic I was experiencing with this investor? What if we could have called attention to the eros and inquired how it might aid our work relationship, rather than distort it? What might have been transmuted and reclaimed for each of us?

*Lara writes of a later scenario: I was working with a male practitioner that was also older than me. I was seeing him for somatic trauma resolution work that involved touch. There was a built-in power differential because he was in the role of teacher and I of student. However, we were also explicitly exploring power in our work. After one of our sessions I realized that there had been a breach of consent. Our agreement was that there would be a check-in along each stage of touch, in this instance he took the session deeper and failed to check-in at a key threshold. As I processed this after the session I felt rage and went into a space of distrust of this container that was meant to feel safe. In this instance there was also a third person, a woman, as part of the team. My discomfort and fear began to mount and I knew it was essential to voice what I was feeling. After the session, I reached out, by phone, to the woman on the team. I told her that I felt there was a breach in integrity and how I was feeling about it. She honored my experience while also taking the frame that this might be an important healing opportunity as we work through it together. We agreed to talk about it in person during our next session. A few minutes after I hung up with the woman I received a phone call from the male practitioner. The first thing that he said was, "I am so sorry." He took full responsibility saying that while it was not his intention, it seemed there was a misunderstanding and misstep on his side. He assured me that his highest priority was my safety and that we would make it our work to repair this breech in our next session.*

**Developmental Reflection:** The first example shows us blatant untransformed eros within the context of unilateral power. Lara and her potential investor occupy different developmental levels. The man was either unconscious of his power or manipulatively wielding it, while Lara was conscious of what was occurring but chose not to address it. In an unintentional imitation of the earlier work with her female colleague described above, she was engaged in people pleasing and, again, avoiding conflict (not least because she correctly intuited that investors don't wish to be troubled about their bad behavior). We might say that nothing can be done in such a situation but to grin and bear it. Or at least grin and bear witness. Regardless of how he received it, Lara can dialogue with herself about it. And sharing about it in writing, as she does here, shows that transforming the experience for herself, in service to others, honors the boundaries that arise with eros. Anger is an impulse here to "make right." All nasty experiences can be composted to allow new growth.

In the second example, we see a further developmental advance toward mutual power in relationship. (Later stages do not mean that there are no problems, merely that they become composted more quickly.) What Lara had experienced as unilateral power gone awry became a profound healing experience. There is a shift in Lara's development, which we see clearly in the timeliness with which she voiced her experience and the maturity toward the practice of mutual power which she exercised, and in the way that this allowed the man to take responsibility. Here, the rupture was also an opportunity to repair – not only the given relationship, but also to consolidate learning from the previous times in her life where her boundaries were violated and she was unable to speak up, and/or the other party didn't take ownership of their role. Lara notes the importance of having the presence of a third trusted person.

Organizations, or organized groups of independent entities, are uniquely poised to lead this change in the culture of power because of their very nature, beginning with a shared purpose.

Inviting the conventionally personal sphere into our professional lives is difficult, in part because when we do this, we risk feeling the things that we most want to avoid – embarrassment and shame. It requires developing a new set of relational skills. Just as organizations organize around a specific mission statement and explicit values, they can also create structures for more transparent and participatory ways of relating. Shared conceptual maps, a common language, agreements and clear practices all help create the necessary scaffolding to bring objectivity into the interpersonal space. In other words, the organizational culture can build the trust and support for a more conscious relationship with what we feel, what moves us and how we communicate about it. In this way, eros is released from the dungeon of repression and liberated as creative expression and authentic connection.

When we are no longer afraid of or denying eros, it begins to mature. Instead of desire being relegated solely to the realm of sexuality, we can see how our attractions point to the ideas, projects, people and values that bring us most alive. We learn how to be better in relationship with each other and with our own wants, needs and desires. Instead of unconsciously dis- charging the fiery energy of eros, we can allow it to shape us and our connections in new and surprising ways.

Questions to ask when eros arrives: What is this creative tension giving birth to? What is the most generative way for- ward?

## 3. Social Eros.

We recognize, of course, that all of this is easier said than done. Eros is disruptive, it beckons – and sometimes shocks – us out of complacency. We are all under-practiced in the kinds of in- timacy, vulnerability, trust, capacity and risk that navigating a re- lational field infused with eros requires. Eros is not something that can be measured, quantified or controlled by the logic of the rational mind alone. Eros exists in the realm of mystery.

We might take refuge in the realization that eros is not just personal, or even interpersonal, but part of the evolutionary force of nature. When explored with this in mind, we can per- ceive the longings and disturbances of eros from an even wider perspective and inquire about a greater purpose. Eros changes us. And, since something must be sacrificed during this alchemi- cal learning, perhaps we might let go of an old part of our identity, the way we have always done things, a feeling of knowing the an- swer or having a clear plan. Perhaps we can finally let go of all of those things!

If there has ever been a time to put it all on the line, this would be it. Our current socio-ecological emergency requires us as a species, and as a planet, to make a great developmental leap in order to match the complexity of what we are faced with. It is time to step into the fire and to sacrifice what we have known, in the service of new ways of working, of relating and of living that can move us forward through hardship and even collapse, and into a new kind of thriving.

**Developmental Advance:** And now we take our own inner work, and our interpersonal work with one and another, and also the work of our organizations, and we ask what is the biggest way that we can use all of these resources to be in service to our community, our society and the planet. We become participatory agents in hospicing and midwifing the Great Turning/Work. Eros asks us to risk it all, for radical creativity and the greatest expression of love that we can imagine.

We see the role of such collective inquiry in stabilizing the new structures of power we need to see in action. A more sustainable – and intimate – approach is one where we are experimenting and practicing in smaller configurations, all the while attuned to and connected to our place within the larger living systems of the earth. For example, we may be part of a team whose purpose is to make progress on an initiative. The initiative has a larger ecological and/or social implication, while also rooting the participants in the change effort themselves. The team has practices built in for working with personal and collective inquiry intended for developmental growth. The team is enacting both inward and outward evolution. We can visualize overlapping and expanding circles of self, relationship, organization, community, society and ecology.

## Calling more communities of action inquiry/practice

In his book, *The Social Labs Revolution* (2014), Zaid Hassan describes social labs as experimental approaches aimed at addressing the root causes of complex systemic challenges. Social Labs are meant to design a new approach to today's rapidly changing and emergent social challenges, challenges that cannot be met solely by long term strategic planning because of their inherent instability. For example, Hassan writes about his participation in the early phases of The Sustainable Food Lab, which began in 2004. This lab largely derived from the work and process developed by Joseph Jaworski and Otto Scharmer, who were also early participants in the lab. The Food Lab sought to reimagine the world's largest industry, agriculture. This enormous task began with a single question: How is it possible to meet the world's food needs while maintaining a healthy planet? Today the Sustainable Food Lab has become an independent organization implementing large-scale sustainability in the mainstream food system, with more than 13 current initiatives.

What these communities and their various configurations have in common is a holistic approach to practical inquiry. In this, they ultimately harken back to William James' philosophy of Pragmatism, but they have taken many forms and have had many names during the years since James developed his philosophy. (They are sometimes called Communities of Practice [Lave and Wenger], S-Labs [Scharmer], or co-labs [Bradbury and Associates, 2017].) The efforts of some communities engaged in such "Action Research," to use an umbrella term for them, have rippled out in various ways, both small and large. For example, the initial inquiries of Jaworski and Scharmer in the Food Lab led to insights in articulating a practice of Action Research now known as Theory U, ultimately leading to experiments in response to complex dynamic problems. (Theory U is in fact a decades-old paradigm that included Socio-Technical Systems, a form of inquiry credited with bringing democracy to work-life since the '70s; see Bradbury, for a global overview of Action Research, including Scharmer's.)

## Key practices: Inquiry and meditation

Because we live in a time of climate change, and the possibility that our species will not survive, more people, especially those with control over the lives of others, must develop and move up the ladder to action-logics with larger perspectives. Unfortunately, developmental research suggests that, for more than half of the adult population, personal development ends by age 21. Of those who do transform after that, over half transform only once, and only a very, very small percentage transform the three further times that current research suggests is possible.

For those of us who sense that adult development is part of a lifelong inquiry process that leads to greater integrity and mutuality, as well as to more sustainable timely action, one practice we can cultivate for our work (and/or the Great Turning) is to write in a disciplined way about our early years, to see, to feel more deeply into, and thus to transform the seedlings of our current troubles. For this, it helps to feel more stable, and for this meditation is helpful. The unexamined life, as Socrates suggested, is not worth living, though we may have to shut off our social media feeds for a while to engage with ourselves fully enough.

# Conclusion

As we stand in this gap, the Great Turning between actuality and potential, we ask ourselves and our readers how to re-imagine work as a means to develop ourselves and as an activity that contributes to the world of our aspirations. We assert that this transition will include a new dawn of human creativity. It will have at its center an eros-infused creativity that no longer belongs solely to the privileged, one that becomes the way of life for all, as time, energy and resources are freed up from the way they are used by modern industrial market systems. It's possible to dream into a future where work is an evolutionary leap. Making a living becomes making a life, where our work is to participate in a co-creative endeavor, one that is inspired by and in response to the cycles of life in which we all participate, one that cares for these cycles and sustains them as we make our life and our living. Let's get to Work.

Chapter 2

# Understanding Self and Others for More Wholeness in Teams

*Concern for wholeness requires moving beyond shallow appearances and symptoms. It requires moving into fuller meanings, deeper causes, greater complexity, subtlety and ambiguity.*[25]

How can we live aligned with our personal life purposes, bringing our whole being into the workplace, collaborating in a joyful way and still achieving the most effective performance possible?

In the discussion about self-organization and self-management wholeness is named as one of the fundamental principels to achieve this. Wholeness is *"the quality or state of being without restriction, exception, or qualification"* (Merriam Webster); it can also be a state where body, mind, and soul are in balance with each other. It does not mean something has to be perfect to be whole, only that all relevant aspects of life are ac-

---

25   Tom Atlee, *The Co-Intelligence Institute, co-intelligence.org/I-wholeness.html (accessed April 1, 2019)*

knowledged and integrated. Like the gold-filled cracks in a Japanese Kintsugi pottery, even a human being can be whole again after having had physical and emotional injuries – or at least one can strive towards wholeness and begin moving along a healing path. Every hurt or failure we have gone through can strengthen us and let us find new possibilities for meeting our daily-life challenges. Wholeness can also be experienced as the interconnectedness in a collective and in trusting relationships.

One important ingredient for wholeness might be the transformation, growth and development of our consciousness, which can be achieved through different methods – for example, cognitive training, communication skills, nurturing relationships, meditation.

With the higher consciousness that comes with such wholeness, we are able to integrate more complex information into our system and even increase our sensory awareness, and we can make more intelligent decisions, maintain equanimity, and understand our own thought processes, emotions, and behaviors. Through all of these things we can build an accurate and effective model of reality. Our courage and compassion might increase, and we might find inner peace and enhance our intuition. All this can lead to a healthier life, more integrity and better relationships. In turn, these things will lead to better productivity in the workplace, as people will feel better and work better if they are coming from a place of wholeness. The key thing to recognize here, though, is that productivity is not privileged as the whole point of this enterprise; rather, it's a by-product of an approach that is ultimately concerned with the quality of our relationships and our lives.

# Growing Consciousness

For the last 19 years I have learned and practiced different forms of meditation, and the simplest form is currently very much in vogue, going by the name "mindfulness." More and more companies are including some kind of mindfulness training in the workplace. This is because the benefits of mindfulness have been so well documented in the past few years, it feels unnecessary to try to convince anyone of its benefits these days.

Mindfulness techniques and meditation can help you become more aware of your overall thought and behavior patterns and help you become more conscious of what holds you back, limits your joy, and sometimes even causes you pain. But with mindfulness alone you might not be able to capture those aspects of your psyche which are difficult to see during contemplation or introspective practices, but which exert an enormous influence upon your perceptions, your reactions, and the way you make sense of the world.[26] Fortunately, there are ways we can explore these fundamental but largely hidden part of ourselves, as I will show in good time in this chapter.

While I assume that the topic of the book might attract readers who are advanced in their path of self-development and spiritual practice, I still find it important to include the people who are just starting to sense that there is something deeper behind human relations than is generally acknowledged in the culture at large, people who have begun searching for a new way of living in deeper connection with this hidden something but have not yet encountered some of the ideas I'm bringing forward in this book. Of course, many middle-aged adults have started some kind of deeper exploration of the mind, the psyche, and sometimes even

---

26  *Full Spectrum Mindfulness, online course, https://integrallife.com/full-spectrum-mindfulness/ (accessed April 1, 2019).*

68

the body, but this usually doesn't begin until people are already in their late twenties or early thirties. Imagine if we have had the opportunity to start earlier in our lives?

In public schools we usually don't learn much about how to explore our own true nature. We learn how the organs in our physical body work, we learn to speak and write properly, we learn what happened in history, and we learn many other things that most of us will never use after graduating. I believe it would be much more useful and important to encourage the individual talents that are latent in all children. And because the true "genius" within a person can only be explored in self-inquiry, children should be taught these skills, which only in the last few years have become a subject in some progressive schools. Classes in Mindfulness, Yoga and Emotional Management are becoming more popular but are overall still very rare in public schools.

As things stand, most young people have to find meditation courses themselves, or build communities where they have a shared and safe ground of participatory learning, and where they can get genuine feedback from kindred spirits. Many of the so-called millennials grow up in highly technological environments, but they are also a generation that is emotionally very open and receptive to spiritual experiences, and they are often very attentive to the ecological balance on our planet. Many of them seem to have a natural world-centric or even cosmo-centric perspective and see themselves as part of a bigger eco-system.

## Who is My Self? What is My Work?

I don't remember when I first asked myself "who am I" or "why am I here," but it was definitely at a very early age. Often I felt that I did not fit in in this world, and I looked for confirmation from others and tried to improve my surroundings. As there were obviously others involved in my experience of life, and as I often felt dependent on them, I supported the people in my surroundings by trying to help them have spiritual experiences, too. I didn't always feel the same support from others, so I stumbled alone through numerous challenges, and eventually this led me to me to try being self-employed at the age of 24, as part of a collective of freelance visual merchandisers. Since then, to this day, I have never found employment that has truly fit my needs for professional and personal self-realization, that has let me work with other people with mutual emotional support. This is one of the main reasons I am exploring the topic of this book – it arises out of a real need that I have felt for years, one that I assume others have felt as well.

But before I move forward, I want to look at the present situation and why it doesn't fit well with my needs, and the needs of so many of us. I'll start by pointing out something obvious, that many if not most companies expect their employees to have emotional stability during working hours, and that employees have to make sure that they perform well and do exactly what their job description says, no matter what. I have always found it much more important to be able to bring my whole self to the workplace, whether or not I am perfectly stable at the moment. Often, in jobs I have had, when I have brought up innovative ideas, or seen possible ways to make a working process more effective, I have gotten the response that this is none of my business and I should just concern myself with what I am paid for. Only a few bosses have supported me in my creativity — and for them I always performed much better, with better financial results in the end.

My favorite example of a boss who encouraged my creativity happened when I was working closely with the general manager of a furniture store where I worked as a visual merchandiser when I was 22. From the beginning he paid me 7% more than I asked for, and he gave me, in addition, a grant to help pay for evening classes which I had just started three months before. He gave me a lot of freedom in my creativity and even approved an innovative project for a fancy Christmas market that I pitched to him. The market ran from the end of October to the beginning of January, and the revenue surpassed the building costs within the first three weeks. It was a major success and continued to run for years afterwards, even in other branches of this furniture company. This is just one example of how empowering employees, without directly thinking about outcomes, can lead to really great outcomes.

## An Integral Map of Experience

I really believe in the potential of people, and I am sure that everybody can do better when their full potential is acknowledged and valued by supervisors. But how can people evolve their own potential or discover their own personal genius?

There is, of course, no one simple answer to that question. But I would like to suggest a framework has helped me understand the complexities involved in this important question, and to navigate between different vantage points, and to find one's own location on this comprehensive framework or "map". This map is called AQAL and it was first introduced by the American philosopher Ken Wilber in the late '90s:

*AQAL (pronounced ah-qwal) stands for all quadrants, all levels, all lines, all states, and all types. These five elements signify some of the most basic repeating patterns of reality. Thus, by including all of these patterns you 'cover the bases' well, ensuring that no major part of any solution is left out or neglected. Each of these five elements can be used to 'look at' reality and at the same time they represent the basic aspects of your own awareness in this and every moment. You do not have to use all of these distinctions all the time. In fact, even using two of these elements can make your approach to analysis or solution building more integral than many others. However, having all five of them in your 'toolbox' allows you more capacity to respond to the complexity of our world and provides a place for including the essential aspects of any given situation.*[27]

---

[27] Sean Esbjörn-Hargens, An Overview of Integral Theory — An All-Inclusive Framework for the 21st Century, https://integralwithoutborders.net/sites/default/files/resources/Intro_Integral_Theory.pdf (accesed April 1, 2019).

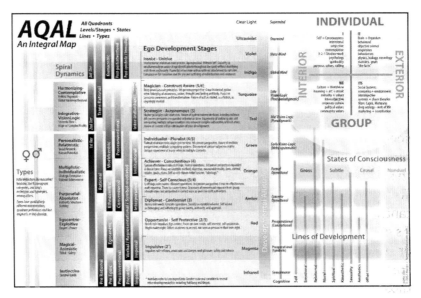

*Figure 1: Comprehensive AQAL Chart by Steve Self from kenwilberfund.org*

It is helpful to have a map when you have a goal and don't know the way. Indeed, even if you don't have a clear goal, the integral map can support you to understand certain situations much better, because it helps you to look at them from different angles. And the more detailed the map is, the more possibilities you will have for finding your way. Of course, the map is not everything, and it means nothing without lived experience in the territory itself. Only by bringing vibrant ideas and thoughts into action in the field can you really test your integrity and find out if you can walk what you talk.

# Three Basic Perspectives on Life

To understand oneself and others we can consider different vantage points, to see our various views and opinions. These perspectives correspond to what we mean when we say "I," "you" or "it." Let me explain this in some detail, since it's such an important idea.

First of all, at the core of this model lies the First-Person perspective, where I look from inside myself. The good thing here is that nobody can disagree with me about what I perceive from this angle, because there is nobody but me who is witnessing it. To be able to speak from this First-Person perspective is important, in order to be able to express my feelings, wishes and needs. As other people won't be able to see what my deepest fears are, or what might really bring me to life, it is my responsibility to learn to speak from the "I," to communicate my perspective to those around me. To properly use "I-language" in daily business might be one of the most important steps for deeper human relations, as it is the first move towards deeper integrity, and authentic communication.

The Second-Person perspective is the one where I go in connection with others and become able to perceive a genuine "You". This can be another person, or any being, or everything in nature that I am aware with all of my senses. This way I can be in "conversation" with people, animals, trees, stones or even with any spirits I believe in. Anything that I might encounter face-to-face I can think of as fitting under the category of "You." If I am open to the outside world, I can get into connection with a wider range of the stream of life, which can then touch me from inside, allowing me to be able to feel new sensations and emotions. From this point of view, I am even able to listen to my opposites, to hear what they have to say — not just in words, but also "between the lines," and in their bodily expressions. It gives me the possibility of actively listening to and perceiving the Other in complete fullness.

Looking at things from the Third-Person perspective, we are able to see the "It" side of life, like the dynamics between two people in a conversation, or even a group, and we can see the broader themes or patterns in the tension that we might have with somebody else. This is very much like how it is when we see the world from the top of a mountain, or from an airplane: we have an overview of the situation and can see things which are otherwise hidden. We create a distance from the objects in view, like a scientist looking through a microscope, or an astronomer looking at the stars through a telescope. This sort of objectivity often brings a different kind of understanding to situations than we might have from a purely subjective or first-person perspective, especially if they are situations where we've been stuck, or ones that have been troubling us for a long time.

Best of all, we can learn to consciously move between one and another of these vantage points, and to use them in our daily meetings. Every situation can be looked at from all three angles, whether it's a challenging or a joyful one. The more I am able to see the world from different perspectives, the more I am able to perceive, in terms of really understanding the present moment.

## Seeing the World from Different Altitudes

Perspectives can also change by changing the "altitude" of the view point – like I suggested above, with my airplane metaphor. It makes a difference if I look at a place from street level, from the roof of the house beside it, the church tower or other highest point in the village, from the hill nearby, or from an airplane. Different aspects of the view will slide in and out of focus, depending on one's altitude. And, just as it's possible to be aware of the three different perspectives discussed above, it is also possible to learn how to view things from various altitudes, and to move back and forth among them.

In Integral theory, the idea that people can progress through a whole series of developmental stages is crucial. Over time, the idea goes, a higher altitude brings a wider perspective and an improved overview – not just of the situation at hand, but in terms of a general, broader or "higher" state of being, if you will. As our perspective evolves and changes, we progress through a recognizable series of increasingly complex perspectives. We can get stuck at any stage, and we can inhabit any given stage in both healthy and unhealthy ways, but if we continue to evolve our perspective, the pathway has clear markers and a clear trajectory. Interestingly, from the first-person perspective alone, we would be unable to see these stages, but from the third-person perspective, and with the right "map," we can see them very clearly.

To understand these developmental stages, we can draw from any of several different models, all of which are good. Indeed, the term Teal, which has become so popular recently, comes from one such developmental model, the Wilber-Combs Matrix, which uses a complex system of color coding to name the various levels. However, for a basic understanding of these stages or levels, I will draw from Spiral Dynamics, one of the clearest and most popular models. Spiral Dynamics, like Wilber-Combs, uses colors to name the various stages, but this model shifts back and forth between warm and cool colors, whereas

Wilber-Combs follows the color wheel, for the most part, with colors in the blue-green range being among the highest.

Spiral Dynamics begins by recognizing that humanity has gone through several shifts since the first emergence of the Homo Erectus some 100,000 years ago. Through changes in how people acquired or grew their food, increases of complexity of family and culture, a series of stages, levels, or waves of con- sciousness rose up and continued developing. The transforma- tion from one stage to the next happens, to put it simply, when the environment changes and the individual — or organization, nation, etc. — is forced to develop a higher, more complex, or more comprehensive consciousness in answer to the needs of the changed situation, or when the individual or group has simply lived out the current stage. Finally, everyone who manages to continue evolving passes through the same various stages along the way.

In the Spiral Dynamics model, these developmental stages – also called "value memes" – are pictured as a spiral, or as concen- tric circles in different colors, oscillating from warmer to cooler tones, the warm ones indicating that the developmental focus is generally on the individual or individuals and the cooler ones on the group. Each round on the spiral includes and integrates all smaller, previous circles.

The development starts with beige (color of the Sahara), and moves from there into purple (chief of the tribe), red (hot- blooded), blue (sky), orange (liquid steel), green (forest), yellow (sun), to turquoise (ocean). The next stage, which is just starting to appear, has the color coral, and is little studied yet, as there are so few individuals who have reached it. It's important to stress that idea that when we say individuals or groups are at one of these stages, we don't mean they have left behind the previous stages, or that they don't have any contact with higher stages. Indeed, it's often said that a person has his or her "center of gravity" at a particular stage, not that he or she is fully contained by it.

What follows is an outline of the Spiral Dynamics memes, together with a few brief hints about what individuals and groups with their centers of gravity in each given stage tend to focus on:

- Beige: archaic, survival
- Purple: magical, tribal, blood ties, ancestral spirits
- Red: egocentric, power gods, heroes, empires
- Blue: mythic order, hierarchical structures, roles and rules
- Orange: reason, rationality, scientific, achievements
- Green: pluralistic, egalitarian, community, sensitive
- Yellow: integral, flex-flow, systemic, multi-perspectival
- Turquoise: holonic, collective intelligence, universal

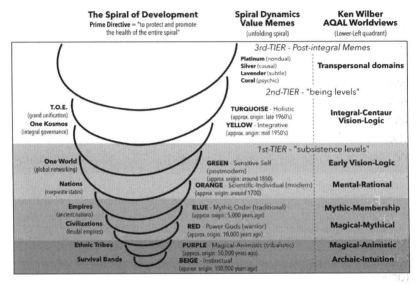

*Figure 2: Spiral of Development - Spiral Dynamics/Ken Wilber*

According to Ken Wilber, every further development "transcends and includes" the previous developmental stages. In other words, it is going beyond the previous stages (detachment, differentiation) and at the same time comprehending it, but from a new perspective (included, integrated). However, Wilber is also careful to note that, though this movement goes "upward," it can occur that the development does not proceed in a healthy way, and some previous stages may not be integrated correctly. This sometimes shows up as a kind of "stuckness" that can hinder further development, causing some parts to become frozen, not continuing to evolve, and thus being out of sync with the rest of the development of the individual or group.

As I mentioned above, in collaboration with Allen Combs, Wilber has developed his own developmental model, one in which the developmental stages are named using a slightly different set of colors, more inspired by the rainbow or the color wheel.[28] It is important to note that people are not types in this model, as they are in the Enneagram and some other models out there, but all the stages are in all of us. We live and move through these stages, depending in our capacities. Wilber and the others who have studied human development simply provide us with maps of the territory which, as humans, we cannot avoid living in.

For more details about Spiral Dynamics see the work of Don Beck, as well as Wilber-Combs, and the work of other scholars with similarly complex models of adult development, like Susanne Cook-Greuter (mature ego development), Robert Keagan (orders of consciousness), or Bill Torbert (action-logics).

## In Relation Reality Becomes More Real

Though Spiral Dynamics is a model rooted in developmental psychology, it is vital to see that it's not just about individuals but about groups as well, and ultimately it is also about how people relate to each other. This is crucial, if not necessarily apparent at first glance. Indeed, as the philosopher Martin Buber — who dedicated most of his life to exploring the topic of dialogue — stated in his book "I and Thou":

> *He who takes his stand in relation shares a reality, that is, in a being that neither belongs to him nor merely lies outside him. All reality is an activity in which I share without being able to appropriate to my self. Where there is no sharing there is no real-*

---

28  *Wilber stages and colors (see also figure 1 and 2): Archaic-Intuition (Infrared), Magical-Animistic (Magenta), Magical-Mythical (Red), Mythic-Membership (Amber), Mental-Rational (Orange), Early Vision-Logic (Green), Middle Vision-Logic (Teal), Late Vision-Logic (Turquoise), Illuminated Mind (Indigo), Intuitive Mind (Violet), Overmind (Ultraviolet), Supermind (Clear Light).*

*ity. Where there is self-appropriation there is no reality. The more direct the contact is with the Thou, the fuller is the sharing. The I is real in virtue of its sharing in reality. The fuller its sharing the more real it becomes.*

These words may sound a little strange, as they were first published in German in 1923 (English translation 1937), and the language itself was meant to challenge readers, possibly even to make them have to slow down to appreciate what the author was saying. What's important for my purposes is that one of the book's major themes is that human life finds its meaning in relationships. And that is what my experience has shown me, as well. I can have the best visions and ideas, but they only come to have meaning when I share them and bring them into connection with others, to help us meet life's challenges and savor its opportunities. A vehicle can only gain traction when the rubber hits the road — as long as it isn't a hover board.

Here, life starts to get interesting. When people come together, open to learning, willing to develop, interested in growing and coming together, then a commitment to connection seems very important, as part of that path. I cannot reveal my full potential when I step away from a process as soon it becomes difficult, or whenever I feel drawn to something that is more fun. That doesn't mean that I should never follow my impulses, but perhaps it does suggest that to know the source of the impulse is crucial. Is it my self-righteous ego that is offended or not interested, or is it intuition from a source that is greater than my ego, something that comes from my higher Self, my deepest and truest Self, that tells me to walk away from something?

Just like we do when we work out physically, we need to exercise our inner selves. It's important to take the time to practice really knowing ourselves from the inside, to develop the connection to the source of intuition, to develop self-confidence and trust in our inner authority. This can be achieved through meditation, contemplation, mindfulness, or inquiry. And we need the same kinds of practice in order to really listen to other people, to share authentic feelings and motives, and to give and get constructive feedback. Feedback, whether it is challenging or appreciative, can really help us to grow into bigger versions of ourselves. Sometimes it can also be helpful to see the outside world as a mirror of the self, either when we admire somebody for his or her abilities, or when we get triggered by mean behavior or bad attitudes from others. Both can be a sign that there is something in what is going on to learn from, for all of us. Both have to do with what's inside us, not just what is going on outside.

## The Opportunities in Conflicts

Triggers, especially, contain a big potential for growth, and we should pay attention to this and learn from it. As Robert Kegan writes, in his book In Over Our Heads (1994): *"Conflict is a challenge to our pretense of completeness."* So even conflict or disagreement can be a chance for transforming oneself and for achieving greater wholeness. Sometimes all it requires is a good mediator who can hold the space for the process. When different perspectives clash and create a divide, it's often because the parties come from different reference points or identify with other values or ideologies. So sometimes we first need to clarify where someone is speaking *from*, before a shared truth can be found, or a shared understanding of what is important for the process we

82

are both in. In teams who are working close on the same project, this is an extremely important point. Otherwise, they may never find a "We-Space" where they can work together, coming from the same basic place and moving towards the same basic vision.

The integrally informed Zen teacher and experienced mediator Diane Musho Hamilton has developed in her work many creative responses to working with conflict. In her book *Everything is Workable–A Zen Approach to Conflict Resolution*, she writes:

> *The simple, self-evident truth is that, however difficult, conflict is intrinsic to our human experience—in other words, it isn't going away. To learn to transform conflict, we must let go of the notion that something or someone is wrong or bad. This belief creates fundamental resistance, and it is the first obstacle to work with conflict. We can shift our point of view to see that our conflicts, like dreams, may possess an elegant intelligence that expresses truths that we may not want to see clearly. For example, an old pattern needs to be abandoned or a relationship needs to grow or change. We can, with practice, learn to see this intelligence at work and respond creatively and constructively. The conflict isn't the problem; our respond to it is.*

Active listening is an important part to start a conflict resolution. Genuine interest in the world of the other, where they are standing and what their position on an issue is, opens the toolbox of possibilities. But sometimes one of the conflicting parties is building up a wall and is not open to listening and sharing their perspective at all. Here a third person as a mediator, or the whole team as witnesses and supporters, can help to solve the issue. Granted, there are several good methods for groups to deal with such group dynamics without hiring an external professional, but each of them requires the willingness of all those involved to apply the principles and to trust them.

# The Power of Vulnerability

*"Wholeness doesn't come from trying to be whole, from striving for wholeness—but from accepting brokenness and incompleteness. Wholeness only ever arrives as a surprise."*

*- Hanzi Freinacht*

To support shared understanding, there are several practices which have already been at least partially applied to teamwork. They include Action Inquiry (Torbert), Transparent Communication (Huebl), Circling (Sengstock), Focusing (Gendlin), Voice Dialogue (Stone), Encounter (Rogers), Dialogue (Bohm, Isaacs, Senge), Possibility Management (Callahan). Most of these forms of dialogue use a kind of intersubjective mindful container in which people can be more open-minded and vulnerable. This seems important to me – to create a more intimate and safe space where one's own actual experience of reality can be shared freely, and where all participants are interested in the worlds of the others.

Vulnerability and intimacy in a corporate setting may seem scary for some, but my hope is that, through this book, the reader

84

will see why these ideas and practices are important in helping us create more constructive means of collaboration and helping us to co-create a thriving future. Brené Brown, a research professor and author of currently 10 books has spent the past two decades studying courage, vulnerability, shame, and empathy. She says showing vulnerability needs a lot of courage, but it leads to more authenticity and connection between the involved people.[29] Laying down weapons and shields can be a first step in bringing people together. When we dare to show our weaknesses, the opportunities are greater to find synergies, to support each other to find solutions, to do the work we do jointly, and to put our strengths together.

This could, of course, result in some very emotional moments during meetings, or it could bring up some tensions or hidden feelings between team members, and particular attention should always be paid to that. There should be room, and time, for processing such issues. Bringing certain issues to the table and making them conscious can lead to healing and wholeness, for both the individual and the organization. This seems like something well worth the time it might take to develop the necessary skills.

29   Brene Brown, https://brenebrown.com (accessed April 1, 2019).

Chapter 3

# About Vitality and Polarities

..................................................

*What brings people together? What makes them willing to find others to work together with towards the same goals? And what are the dynamics that cause good collaboration, apart from just having a common purpose? How can we make the dynamics between people visible, to help us to make conscious rather than unconscious choices, and take actions that serve every stakeholder of the organization, and have a positive impact on future innovations and generations?*

I find these questions fundamental for every team or organization, because answers to them may have a huge impact on how we create our workspaces and structure our organizations. In this chapter I would like to get to the bottom of these questions, and perhaps suggest some answers, or where we might look to find them.

One of the essential factors might be our sexual energy and basic vital force. Philosophers, theologians and scientists have explored and studied this life energy for centuries. They have had many insights into it, insights which often paint very similar pic-

86

tures of the phenomenon, but which use different names for it, mostly based on cultural and ethnic differences. What we know for sure is that there is a force that lets cells reproduce and re-generate, which causes our organs to work even without thinking of them, and which drives us to procreate, for the survival of the species. The same prime source of life and creative power is used in our muscles, and in our ability to use willpower to achieve something.

Around 1900 George I. Gurdjieff, an Armenian born mystic, philosopher, and composer, did some work on why and how to become conscious of our sexual energy.

> *Sex plays a tremendous role in maintaining the mechanicalness of life. Everything that people do is connected with 'sex': politics, religion, art, the the-ater, music, is all 'sex.' . . . What do you think brings people to cafés, to restaurants, to various fetes? One thing only. Sex: it is the principal mo-tive force for all mechanicalness . . . Sex which exists by itself and is not dependent on anything else is already a great achievement. But the evil lies in the constant self-deception.*[30]

The French philosopher Henri Bergson named the impulse of life *Élan vital*, and the Greek philosopher Plato used the word *Eros* to refer to one of the four forms of love and an inspiration for seeking truth. Psychologists have also been very interested in this phenomenon. While C.G. Jung used the term *Eros* to describe the desire for wholeness or interconnection, Sigmund Freud used it to describe the 'will to live' and used the word *Libido* to de-scribe an erotic energy or force of the unconscious parts of our

---

30 Gurdjieff discusses the misuse of sexual energy in extended conversations with his students recorded by P.D. Ouspensky in *In Search of the Miraculous: Fragments of an Unknown Teaching* (New York: Harcourt, Brace & World, 1949), pp. 254-255.

psyche, which can be used consciously through sublimation. The Taoists call this vital essence *Chi*, which is the animating factor in all living things, and in the old Vedic scriptures, *The Upanishads*, the primal, instinctive or evolutionary force is called *Kundalini*. Many scriptures assume that this raw, foundational energy is normally dormant, and it can be activated and cultivated in many ways. It's not a measurable physical energy, nor an electrical or magnetic force, but a kind of raw potentiality which can be harnessed, even modified. In Tibetan Buddhism this energy can be awakened through the practice of Tummo, translated as the Inner Fire that *"increases the wisdom, burns the ignorant mind of the brain and gives realization and liberation from the darkness of unawareness."*[31]

In the late 1920s, the Austrian scientist and psychoanalyst Wilhelm Reich named this energy *Orgon*, and he was even able to objectively measure the movements of this energy by using a very sensitive millivolt meter attached to the body. He originally observed a bio-electrical charge whose flow within the body could be visibly seen as waves, which he was able to observe with his instruments as they were passing through the bodies of his patients, especially when they were experiencing intense emotional breakthroughs. You might have experienced this lightning-like discharge of energy yourself, when a cold shiver is running up and down your spine, or your arm is twitching when somebody mentions a specific topic, or when your whole body starts to shake when you lie on the floor after a strenuous workout. Indeed, Tension & Trauma Releasing Exercises (TRE), a therapeutic method created by American therapist David Berceli, harnesses the body's natural "neurogenic tremors" as a way to reduce stress, unload tension and decrease the intensity of PTSD symp-

---

31  Dr. Pasang Yonten Arya, *Tibetan Tantric Yoga*, 2009, http://www.tibetanmedicine-edu.org/images/stories/pdf/tibetan_yoga.pdf (accessed April 1, 2019)

toms. In other words, in countless ways lots of spiritual and scientific thinkers have already pointed to the tangible existence of this life force.

## Flavors of Life

Even if the concepts of the life-force differ slightly, the link is an energetic dynamic that generates some kind of movement, or current, either mentally, subtly or physically. The dynamic is provoked by the attraction between opposites (at least two of them, as in a polarity). Using the image of a battery, we can think of the current as alternating between the positive and negative poles during charging, or perhaps as a flow that continues outside the physical body when connected with another "unit." Such poles could be located in the human body as well. According to the work of Wilhelm Reich for example, the female body is positively charged in the heart, and negatively in the genitals. The male body has the opposite set-up. His genitals hold the positive charge, and his heart the negative. In the Hindu chakra system, the current flowing on one side of the body is positive and on the other negative, causing each of the chakras along the spine to revolve like the rotor of an electric motor, oscillating between the opposing poles of two magnets.

Clearly, then, there's good reason to understand much of what happens inside of people in terms of such polarities. But we have to be careful to see these energies not just as separate and opposed but also in terms of what binds them together. Here we should think along the lines laid out years ago by Alan Watts in his book *The Two Hands of God*, where he gives an excellent illustration of polarity, and of what unites the two poles:

*Polarity is something much more than simple du-
ality or opposition. For to say that opposites are
polar is to say much more than that they are far
apart: it is to say that they are related and joined
— that they are the terms, ends, or extremities of
a single whole. Polar opposites are therefore insep-
arable opposites, like the poles of the earth or of a
magnet, or the ends of a stick or the faces of a coin.
Though what lies between the poles is more substantial than the poles themselves — since they are
the abstract "terms" rather than the concrete body
— nevertheless man thinks in terms and therefore
divides in thought what is undivided in nature.*[32]

Applied to human connections, we can say that what is going
on between two or more people is as important as the individuals
themselves, and these interpersonal connections can be as man-
ifold and diverse as the people themselves are. Each relation can
have such a unique flavor, and some can taste better than others.
But isn't that what makes life interesting? M. C. Escher writes
about how monotonous a world without difference would be in
his essay "White—Gray—Black":

*Life is possible only if the senses can perceive con-
trasts. A "monotonal" organ sound that is held too
long becomes unbearable for the ear, as does, for
the eye, an extended solid-color wall surface or
even a cloudless sky (when we are lying on our
backs and see neither sun nor horizon).*

Moreover, Buber speaks about das Zwischenmenschliche (the
interhuman), or the "in-between space," as a "zone" or a happen-

32  Alan Watts, *The Two Hands of God-The Myth of Polarity*, https://openlibrary.org/books/
OL22127855M/The_two_hands_of_God (accessed April 1, 2019)

90

ing where whole humans are meeting. While Buber characterizes the interpersonal as stimulus and response reactions within a context of shared meanings, in interhuman relationships the other is not seen as an object but as a partner in a living event. This can happen even between people who know nothing about each other. Far more than sympathy, the meeting affects each person's attitude and has a direct influence on the relationship.

Recently, researchers Hilary Bradbury and Benyamin Lichtenstein have expanded on this part of Buber's work in an article on interpersonal relations within organizations, and they characterize it in terms of an organizational and systemic context.

> *Taking a relational orientation suggests that the real work of the human organization occurs within the space of interaction between its members. Thus the theorist must account for the relationships among, rather than the individual properties of, organizational members. Similarly a relational theorist will be conscious of the impact of her/his research on what is being researched, and too on how that research impacts her/himself. Such a scholar enters an organization as if it were an extended set of relationships. S/he thereby places more attention on the "space between"—the space between subject and object, subject and research, researcher and subject, and the reflexivity of the research process itself.*[33]

In other words, when people meet, the space between them, and how and why they connect, has to become a vital area of interest for those planning the basic structure of organizations.

---

[33] Hilary Bradbury, Benyamin M. Bergmann Lichtenstein, *Relationality in Organizational Research: Exploring The Space Between . Organization Science 11(5):551-564, 2000,* http://dx.doi.org/10.1287/orsc.11.5.551.15203 *(accessed April 1, 2019)*

Failure to take this into account can lead to failures at all levels of an organization.

In private life people mostly come together because they have some similar worldview or common interests. Based on that, they can build strong relations and friendships. In a working environment, however, it is often not so easy to choose one's colleagues, especially given that employers look for skillful and diverse people rather than ones they think will have mutual sympathy with each other. It's just taken for granted that they will find a way to work well together. Many employers think that if their employees have enough diversity of knowledge and skills, this is enough to ensure that projects will work, new ideas and innovations will be created, and they don't need to be in any way concerned about whether or not their employees are having a good experience at work.

Such an approach can completely fail to take into account this in-between or interhuman space that is so important to the success of just about any endeavor. Indeed, sitting in the same room with somebody I have a lot of tension with, all the while trying to keep a smile on my face, while trying to make important decisions or to create innovative ideas, can be incredibly hard work — much harder than the same work done with people I get along with more easily. Releasing this tension and finding some basis of mutual understanding and appreciation is key for real co-creation. The tensions can exist between the people, but they have to be acknowledged and worked with, and not hidden away – as if that ever really works. Somehow, some way, the in-between space between people simply has to be taken into account in building organizations.

## Putting it on the Table

Of course, in any team there might be people I feel more or less close with and others I don't. There's nothing wrong with that; it's only natural. But if I truly want to create something together with the others on the team, something which is informed by the full potential of our collective intelligence and higher purpose, the issues between us need to be addressed and processed before we can move forward and really accomplish something. I mean issues like personal problems, unilateral or mutual dislike, tensions that come up while collaborating, or even sexual attraction – when things like this come up, they simply have to be put on the table. Now, to do this requires a lot of courage, and it also requires communicating in a way in which we can express ourselves fully, without hurting others, and without it pushing us further apart rather than bringing us closer. It is a chance to create a space of trust where new ideas and innovations can flourish, and it has to be handled with care.

It can also be a space where more vitality can emerge, as we keep the conversation moving and do not get stuck in old stories or habits. Being honest with each other and truthful to oneself doesn't have to be so serious — it can be fun too, and playful. This is essential. Though this is the corporate world and we are all serious adults, we cannot forget how to play. Bringing play into team building can give us a chance to focus some of our attention on the interhuman aspect of the team, to get to know each other and to play with our dynamics at a a time when the serious business of running the company is set aside for a while. If at least some of the time we allow the conversations between us to be a game – not deviating from the rules of the organization, and informed from all that we know, what we love and what we value – it can be a game in which there will only be winners.

As long as we have aces up our sleeves, or hidden agendas, trust cannot grow, and fear of being cheated, betrayed, harassed, or side-tracked will remain, and it will influence our relations with other team members. With more openness, honesty and authenticity, more intimacy and trust can develop between the co-workers, and the collaboration can be lifted to another level.

## A Vital Dance Between Eros and Power

Looking back to earlier stages of human development, we can see a big difference between Eros, as a form of love and constructive energy, and Power, as the suppressive and destructive force in the dance of life. But these too are polarities, in the sense in which Watts describes polarities in the quote above. We cannot have one without the other, and to focus too much on the one is to damage it, to make it something pathological.

Whoever has had experience of dancing the Tango can relate to that, and to the push and pull that often comes with polarities, especially at first. In Tango classes, during the first few lessons, one often sees the two partners fighting about who is responsible for the missteps. The masculine part starts to blame the feminine for not being able to surrender, and the feminine blames the masculine for not being able to lead. (One partner always wants to push the other into going where he or she wants to go.) But as soon as the dancers have learned the basic steps, they can relax, and their bodies can take over the movement. The struggles become fewer and the dance takes on more and more of a natural flow, a flow that comes with being truly together, united in the dance and one with each other. Suddenly even the rhythm of the music becomes one with the two dancing partners, and at a certain point it isn't obvious anymore who is leading, or even what is moving them. In that stage the movement comes from the touching bellies — no thinking is necessary. The next step is sensed and communicated via the connection, through the lower chakras.

Hilary Bradbury and William Torbert try to explain how this works in any human context in their book *Eros/Power: Love in the Spirit of Inquiry*. They explain it using a developmental theory of eight "action-logics," which show *"how we humans can transform during a lifetime."* The two take us on a journey of inquiry through an analysis of their own relationship, as doctoral student and supervisor, a very delicate power difference, and they show how the balance of Eros and power has worked in their relationship. To do so, they outline some key connections between the two terms:

> *We define eros as the soul surging forth to know the other, to learn from and grow with and through that other, a surging that brings with it love. We like Jean Houston's definition of eros as the principle concerned with the interrelationship of psyche and nature (soul and body), with symbiosis and the connection between all things. And so we wonder what will happen when inquiry transforms the connection between eros and power among humankind, allowing our democracies to grow toward real partnership, at least enough to save us from our current unsustainable path. We suggest that Eros/Power is the kind of revitalizing experience of intersubjective flow that occurs when love*

*and power conjoin though inquiry in the midst of relating between persons.*

*We believe that a taste of Eros/Power is the hallmark of a life force fully breathed, a taste of our deepest aspirations in which collaboration, mutuality, learning and creativity arise in relationships. Taken together, our mutual powers, which so few people today intentionally exercise, manifest what we call Eros/Power.*

And, further, they write in their introduction:

*In this book we suggest that relationships between women and men (or more precisely between the feminine and the masculine that embodies us in different measure) can lead an evolutionary leap. But are we up to it?*[34]

I believe that we are not only up to it but primed for it.

Perhaps, over the centuries, we have gone through a long personal and collective development in which Eros is finally ready to be fully seen, not just as something sexual and nothing but sexual, but as a force that can generate and allow a mutual empowerment, where love and intimacy can flow organically in the boardroom and not just the bedroom. In that state of flow, in deep connection, the organic consequence is co-creative. We can recognize and acknowledge the potential in the other and we can empower others to be bigger versions of themselves. Relationship itself is becoming evolutionary. And now is the time for it to take a big leap, and to become conscious of its nature *as* Eros, in all its fullness.

34 Bradbury H., Torbert W., *Eros/Power-Love in the Spirit of Inquiry*, 2015, http://www.erospowerjourney.com/book.html (accessed April 1, 2019).

Chapter 4

# Feminine vs. Masculine Behavior at Work

·····································································································································

*How might teams be put together so the diversity of genders and emerging energetic polarities can be used for co-creation?*

In talking about Masculine and Feminine behaviors, it's useful to remember right from the beginning that gender studies distinguish *gender identity* from other gender-related concepts, as part of an attempt to distinguish this identity from physical male-ness or female-ness. The other gender-related concepts include such things as *gender roles*, which are shared expectations of behavior given one's gender, *gender stereotypes*, which are shared views of personality traits often tied to one's gender, and *gender attitudes*, which are the views about others or situations commonly associated with one's gender.

Beginning at a very early age, people start to identify themselves based on social constructs and definitions, many of which lie along a feminine-masculine spectrum, some being more feminine, some more masculine, and some perhaps a mixture of the two. One can be a female and see herself as masculine, or male and see himself as feminine, but more often than not much of what makes up a person's identity fits with the prevailing view of their gender within the culture at large. This identity guides much if not most of their behavior. When I sometimes speak here of men and women, I mean this personal identification rather than their physical sex.

The typical western distinction between the two gender identities is nearly summed up by sociologists Jan Stets and Peter Burke in the following passage:[35]

> *Masculinity is associated with big power, often forceful, result-oriented, competitive, while femininity is related to personal connection, collaborative work, main attention is to the process rather than the result and supportive.*
>
> *It emerges as a pattern of female nurturing (femininity) that is associated with harmony, helpfulness, and humility, and a male assertiveness pattern (masculinity) that is associated with aggression, exhibition, and conceit once applying to the national culture as a whole.*[36]

While the qualities associated with each gender identity are clearly distinguished, what's important here is that masculinity is not strictly male, and femininity not strictly female. Sociologists like Stets and Burke are quick to point out that actual individuals can reside anywhere along the spectrum, regardless of physical gender.

More than just a social construct, the Masculine and the Feminine are archetypal energies that are accessible no matter

---

35  Jan E. Stets and Peter J. Burke, Femininity/Masculinity, Department of Sociology, Washington State University, pp. 997-1005 in Edgar F. Borgatta and Rhonda J. V. Montgomery (Eds.), Encyclopedia of Sociology, Revised Edition.

36  Priscila Putri, Masculinity and Femininity as Culture in Project Management, 2011, https://www.academia.edu/1466096/Masculinity_and_Femininity_as_Culture_in_Project_Management (accessed April 1, 2019).

what physical gender you are, and they have been observed, witnessed and written about since the beginning of human history in ancient wisdom traditions all over the globe. We see over and over the Feminine as a symbol for life and communion, the Masculine as a force for presence, action and agency. And, of course, we can still see this in various forms in our daily life.

In the old Chinese tradition, they named these principles Yin/Yang, which seems less personified, less associated with a particular gender or sex. The eastern philosophies don't look at these two as separate, like we do so often in the west. Yin/Yang is one, and it only takes on the characteristics of one more than the other when polarities are necessary, or out of balance. Moreover, in Hinduism as well, Shiva and Shakti, the two sides of the polarity, are often pictured as godlike figures, but actually they embody the same masculine and feminine principle. In short, the polarities tend to line up in this way:

| The Masculine Archetype | The Feminine Archetype |
| --- | --- |
| - Focus on Self | - Focus on Others |
| - Outcome Oriented | - Process Oriented |
| - Competitive | - Collaborative |
| - Structured | - Flexible |
| - Facts and Data | - Intuition and Emotions |

Stereotypes (men are masculine, women are feminine) undermine gender balance while archetypes (the Masculine and the Feminine, each of which applies to all) support gender balance.

The corporate world seems to have been out of balance for quite some time now, and this can easily be seen in terms of the

100

polarity. We saw the breakdown of a Yang-dominated system in 2008, and it was the masculine way of doing business that led us there. And most of the attempts to fix the broken system have been based on the old patriarchal habits, too, whether they are carried out by men or by women. Indeed, because women can be masculine, many women have taken on a masculine attitudes and behaviors, like armor plating they can put on in order to survive in the patriarchal world (which seems unhealthy for our system, too).

Carl Jung showed us a way to understand this, when he called the opposites within man and woman the anima and the animus.

> *By the anima he meant the feminine component in a man's personality, and by the animus he designated the masculine component in a woman's personality. He derived these words from the Latin word animare, which means to enliven, because he felt that the anima and the animus were like enlivening souls or spirits to men and women.*[37]

One of the first things that strikes me about this idea is its vitality, its liveliness, which might show us the way to a more vibrant kind of collaboration, if we somehow use this anima or animus power in our daily encounters. But there is more to it:

> *Unconsciously sensing this, many women today have fallen into the trap of becoming 'anima provokers,' operating in a perpetual adversarial mode, mistaking the fact that they can 'rattle' a man by being aggressive as a sign of their own strength. In*

37 John A. Sanford, *The Invisible Partners: How the Male and Female in Each of Us Affects Our Relationships*, 1980.

*reality it is simply a demonstration of male weakness. What is really happening is that the man's feelings function, which is connected to his female (anima) side, suddenly senses it is not safe to be open with this person and an inner struggle takes place as he tries to reidentify with his masculinity. In an incongruous state of affairs (perhaps also divine justice), men now desperately need training in how to not let themselves be dominated by the male side of women!*

*Deep down, women hate it when man become weaker than 'their' male side. At the same time, a woman can become addicted to provoking a man into falling under the influence of his anima and momentarily exhibiting confused behavior.*[38]

This suggests that both women and men play relatively equal parts in many aspects of this power-game. It's up to men to have the courage to make a step back when they are triggered by a tough woman, and to show their vulnerabilities and their softer sides, while women can use their feminine intelligence to provide men with a safe place where they can lay down their weapons.

Sallie Krawcheck, author of *Own it: The Power of Women at Work* and Co-Founder of Ellevest, an investment platform for women, names a few powerful qualities that women bring to the workplace, *"such as risk-awareness, relationship focus, ability to see problems holistically, learning orientation, long-term perspective, and focus on meaning and purpose."* She raises a voice for gender diversity and claims that *"more gender diverse leadership teams can lead to higher returns on equity, lower risk, greater customer focus, in-*

---

38 John Maxwell Taylor, *Eros Ascending-The Life-Transforming Power of Sacred Sexuality*, 2009 (p 406).

*creased employee engagement and greater innovation."* Further she mentions an important point, *"diversity is not bringing together a bunch of people of difference and training them to behave the same way."* Krawcheck sees that the power of diversity does not lie in the different ways that the people are to begin with but in how they manage to bring their various strengths together in a shared, co-created workplace.

Research shows that, among the people who emerge as leaders, male leaders are judged to be more effective than women leaders, but that this often has to do with prior gender-based expectations rather than results. Men and women can achieve the same results and accomplishments, but the perception of their effectiveness is different. In *Women in Leadership: Legacies, Opportunities and Challenges*, the business professor Anne Cummings makes a very illuminating observation about this:

> *Men tend to be more task-oriented while women take on a more interpersonal style of leadership. Therefore, a 'masculine' style tends toward assertive and task-based behaviors, while a 'feminine' style is more relationship oriented and 'democratic.' Additionally, Cummings noted, men tend to take greater intellectual risks and have higher self esteem, whereas 'women are coping' and tend to be more efficient when it comes to solving problems.* [39]

Of course, all of this behavior is relative and most of us have a multitude of styles. According to Cummings people in general are slightly more feminine in their behavior traits than

[39] *The 'Masculine' and 'Feminine' Sides of Leadership and Culture: Perception vs. Reality*, Wharton University of Pennsylvania, Oct 05 2005, http://knowledge.wharton.upenn.edu/article/the-masculine-and-feminine-sides-of-leadership-and-culture-perception-vs-reality/ (accessed April 2, 2019).

they are masculine. We just have often the expectation that a person will act a certain way based on his or her gender and fit into their 'role.' When someone does not meet that expectation, a leader can be perceived as less effective, regardless of their real capabilities.

Other researchers into gender role expectations point to similar problems:

> *The traditional image of a successful career is an upward progressing path, generally associated with masculine values. A person pursuing a management career has traditionally been depicted as a white heterosexual middle-class man, with specific qualities suitable to the task, such as rational decision-making, autonomy, competitiveness, agency, ambition, and leadership skills. This tacitly accepted management theory that is used in practice has strongly influenced both research and work in the organizational world. Adopting such a perspective has meant that women have not been considered as suitable and competent for leadership positions as men.* [40]

In other words, men are judged to be more efficient leaders precisely because the qualities associated with leadership are those associated with men, not with efficiency. What is more, women who do tend to succeed in this world do so by taking on those same masculine qualities. There is very little room for the Feminine in this, even if there is sometimes room for females.

40 Jeff Hearn, Anna-Maija Lämsä, Ingrid Biese, Suvi Heikkinen, Jonna Louvrier, Charlotta Niemistö, Emilia Kangas, Paula Koskinen, Marjut Jyrkinen, Malin Gustavsson and Petri Hirvonen, *Opening Up New Opportunities In Gender Equality Work*, Hanken School of Economics, 2015.

## Men Need Goals, Women Care for the Rest

In a study at Leicester University 2015, the researchers found out that goals, even when not rewarded, can help men to focus and do their tasks more effectively, while women performed better when there were no specific goals set. And, interestingly, other research has suggested that people focused on goals are more likely to fail than others who have, instead, a steady system they have applied to fulfill their tasks.[41] A system could be – to use an example having to do with dieting – to stick to a certain diet and eat right instead of having the goal of losing twenty kilos. In business, making a million dollars is a goal, but being a serial entrepreneur is a system. Goal-oriented people exist in a state of continuous worry, as it might be that things never work out and they never reach the goal. Systems people succeed every time they apply their systems, in the sense that they did what they intended to do. Such people feel good every time they apply their system and are better able to maintain their personal energy.[42]

I can think of other analogies for this kind of thing that might be useful to illustrate my point here. For example, when it comes to shopping, the two genders tend to approach the task in remarkably different ways. It's easy to see how a man typically enters a store with a seek-and-destroy mindset: "I need two new shirts, a tie and shorts, and then I'm out of here!" Women, by contrast, typically will have things on their list, but they inevitably also look for other possibilities. They look at many things in the store, perhaps thinking that "Stephen would like this!" or that "this might work for Claudia." Women often shop with a friend, and they pay attention to ambiance, texture, and sounds. And we

41  University of Leicester Press Office, Men more likely to achieve targets if they set goals, July 8, 2015, http://www2.le.ac.uk/offices/press/press-releases/2015/july/men-more-likely-to-achieve-targets-if-they-are-set-goals (accessed April 2, 2019).
42  Scott Adams, How to Fail at Almost Everything and Still Win Big: Kind of the Story of My Life, 2013.

can also see the same basic kind of behavior in sexual encounters, where men are often focused on ejaculation, whereas women often focus more on the pleasure of sensual touch and the slow build-up of ecstatic energy. There are probably countless similar analogies, all of them having to do with the difference between a goal-oriented approach and one that has to do with a kind of system that has no particular goal it is moving towards.

Putting all of this back into a business setting, we could say that masculine managers could benefit by a more mixed approach, one where they acknowledge the feminine qualities of team-building and systems strengthening, and reward those who practice it, while the feminine leaders might recognize that the guys on the team need the satisfaction of having something to strive toward, and create a process to measure and reward progress. I see no reason why both approaches can't be equally honored, and I can see every reason for having a mix of both approaches, a balance of both.

Having a goal is very healthy, as we all need something to work toward, but to have a more general purpose in life is what keeps you going, keeps you getting up out of bed every morning. This is the point of a wonderful old saying by Seneca, *"If one does not know to which port one is sailing, no wind is favorable."* And, if we choose to think about it this way, it goes without saying that the way we achieve the goal and how we are working towards it is just as important. The masculine way is more about the strategic alignment towards the goal, while the feminine way can help support this by noticing the environment during the journey and by keeping the crew and stakeholders happy. The feminine is a crucial component in a healthy human environment, and when companies have a good balance of masculine and feminine strengths, they are better able to serve all their customers, and the employees of each gender thrive. Burnout, for example, happens mainly in strongly masculine companies, as hard work and long hours are a source of pride, which is based on the masculine competition mentality. More balance will surely equal less burnout.

## A Culture of Equilibrium rather than Quotas

Ultimately, a big part of my argument here is simply an argument against extremes. An extremely masculine company, for example, feels like a mindless machine where employees become mindless cogs. On the other side of the coin, overly feminine companies often disenfranchise men and face the risk of losing ground, as they might not be competitive enough. So, for a healthy organization, the balance between masculine and feminine energy is much more important than reaching quotas having to do with the number of women working in the company. What benefit is there when a company employs, for example, 70 percent masculine women, while the rest of the employees are a mixture of masculine and feminine men? It is still an imbalance of Yin/Yang.

It is interesting to note, too, that masculine and feminine can be used not only for classifying individuals but also cultures. Geert Hofstede did some work on national cultures in the 70's and defined 6 cultural dimensions,[43] which one can use to measure cultures in terms of masculinity versus femininity. In "masculine" cultures, "...*gender roles are clearly distinct: men are supposed to be assertive, tough, and focused on material success, whereas women are supposed to be modest, tender, and concerned*

---

43  https://en.m.wikipedia.org/wiki/Hofstede's_cultural_dimensions_theory (accessed April 2, 2019).

107

*with the quality of life. In 'feminine' cultures ... gender roles overlap: both men and women are supposed to be modest, tender, and concerned with the quality of life."*[44] Hofstede's work on national cultures can only partially be applied to companies, though I find it valuable in this context to do so, at least to some extent. Perhaps, for example, the blended quality of the "feminine" cultures reflect the healthy blend of Yin/Yang desirable in a healthy organization.

The culture and style of organizations will have an influence on how, why and when things are done, and on who does them. The culture within an organization is reflected in the way that people perform tasks, set objectives and administer the necessary resources to achieve them. Culture affects the way that people think, feel, act and make decisions, in response to the opportunities and problems affecting the organization. An equilibrium of masculinity and femininity in the culture of an organization is very important in most areas, such as decision making, conflict resolution, or communication between stakeholders.

> *Masculinity and femininity as culture have unique characteristic. Masculinity is associated with strength, aggressive and task oriented while femininity is more focused on sharing emotions, democratic, cooperation and communication. Although both seems like contradicting with each other, it is important to combine both cultures when managing a project in particular in resolving dispute or crisis in an organisation. The case study in Taiwan construction industry proves that even though construction industry has always been associated*

44  Geert Hofstede, *Cultures and Organizations: Software of the Mind*, 2005, p. 117

108

*with masculinity, femininity approach is also effective when it comes to conflict resolution.*[45]

With globalization and the mix of cultures that comes with it, a major challenge in developing intercultural management competence is the fact that there is no "one way" to lead, especially in bigger corporations. Many companies need to face the fact that the leadership styles they have been practicing might not be suitable for the cultures in other countries, or for employees of diverse nationalities within the home-country office. Research suggests that managers have about four to six months to socialize a new employee into the company's culture; if it isn't done within this window of time, problems usually happen. Executives are therefore advised to promote social integration and networks within their own companies' cultures, or to invite new employees for an informal lunch, to share with them some of the less-than-obvious behavior patterns within the company. Of course, this might be a more feminine role, as it needs empathy and intercultural communication skills, but it's important that managers learn how to take on such a role with new employees.

108

45  Priscila Putri, *Masculinity and Femininity as Culture in Project Management*, 2011; https://www.academia.edu/1466096/Masculinity_and_Femininity_as_Culture_in_Project_Management (accessed April 2, 2019

Chapter 5

# Intimacy vs. Sexual Relations in Teams

*"We tend to think of the erotic as an easy, tantalizing sexual arousal. I speak of the erotic as the deepest life force, a force which moves us toward living in a fundamental way."*

– Audre Lorde

*How can we provide a safe working environment where intimacy between co-workers is fostered without exaggeration, over-exploitation, and suppression of the driving forces? What are the possibilities to express attraction or reluctance to other people, so that they are not hurt in their feelings, and so that a further constructive collaboration is created, maintained, or promoted?*

At this point, I think we need to be crystal clear about distinguishing a kind of general intimacy from sexuality and sexual behavior. Intimacy can include physical closeness between people, but it can also be a state of emotional closeness. One can have this kind of intimacy with other people with-out having sexual relations with them.

Close platonic relationships between colleagues have al-ways existed, but a more conscious attempt to understand ex-actly how this works has emerged in the last few years. It has started to become a popular research topic, and it has even found its way into the popular media, leading to such recent coinages as *work marriages* or *work spouses*. These special friendships with a person at work are characterized by *"a close emotional bond, high levels of disclosure and support, and mutual trust, honesty, loyalty, and respect."*[46] A 2006 workplace survey by Dawn Sagario found that 32 percent of workers say they have an *office husband* or *of-fice wife*.[47] In the yearly Office Romance Surveys by career web-site vault.com, which they have been doing since 2010, results show that up to 44% of workers have such relationships with their co-workers.[48] Relationships like these can have profound effects on employee happiness, productivity and loyalty. In fact, the only real downsides are that it might make other employees jealous, and if one of the work spouses changes his or her job it might feel like a divorce.

In the corporate world it is not very common that people touch each other, and generally it isn't considered appropriate to make even an appreciative gesture like putting a hand on an-other's back. Moreover, when a straight man knows that his male colleague is gay, he might feel some resistance towards any kind of touching. This is generally the case, even though it has been proven that touch can have healing power, when it comes from the heart and is meant in a loving and caring way. Indeed, during

46  Renuka Rayasam, *Having a 'work spouse' makes you happier*, November 7, 2016, http://www.bbc.com/capital/story/20161106-having-a-work-spouse-makes-you-happier (accessed April 2, 2019)

47  https://en.wikipedia.org/wiki/Work_spouse (accessed April 2, 2019)

48  *Work Is for Lovers: Vault's 2017 Office Romance Survey Results*, http://www.vault.com/blog/workplace-issues/work-is-for-lovers-vaults-2017-office-romance-survey-results (accessed April 2, 2019)

an online call a friend recently said something like *"the more nerves are touching each other, the more we can communicate together."* And the nerves can also be our subtle senses in the magnetic field surrounding us, the evidence of which more and more scientists are confirming.

This comes in connection with the other aspects of intimacy, which include trust and benevolence, where people are sharing their private life openly with colleagues, expressing feelings authentically, or showing vulnerabilities. In such relations, very often there are no signs of flirting or being overly sexual, but they can often be perceived as very creative and inspiring alliances, or collaborative partnerships, where even the most difficult personal things can be discussed. In my life I have sometimes experienced situations where supervisors shared very personal things with me, because they felt that I was really interested and noticed that I was listening actively to their story. As the organization researcher Ronit Kark puts it:

> *Intimacy is a form of close relatedness in which an individual shares his or her innermost emotions, experiences, and thoughts with the other and experiences empathic responsiveness, a depth of understanding and a sense of shared meaning. Researchers and psychological therapists have systematically articulated that true intimacy with others is one of the highest values of human experience.* [49]

According to Sexton and Sexton (1982) *"the word intimacy is derived from the Latin intimus, meaning* inner or inmost. *To be intimate with another is to have access to, and to comprehend, his or her*

---

49 Ronit Kark, *Workplace intimacy in leader-follower relationships. Oxford handbook of positive organizational scholarship*, 2011. ch. 32, pp. 423-438.

*inmost character"*. Intimacy is sharing what is innermost with others (Popovic, 2005), and involves *"seeing"* and being *"seen,"* by having an empathic perception and a depth of understanding of the other. Intimate relating is made up of positive behavioral components that are not merely ideational but have an outward manifestation. It's a style of communication in which both partners experience a sense of shared meaning.[50]

Schaefer and Olson (1981) have developed the Personal Assessment of Intimacy in Relationships (PAIR), as a tool for educators, researchers and therapists which provides systematic information on various types of intimacy:

- **Emotional Intimacy** – the experience of closeness
- **Social intimacy** – the experience of having common friends and social networks
- **Recreational intimacy** – a shared interest in hobbies and a mutual participation in recreational events
- **Physical intimacy** – the experience of sharing general affections. (e.g. a pat on the back, an affectionate handshake, a friendly hug, and looking one in the eye)
- **Intellectual intimacy** – the experience of sharing ideas
- **Spiritual intimacy** – the experience of showing ultimate concern, a similar sense of meaning in life, or religious faith
- **Aesthetic intimacy** – a closeness that comes from the experience of sharing beauty[51]

Looking over these different kinds of intimacy, it's easy to see how people working closely together in a business will be likely to have at least some forms of intimacy together. Indeed, it's hard to imagine them not having any.

---

50  *Ronit Kark, 2011*
51  *Assessing Intimacy: The Pair Inventory, Mark T. Schaefer and David H. Olson, Journal of Marital and Family Therapy, Volume 7, Issue 1, January 1981, Pages 47–60*

The benefits of intimacy in the workplace are perhaps most clearly stated in an article originally published in 2011 by Zeynep Tozum, MA, PCC, a Turkish born executive coach and consultant. Describing her own awakening to the value of workplace intimacy, she says:

> For most of my life in the corporate world, I considered 'intimacy' an inappropriate word outside the realm of family and friends. In recent years, however, I discovered a link between building meaningful relationships in the workplace and hard-core performance: the more intimacy we have with our colleagues, the more we will enjoy what we do, produce radical ideas, implement them with speed – and enhance our overall business performance. At the same time, intimacy is hard to define, easy to fake, and risky to engage in without skills. And yet, it works when truly appreciated and nurtured.[52]

Tozum is clearly aware of the potential pitfalls of workplace intimacy, but she strongly suggests that it can foster the best kind of creativity, and she suggests how it leads to productivity, without productivity itself being the sole focus. Indeed, she concludes her article with a kind of call for nurturing such intimacy by really creating a culture of trust and mutual respect in the workplace:

> For intimacy to survive, grow, and benefit the business, it is not enough for individuals to be willing to engage and manage intimacy in the workplace. Leadership of these businesses needs to deploy strategies to foster integrity, respect, and caring for

52 Zeynep Tozum, MA PCC, Gestalt Review 15(3):225-238, 2011, On Intimate Ground:A Gestalt Approach to Working with Couples (1994), Edited by Gordon Wheeler and Stephanie Backman, Intimacy: Why Do We Need More of It in the Corporate World?, http://bestwork.biz/sites/default/files/Zeynep%20Tozum%20Article%20for%20The%20Gestalt%20Review%202011.pdf (accessed August 22, 2021)

114

> *others as elements of their culture. In this way, intimacy can find a context and be cultivated to support business results. What often stands between high performance and poor performance is not the lack of technical capacity but, in the absence of trust and support, the pressure of surviving without failing or being ridiculed. Some may say that they are not interested in bearing their soul in the corporate context. I came to see that, as long as we are discriminating about when and with whom, we can afford to do so with benefits. Investing into knowing those with whom we work, and letting them know us, can be transformative in terms of our creativity and performance, that is, in connecting thoughts and power for focused delivery.*

What Tozum calls for here is a culture of caring within the organization, a way of focusing on opening up to each other rather than just focusing on the bottom line.

And Andrew Kakabadse, co-author of *Intimacy: An International Survey of the Sex Lives of People at Work*, has another perspective on that topic:

> *I think intimacy should fall into the category of diversity and at the moment we seem to have interpreted diversity as a gender issue — it's not. Diversity has many meanings in many organisations and one of them is people forming personal relationships in the workplace simply because they are number one overworked; number two they have*

*very little time to spend elsewhere; and number three the demands of work push various people together. So I can see intimacy just naturally coming out because of the pressures of work today.*[53]

In other words, intimacy in the workplace will happen. What many are starting to realize is that we need to be more conscious of how we cultivate this intimacy, so that it has the most possible benefit for employees and for the companies they work for.

## Destructive Sexual Behavior

As soon the interest in another person is driven by pure physical attraction and/or the sex drive, the relations are often more superficial and will not have a long lasting and sustainable quality. And when an inequality of power is involved, like the typical boss and secretary affairs, it might lead to confusion rather than to creative and constructive outcomes.

Men, especially, tend to follow their primal instincts very quickly, and they can be trapped by the unconscious stereotypes they have about women (often coming from watching too much pornography, from a very young age). Women are regarded as fair game for men with a strong sex drive, and every woman with sexy clothes seems to be available for everything. Some men make offensive jokes, vulgar expressions, demeaning comments, or even obvious advances. These are surely very generalized judgments but, still, many people, not just women but men as well, will agree with me about this.

The issue of mutual consent becomes important here. Even if the "object of desire" seemingly returns the feelings, it is not a

---

53  Andrew Kakabadse, *Knowledge Interchange Podcast*, Cranfield School of Management, 2008, http://www.digitalpodcast.com/feeds/52247-the-knowledge-interchange-cranfield-school-of-management (accessed September 23, 2017)

carte blanche for irresponsible action. Sometimes there are unconscious power games going on, which become more conscious only through an open dialogue about personal interests and expectations. And even if two people feel a mutual attraction and have some kind of feelings for each other, does that mean they have to go to bed together or become a couple? Or can it be, just as easily, something more like an invitation to work together on a project, which could be more fulfilling and beneficial for more people than just the two individuals involved in the attraction? If it is the former, which tends to be very private, only the two people benefit, and others are most definitely left out.

Sexual attraction can also be destructive, then, in terms of who doesn't get favored because he or she is not the object of the attraction. People a manager finds attractive might be more likely to be favored, to be awarded the best jobs the manager might have to assign, so that, in a very real sense, all the others get punished because they don't conform to the manager's sense of beauty and goodness. Sometimes the "beautiful" people get better ratings when it comes time to choose the employee of the year. Or sometimes people feel jealousy when their favorite colleague is occupied too much with somebody else, simply because that person is attractive to him or her. We want them around as much as possible, but someone with more power is able to occupy their time. The resulting behavior that can stem from such a situation will block the smooth flow of energy in any collaboration, which could better be used for creating something together, in a pleasurable way.

# Constructive Eroticism

Wherever Eros is alive, that situation is erotic. But we tend to confuse the erotic with the sexual, when actually it has a much deeper meaning. As I said above, Plato used the term Eros for the inspiration for seeking truth, and Jung used it to describe the desire for wholeness or interconnectedness, and Freud as the general "will to live." None of these visions of Eros reduces it exclusively to sexuality. I believe we should follow the examples of Plato et al and return to a more inclusive vision of Eros, one that includes the full spectrum of what this powerful force has to offer.

Indeed, when we see it fully, Eros isn't even just a force, or form of energy, it is also space for love, desire and creativity. Whenever I feel love for somebody, experience desire for something, or when creativity is expressed in a liberated way, it is a form of eroticism.

Evolution is happening because of Eros. Lower life forms are attracted to higher potentials within themselves, and ultimately to higher forms of being. The more we are attracted to something, the more possibilities emerge for us to get it, to be with it, or even to become it. Consciousness becomes form when Eros awakens. Teilhard de Chardin wrote that, with the advent of modern scientific thinking, *"evolution is becoming conscious of itself"*, and Eros is the driving force behind that path. Alan Watts eloquently says very much the same thing:

> *Through our eyes, the universe is perceiving itself.*
> *Through our ears, the universe is listening to its*
> *harmonies. We are the witnesses through which*

*the universe becomes conscious of its glory, of its magnificence.*

This hopeful prognosis will require matching our growing external power with an equally great interior sense of responsibility and capacity for spiritual guidance.

How then, can we create an erotic or evolutionary organization? It might be through making the ebb and flow of Eros more conscious, through our relationships, through ways of being together in daily meetings that include a fuller range of feeling and emotion, and perhaps even through the design of our workplaces. Nature can often be a good teacher for things like that, when we are able to receive the teachings. And the more we let Eros flow in and through us, the more we will be able to be inspired by nature's teachings. Life becomes a co-creation between our individual will and a shared higher purpose.

## An Erotic Corporate Culture

Culture cannot be re-created from one day to the next. It will be generated by us, as a sum of all our actions, behaviors and collective mindsets. What would a corporate culture look like if it were more open to Eros, to the fullness of human experience? It might be found only in the ways people work together in an intimate way, knowing of the power of Eros in and between them.

We know, for one thing, that proximity is a key element in the formation of communication ties, which are such an important part of intimacy. For years, big US companies like Microsoft and Amway have used community strengthening methods to empower their employees. Methods which come out from tribal or mythical stages of consciousness, like inviting an inspiring success guru to give a speech on stage to motivate the people in the audience or singing of the company's "anthem" together whole-heartedly.

According to a recent study published in The Harvard Business Review, *"the time spent by managers and employees in collaborative activities has ballooned by 50 percent or more"* over the last two decades, and in many companies more than three-quarters of an employee's day is spent communicating with colleagues. And the authors go on to point out that such collaboration needs to be arranged in a conscious way, to maximize its effect:

> *Collaboration is indeed the answer to many of today's most pressing business challenges. But more isn't always better. Leaders must learn to recognize, promote, and efficiently distribute the right kinds of collaborative work, or their teams and top talent will bear the costs of too much demand for too little supply. In fact, we believe that the time may have come for organizations to hire chief collaboration officers. By creating a senior executive position dedicated to collaboration, leaders can send a clear signal about the importance of managing teamwork thoughtfully and provide the resources necessary to do it effectively. That might reduce the odds that the whole becomes far less than the sum of its parts.*[54]

Again, scholarship finds that the right kinds of collaboration produce positive results.

---

54 *Collaborative Overload, Rob Cross, Reb Rebele, Adam Grant, Harvard Business Review, January-Februar 2016, https://hbr.org/2016/01/collaborative-overload (accessed April 2, 2019)*

In Project Aristotle, which began in 2012, Google has focused on building the perfect team, and researchers studying this project have found that exactly what makes a team function well has often been misunderstood. For example, they found that many of Google's top executives' beliefs about how workers can become more productive within teams were not true. They also discovered that the composition of teams doesn't make any difference. Looking at 180 teams from all areas within the company, they had plenty of data, and after sifting through it they found that there was no evidence showing that *"a mix of specific personality types or skills or backgrounds made any difference. The 'who' part of the equation didn't seem to matter."* Google's data indicated that psychological safety was critical in making a team work together well, and that conversational turn-taking and empathy, the behaviors that create this sense of safety, seemed to be a key part of the collaborations they studied. These are the unwritten rules for creating a feeling of psychological safety, the things we often do when we need to establish a bond. And those human bonds matter sometimes more at work as anywhere else.

Google found evidence that pointed to what good leaders already knew, that for a better collaboration in teams, the members listen to one another and show sensitivity to feelings and needs. The study of Project Aristotle sums up the situation nicely in the following paragraph:

> *What Project Aristotle has taught people within Google is that no one wants to put on a "work face" when they get to the office. No one wants to leave part of their personality and inner life at home. But to be fully present at work, to feel "psy-*

*chologically safe," we must know that we can be
free enough, sometimes, to share the things that
scare us without fear of recriminations. We must
be able to talk about what is messy or sad, to have
hard conversations with colleagues who are driving
us crazy. We can't be focused just on efficiency.
Rather, when we start the morning by collaborating with a team of engineers and then send emails
to our marketing colleagues and then jump on a
conference call, we want to know that those people
really hear us. We want to know that work is more
than just labor.*[55]

In short, efficiency is not the focus but the by-product of a focus on genuine communication about real human concerns while working together on business projects.

Of course, doing this requires that we take the time to con-nect on a deeper level, and to learn how to really do this. It re-quires that every member have a willingness to dive deeper, and a certain degree of self-reflection, self-knowledge and emotional intelligence. This might involve, as well, being able to listen to one's bodily sensations and feelings and to see what is triggering them. These are "soft-skills" that perhaps only a small percentage of people have really developed. We need some professional col-laboration managers to support the development of these skills, if we are to evolve better organizational structures.

55 Charles Duhigg, *What Google Learned From Its Quest to Build the Perfect Team*, Februar 25, 2016,
https://www.nytimes.com/2016/02/28/magazine/what-google-learned-from-its-quest-to-build-the-perfect-team.html (accessed April 2, 2019)

Chapter 6

# The Respons-ability of Men

..............................

*A man should dive into the world like into a woman: not out of greed or pleasure, but to kindle more love, more openness and more depth.*

*- David Deida*

I am grateful for the achievements which men and women have brought us in the last few centuries, men and women who had the drive and the will to follow their purpose and arrive at a goal, all of them driven by Eros and most of them not aware of it. There have been many moments in history where Eros was oppressed through patriarchal power structures and could not find its organic flow, or when decisions were fear-driven rather than made out of love and joy. In spite of this, I don't want to blame men for everything, even if men sometimes tend to do strange things when in passionate pursuit of their purpose in life, or of a person they admire. Things like fighting another tribe to secure survival of one's own, occupying another country to get their treasures and resources, or betraying one's own values because of the need to earn money to feed a family. Most events which led to the current economic, social and spiritual crises were based on unconscious impulses, and only more consciousness and awareness can fix any mistakes we might have made in the past.

As a masculine person, I would like to encourage others like me to become conscious of our perspectives on sexuality and our interactions with the feminine, by taking on a new perspective. To encourage this, I will ask the reader to consider a few questions. First of all, have you ever flirted with a colleague at your workplace? Have you ever felt attracted to somebody of the other or same sex in your team? How did you deal with that situation, in terms of your own self, and in relation to this other person? Have you taken the step to openly talk about the issue? What was your primary interest in this person, or the meeting? What has been your experience when you have noticed such situations arising between other people in your organization? Are you aware of any feminine aspects of yourself, and how do you integrate them in your life? And, finally, how do you support women, or the feminine, in your workplace?

Although I am writing here especially about encounters between women and men, what I say might also be true for people of the same sex. Often a strong masculine person, whether a man or a woman, can have the behaviors I describe below. Maybe not so much in the corporate world, as homosexuality is still not acknowledged publicly in most countries. As I sometimes attract gay men myself, I have found a hand on my bottom at least in dance clubs, and I've heard stories of gay men who were stalked and harassed by other men. And a strong masculine woman can overpower and do harm to a rather soft female person. The feminine response to masculine crude behavior and oppression is sometimes silence and too often blind submission. Some more awareness and respect for the feminine in our daily lives would bring balance in ourselves and to our relationships.

As more and more women are coming out with stories about being harassed in all areas of work, we need to raise awareness of the responsibility we men have for this. The boundaries of what harassment or violation means are often not so clear and can be very different from woman to woman. So we need to pay attention to the tiniest sign of insecurity and discomfort in a woman. It might be a little joke for you, or just a short friendly touch, but it might be a violation of her boundaries, or even re-traumatization. Not every friendly smile is an invitation to come closer.

## Lack of Controlled Sexual Urge

Young men, especially, are often carried away by their sex drive, and many don't lose their sexual focus until they reach old age. The power behind this desire is an irresistible force, it is what keeps us searching for our life's purpose, what allows us to focus on a goal, and what lets us go forward even when we are facing obstacles in our path. When we become sexually stimulated, it activates our whole body/mind system, including hidden creative abilities. These thoughts and physical needs often distract us from our mission and keep us from doing our work. The expression of sexual energy is, of course, innate and natural, but it should find an outlet which enriches the body, mind and spirit.

Unfortunately, when this drive is expressed in an excessive and unconscious way, it often leads to pain and destruction, in one's self and in one's relations with others. In the business environment we have seen this too often as sexual misconduct and harassment. And it might be the reason why some people burn out — when workaholics don't realize how they are draining their own energy reserves, or trying to work harder for success.

We all know that sexual energy, when expressed without skill or consciousness, can cause a lot of damage. Especially during puberty, when the hormones are going haywire, some adolescents focus their increasing life force and growing sexual energy on sex with many partners, or they act out in frustration and anger. In most countries, the courts have learned how to deal with such behavior, particularly in the way that the law regards teenagers in ways that are less strict than they are for adults. But the same countries are lagging far behind when it comes to educating teenagers about what they are going through and how they might channel this erotic energy better.

It might be expected that, as we become adults, we will have learned how to behave in a way that we don't act to infringe on other people's privacy, emotions, rights, or bodies. But, clearly, this is not true for everybody. Indeed, men tend to have a longer period of "adolescence" than women, and many men behave like angry and sexually charged teenagers much longer than one might expect, and they remain unconscious of their own actions and their impact on the world. We still have much to learn if we are to harness this tremendous energy and do something constructive with it.

Many years ago, author Napoleon Hill suggested that we can harness these powers much more than we tend to realize:

> *The majority of men who succeed do not begin to do so before the age of forty to fifty, is their tendency to dissipate their energies through over indulgence in physical expression of the emotion of sex. The majority of men never learn that the urge of sex has other possibilities, which far transcend in importance, that of mere physical expression.*
>
> *The desire for sexual expression is by far the strongest and most impelling of all the human emotions, and for this very reason this desire, when harnessed and transmuted into action, other than that of physical expression, may raise one to the status of a genius.*[56]

Hill was right, of course, but far too few of us have learned to do what he asks of us in this far-sighted passage. We men need harness our lust and develop a strong will not to exploit this precious power of Eros. This powerful energy can do so much more than just compel us to have sex or to reproduce, or, worse, cause fear and pain in women, when unleashed in an unconscious way. When the sexual urge is stirring up in you, especially in a working environment, I would invite you to feel it, not as a desire for the other person opposite you, but as a longing for connection, a deeper connection with that creative energy within yourself. Let life pulsate through you, like waves on the ocean come and go.

---

56 *Napoleon Hill, Think & Grow Rich, 1937*

## Slow Down and Smell the Roses

Based on my own experience, and from conversations with numerous men and women, I've realized that the root cause behind so many failed human connections is the craving for instant gratification. The addiction to a fast climax, be it by making money, climbing the career ladder, getting a potential sex partner into bed, or ejaculating quickly and without concern for the needs of one's partner. If you dig deep into your own motives, you may find some truth in what I've just said. But it might not be your fault. Western culture somehow teaches us to value pressure and velocity, and most of us haven't learned something different yet, or we haven't learned it well enough.

The majority of people, both men and women, seem interested in the outcome of a personal encounter rather than in the depths of the relationship as it unfolds in the present moment. Very few have learned to enjoy the moment, and be more interested in the current situation rather than what they can get out of it. This behavior is common in our daily life, when we meet people briefly on the street, in many work relationships, and unfortunately in too many love affairs as well.

For centuries our patriarchal structures have favored and strengthened this behavior, and we all experience the negative consequences of it. The current crisis, which came to a head in 2008, is mainly caused by the lust for power, and by envy, greed, dishonesty and egoism, which are symptoms of this behavior. We, as men, have the responsibility to change this behavior. It wasn't the best way to do things in the past, and it certainly isn't the best way to do things now, or in the future.

What can we actively do, then, to change this? One thing could be to actively slow down, to calm the breath and enjoy every little movement of the body, to notice the subtle "scents" that come to us in each and every instant, to listen to ourselves and each other, and to consciously move into the space between or within our interactions with each other. Of course, truly being in the present moment, noticing what is going on in me, around me, in others, and between us, right now, can be a challenging task. But it is helpful, because it allows us to have a fuller experience of every meeting, and to be able to respond to events in a way that serves everybody involved.

A beautiful practice that I have been doing for many years now is to literally stop and smell the roses. Whenever I see a rose along whatever pathway I am on, I stop, I take a deep breath of its perfume, and I let it unfold in my olfactory cells. Most of the time it feels like a little orgasm, and it fills me with joy and verve for the rest of the day. This slowness and receptivity can be practiced with many other beautiful random things, like the sound of birds, the colors of a field of flowers, or the movements of a swan swimming in a lake.

## Own Your Stuff

Perhaps my most important practice is to own my responsibility, to be aware that every one of us is part of this system that causes the troubles we are in. I can only start with myself, when I want the world to change. This is a great insight that Mahatma Gandhi expressed so well in his often-quoted statement: *"Be the change you want to see in the world."* Seeing and acknowledging my part in the story is the first step.

Being honest and authentic, and sharing one's own experience in an empathic way, is a further move along such a path. It is not about imposing one's own opinion on somebody or dumping all sorts of personal stuff onto other unsuspecting people. Facing each other with direct eye contact, and sharing what is present in the body, and being aware of what kinds of emotions and feelings are happening, what the impact your connection with another person has on that person — all of this can start a deeper inquiry into the meaning of that encounter. And there might be much more hidden in the depths of that meeting space than you had ever thought of before.

In the last few years, I have begun to show up in a more authentic way myself, tying to meet others in the way I have described above. These days I generally tend to meet with people who are longing for deeper connections, whether it happens to be in my circle of friends or in professional environments. In other words, I know I am not alone in searching for a way of finding and exploring deeper connections.

Current research also shows that a lack of human connections is a main cause for many kinds of addictions. It is also a main cause for many symptoms which are nowadays diagnosed as burnout. When people only focus on their work and career, not being willing or able to connect with others in their workplace, life energy and stamina decreases, and people feel powerless and burned out.

Being interested in the vis-à-vis, truly interested and engaged, with an open mind and heart – this is where we can start being able to enter the world of the other. Willingness to open up to different perspectives and worldviews can lead to a broader understanding, not just of the outer world but also of oneself. For that, I need an understanding of my own reactions to certain events, and a careful and measured response to situations which I might never have experienced before. Sounds quite challenging, doesn't it? And, yes, it takes courage to be able to face that challenge. But isn't that what a masculine man is looking for?

## Rein in Your Horses

A salacious joke, a sexist remark, or a chauvinistic statement comes out quick in heated discussions, or when someoone is turned on by another person, or when other masculine/feminine games are going on. Too often it happens that a man wants to be funny but instead ends up hurting a woman with his comments on her appearance or behavior. Sometimes, if I am making a statement about a woman's appearance, she is more offended by it than flattered, even if I think what I just said was a positive comment. Her response depends on many things, like her mood, her openness to me, my own manner and confident demeanor, and certainly the words I have chosen. The same thing happens with very feminine and sensible men, whether they are homosexual or straight.

In any case, it is always good to be as conscious as possible of our actions, and as conscious as possible of the other person's state and situation. If you take full responsibility for your actions, and whatever outcome they might have, then go for it. But instead it might be smarter to be cautious and to approach other people in a more empathic and caring way. When you share your feelings and express how it feels when a certain person is around you, you can't be wrong, as they are your feelings and you are owning them. But problems happen when the other person senses a hidden agenda, or veiled motives or expectations, and suspects there is some underlying hostility behind your friendly mask. As I stated at the beginning of this chapter, if you are interested only in the outcome, and getting it as quickly as possible, and you don't even have the intention of really getting to know the other person, your advances might not be accepted in the way you would like them to be.

You don't have to control your behavior and restrain genuine impulses. It's more about having an authentic humility and a sensitivity to the needs and boundaries of the feminine aspects all of us carry. A good start to learning to be humble is to listen more and talk less, and to just be present with whatever arises in the expression of feminine energy in other people, or in yourself.

## Holding Space for the Feminine

The feminine principle is often described as the kinetic aspect of life itself. Every movement is of feminine nature. On the other hand, stillness, and also determination and focus, are often seen as masculine qualities. Women often don't like it when they hear that feminine expression doesn't have direction. And most people who are interested in gender equality don't even like the separation between feminine and masculine, even though these are principles which have been observed, experienced and even measured for countless centuries. What's more, isn't this dance between the masculine and feminine a lot of fun?

If you, as a more masculine person, can hold the space for the feminine, can stay present, and just witness the expression of pure beauty, and sometimes raw fierceness, you can actively support the shift to a new paradigm, where the Shakti power, as the Hindus call it, can rise and unfold in our collective experience.

You will be surprised about the feedback you might get, when you can just "be there," not immediately responding with words or gestures, not judging, not questioning the feminine spectacle happening in front of you. I've had many women tell me how empowered they felt in moments like this. They often tell me that they can really relax into themselves when they feel seen in this way, and some even felt embraced, even though we didn't have physical contact. The only thing you have to do in such moments is to keep eye contact, and to keep an open mind and open heart. Just listen, observe – and enjoy.

## Chapter 7

# An Invitation to Women

................................................................................................................

*Deep inside every woman is anchored a primal force that is recognized less and less. Especially women suffocate in the vacuum of the current patriarchal behavior coercion. They alienate from their inner strength, their 'Feminine Capital.'*

*- Kaouthar Darmoni*

As much I blame my unconscious masculine brothers for the crisis we are in, I also know that women are involved in the same situation. They too share some of the blame for our failure to communicate openly. I'm sure many women see their complicity in this, when, for example, they have seduced a man, or have just wanted him to find them attractive or to get him to do things for them. Or perhaps some have played the bitchy diva, knowing in advance that this will make the guy angry. For those of you women who can relate to any of these characterizations, I want to invite you to open your mind to the sufferings and worries of men, as much as to your own powers and potentials. I mean the potentials you can even live out in a feminine way and not as a copy of the pathological masculine. From my perspective, the feminine is actually the stronger gender, as you carry the power to turn the heads of men and wrap them around your little finger. Use this power wisely and we can make this world a better place together.

I wonder if any of my female readers have ever been approached by a colleague in a way that felt inappropriate. Probably the answer is yes. Has a man, or woman, expressed their affection, or even antipathy to you, in the workplace? What was the impact in you, what did you feel, how did your body react? How did it affect your further collaboration?

If you are a more masculine woman, you might have immediately responded with a ridiculing joke, or in a defensive and angry way. Or you might not have answered at all, because you were shocked, or you might have just laughed about it out of embarrassment, which could be a sign that you have a more feminine essence. If this second scenario has happened to you, you also might have struggled with it for days, and you may have had self-doubts and even blamed yourself for that situation. Your own response will have a unique flavor, perhaps only a little bit similar to what I have described above. But I have offered up these hypothetical reactions because they are common ones I have experienced or have had described to me by various women.

## This Awkward Moment

In a working environment you might face situations which feel a bit awkward at first. Situations where either you or your colleagues experience emotions which usually get suppressed in that environment, even though these emotions are totally normal and typical in our human experience. When the heartbeat in-

creases, the mind can engage in all kinds of phantasies, and but-
terflies can start buzzing around in the belly, or it can get warmer
in your lap. At times like these our insecurity level rises, and we
don't know what to do with that. When you experience erotic attraction, or sexual arousal, it is usually not the most comfortable
state to be in while in a business meeting.

In meetings with teammates you seek to have good collaboration with, can such emotions as I've described above be there,
exactly as they are, without making you less productive? Can you
allow yourself to feel these feelings, and can you share them with
the colleague who helped stimulate them? You might sense some
discomfort in the room, or an insecurity in yourself, or a tension
between you both. Mentioning your perceptions, or whatever
you feel in that very moment, will have an impact on the other
person – that's for sure. There might be no resonance at all, but
the other person can have a different experience of the situation,
which is easier to express for him or her because the conversation has gone to a deeper level of awareness. Whatever the case,
it is my belief that dropping into this deeper level of awareness
can and will, in the long run, strengthen the working relations one
has with colleagues. Including more of these subtle perceptions
as part of your conversation, even if it feels uncomfortable or
awkward at first, will make a difference in your daily collaboration, and you will be surprised by what's possible from this
deeper place of human connection.

## Harassment or Lack of Social Competence

When a man approaches you in a way which feels inappropriate, it might not be his intention to intimidate or offend you.

Men are sometimes so clumsy or inattentive that they don't know what the outcome of their actions might be. Many men are raised either to emulate their father's dismissive attitude towards women, or they have learned, from how they interacted with their mother, to have an ambivalent relationship to the feminine and therefore to women in general. With the evolution of our cultures and the rise of women in more powerful positions, it still takes most men longer to adjust to these changes and to develop a new attitude and behavior that is suited to the changing situation. For such men, it's often difficult to learn from women, especially when they are doing so in an angry manner. The situation, perhaps, reminds them too much of problems they might have had with their mothers, and so some conflicts are preprogrammed.

The topic of sexual consent has been all over the media recently, and there is a big variance in what this concept really means in the US, Europe and other parts of the world. As I have been trying to highlight the importance of the responsibility that men have to take on regarding this issue, I also want to acknowledge the responsibility women have – to express their feelings and decisions in a clear way, and to make clear where their boundaries are, so that men can understand what a woman wants and doesn't want. And of course this issue is equally important for same-sex encounters as well. The receiving person needs to listen to his or her own feelings and understand them, and to communicate a basic Yes or No in the clearest way possible.

In the workplace, encounters between people will not primarily be explicitly sexual, but attraction and erotic feelings can be fueling much of the energy between people, can be the better part of what's going on below the surface. The more that the communication is clear and transparent, right from the beginning, the fewer misunderstandings there will be. If there is the slightest trace of discomfort, and especially if there is any feeling of being cornered, it would be good to bring that up as soon as possible and deal with it, openly. One might do this, first, by expressing oneself, and, second, by being sure to bring it clearly into the awareness of the other person, who might not be conscious about it.

These two moves are almost the same thing, but I separate them out because the second one is so important. Too often, if the feeling isn't expressed at the time and in a thoughtful way, it only gets expressed later in some roundabout way, as seemingly unrelated hostility at a later date, or even as private regrets long after the fact. The first step, then, is to find the words to express the feeling. But then it's important to make sure what was said has been understood by the other person. Once this has happened, the other person can know what the situation is really like for you, and the possibility of later recriminations and hostilities almost vanishes. And, what's more, a clear channel for open communication is established between the two people — a channel that can be used again on subsequent occasions.

Now, I don't want to make men appear to be nicer than they really are. Sometimes they are not nice at all. Nonetheless, I invite my women readers to find and set your boundaries *and* to stay open and to receive the masculine being in all his imperfection. Receive it, and at the same time communicate what your experience of it is like, in a timely and clear fashion. This way, the channel towards open communication can be established, and the issues that could bring about potential hostilities can be dealt with as they come up, and as they really are. This way we will be less likely to walk away from something with the kind of suppressed anger that so often leads to later hostile situations, ones that are so far removed from what created them that no one really knows what the hostility is about anymore. No one remembers how it began, and whatever discomfort the two people feel seems like something almost God-given, part of nature. By contrast, if the feelings had been acknowledged and expressed right from the beginning, perhaps there would be no lingering discomfort at all. And a channel for honest and forthright communication will have been opened. From there, collaboration becomes much cleaner and far easier.

## Using Your Erotic Intelligence

As a woman you have the power to use your radiance and erotic charms. You can make it a playful game or a serious exploration when you apply what Esther Perel calls your *Erotic Intelligence*. Recently, researchers at Oxford University found that such an erotic appeal can be of tremendous value in professional life, and they coined a term for it, *Erotic Capital*, which they saw as a fourth kind of personal asset, an important addition to economic, cultural, and social capital.

> *Erotic capital is increasingly important in the sexualized culture of affluent modern societies. Erotic capital is not only a major asset in mating and marriage markets, but can also be important in labour markets, the media, politics, advertising, sports, the arts, and in everyday social interaction.*

> *Women generally have more erotic capital than men because they work harder at it. Given the large imbalance between men and women in sexual interest over the life course, women are well placed to exploit their erotic capital. A central feature of patriarchy has been the construction of 'moral' ideologies that inhibit women from exploiting their erotic capital to achieve economic and social benefits.*[57]

If we speak of this force as a kind of capital, which I think makes a great deal of sense, then I would like to see it treated not just in a typical capitalist way, but rather as something to be shared, like an infinite resource, not hoarded or saved like in a bank account. I would like to see this capital treated in ways that are traditionally thought of as feminine, not just from a traditionally masculine perspective. Only if it is put out in the market in all its fullness can it have the power to change the world.

Over centuries men have been afraid of this feminine erotic power and have regulated our work-life so we do not get distracted by it while focusing on goals, careers and success. But if the soft curves of a female colleague can be a distraction, they can be a source of inspiration as well. That's why, in the previous chapter, I challenged my brothers to take responsibility for their behavior when being attracted to their female colleagues. As a woman, it's not your fault when a man gets turned on by you. You should not be forced to cover your natural radiance, to wear trousers, a buttoned-up blouse and flat shoes, so that some guy doesn't go crazy over you. Of course, if this feels natural to you, then you should do it. It might be one of the ways you feel comfortable expressing yourself in the corporate world. But if this

---

57  *Cathrine Hakim, Erotic Capital, Oxford Journal, Volume 26, Number 5, 2010, p. 499-510, http:// www.catherinehakim.org/wp-content/uploads/2011/07/ESR-Erotic-Capital-Oct-2010.pdf (accessed April 2, 2019)*

feels like torture to you and you only do it because your organization asks you to do so, I feel sad about that, and I hope you can find another way to express your feminine radiance. As Perel reminds us, some of these standards are flexible, and all of them are bound by cultural context:

> *In Europe, to sexualize a woman doesn't mean to denigrate her intelligence or competence or authority. Women, therefore, can enjoy expressing their sexuality and being objects of desire, can enjoy their sexual power, even in the workplace, without feeling they're forfeiting their right to be taken seriously as professionals and workers.*[58]

Esther Perel defines erotic energy at work as, *"being alive, focused, present, intentional, curious, expectant and playful."* As much we have a cognitive intelligence or emotional intelligence, we have an erotic intelligence, and it is an important part of us and, like the other intelligences, it can be trained. Perel, it should be noted, is one of many women out there who are encouraging women to develop and increase their erotic intelligence. Others include Catherine Hakim and Kaouthar Darmoni. Darmoni even support women to even embody that intelligence, through her Arabic-inspired "Dance of the Goddesses."

## It Takes Two to Tango

In order for a group to create something together, the various participants all need the ability to lead and to surrender. Leading is the ability to actively hold space for a group, guiding this group through the next steps of an emerging future. Surrender can be seen as a full acceptance to what is present, and a trust

---

58  *Esther Perel, Erotic Intelligence — Reconciling Sensuality and Domesticity, Psychotherapy Networker, May/June 2003, https://www.psychotherapynetworker.org/magazine/article/832/erotic-intelligence (accessed April 2, 2019)*

in following the organic flow of life that emerges in any given moment from a higher intelligence. When you let go and truly give yourself to something greater than yourself, you will possess the full flow of life energy as it presents itself in you and moves through you.

Leading and surrendering are two polarities that can actually work together, synthesizing their unique capacities and becoming a wonderful mode of being. You, as a feminine being, do have a natural ability to surrender to the directional masculine energy. If you cannot give to the masculine polarity the space required for it to guide and direct, the masculine cannot take over the lead, and it might even experience a sense of uselessness. Also, without the masculine taking the lead, you will have nothing to surrender, and you might feel lost and alone.

We, as sentient beings, are neither 100% masculine nor 100% feminine, but always a mix in varying degrees. Both men and women have the ability to lead and to surrender. What I believe we need now is the ability for men to surrender in a masculine way and for women to lead in a feminine way. So my invitation to you is to find a feminine expression of leadership, so the men in your team do not feel mothered, but can grow in their trust in you as a woman who knows the way towards a better future.

Chapter 8

# What Feelings, Emotions and Intuition Have to do with it

*How can one recognize his or her own feelings and emotions, and find more effective ways to manage, express and include these in a working situation? How can one recognize feelings and emotions in others, deal with them and support others to manage them better, themselves?*

In her study *Emotions at Work - Working on Emotions* (2013), Sabine Donauer outlines a trend towards a more dynamic approach to dealing with emotions in the workplace. Donauer begins by exploring how researchers have approached the inner life of workers. To begin with, around 1900 psycho-technical methods emerged (technologies that are intended to influence behavior of the workers and management decisions) which promised to make industrial labor less exhausting and to thereby reduce the workers' revolutionary zeal. By 1925, the new guiding ideas came from characterology and from efforts to build up a "factory community" against class-based solidarity. Around 1940, psychoanalytic models informed new "scientific" theories and approaches to the problems of the labor force, which provided the foundation for the ensuing "Human Relations" paradigm. In turn, the latter was replaced in the 1960s by the Human Resource approach based on motivational theories which had been formulated in the US.

It's interesting to note that, while it was taken for granted around 1900 that workers had a kind of pre-existing tendency to feel joy in work (which could only be troubled by unfavorable working conditions), by the 1970s the Human Resource paradigm was promoting a very different conceptualization: it claimed that job satisfaction was an unstable psychological state which could only temporarily be reached by making the employee master ever newer and more challenging tasks. After fulfilling certain goals at work, new "stretch goals" would have to be found to create a new field for generating positive emotions.[59]

Donauer also writes extensively about current ideas about this topic, some of them based on findings by sociologist Eva Illouz:

> *Intimacy seems to be an indispensable ingredient for efficient and high-performing work in today's working world. Where leaders are empathic, know and understand the personal situation of the employees, where colleagues find sympathy for each other, and bring in their passion for the business, there the coworkers are happy and there is good chance for economic success—so far the picture which results by a view on coaching offers, job ad-*

---

59  Sabine Donauer, *Emotions at Work – Working on Emotions: The Production of Economic Selves in Twentieth-Century Germany*, 2015, https://refubium.fu-berlin.de/handle/fub188/330 (accessed April 2, 2019)

*vertisings, company PR and occupational psycho-
logical studies. If we translate the term 'intimacy'
freely with 'emotional proximity', than this is
asked for seemingly on several levels on the workplace: emotional proximity is rated positively between supervisor and employee (as relationship of
trust and motivation), amongst colleagues (team-
spirit), and in the relation of the individual to their
occupation, which ideally provides fun and contributes to the feeling of self-fulfillment.*[60]

In other words, intimacy is one of the things that helps create worker satisfaction. The old models, about workers' innate
sense of fulfillment, or about stretch goals, are being supplanted
by ideas about how important fundamentally human (intimate)
the relations between employees at all levels are. In a very real
sense, ideas about what makes for a good workplace are empha-
sizing the inner or inward side of things.

## Emotional Intelligence

The inward turn I've outlined above is only part of a more
general trend towards understanding the importance of our
emotional life that has been going on in recent years. Indeed, a
few decades ago, Daniel Goleman, with his bestselling book *Emotional Intelligence*, started a kind of revolution in how we can look
at intelligence, in all its manifestations, including the emotions.
He suggested that we need to think not just about a person's IQ
but also his or her EQ — in other words, not just brainpower but
emotional acuity. According to Goleman, EQ is the capacity to
think intelligently about our emotions and to have our emotions

60  Illouz, Eva, *Cold Intimacies: The Making of Emotional Capitalism*, Contemporary Sociology-a Journal
of Reviews, 2009, https://www.academia.edu/3206428/
Cold_Intimacies_The_Making_of_Emotional_Capitalism (accessed April 2, 2019)

help us learn how to think more intelligently. The first part of this definition clearly involves the ability to regulate one's emotions, to achieve a greater awareness of one's inner self. But emotionally intelligent people also know to regulate others' emotions, and this is an absolutely key part of Goleman's conception of EQ. Numbers and spreadsheets are never the whole story, because much of what goes on even in the most "rational" enterprises involves, at every level and at all times, how we influence each other emotionally. A leader who knows this can be tremendously effective in fixing a bad situation or reinvigorating members of his or her organization, by captivating people, or calming them down. People resonate with people who connect to them emotionally.

Former Morgan Stanley investment banker James A. Runde, in an interview about the importance of emotional intelligence on the career path, gives a good insight into how Goleman's theories might be practically applied in business:

> *What I learned over 40 years is that emotional intelligence is the secret sauce for career success. I say that based on sifting through thousands of promotion decisions and seeing that people struggled not because of their cognitive skills, not because of their work ethic, because everybody has great cognitive skills and great work ethic. But it was either adaptability, collaboration or empathy that caused people to stumble. And there is a way to take your game up on soft skills or emotional intelligence.*[60]

Emotional intelligence is the ability to recognize emotions and understand how they operate, and also the ability to manip-

61 *The Emotional Intelligence Deficit – How It Stifles Careers, Dec. 20 2016, Morgan Stanley investment banker James A. Runde discusses his book on emotional intelligence,* http://knowledge.wharton.upenn.edu/article/the-emotional-intelligence-deficit-how-it-holds-back-so-many-professionals/ *(accessed April 1, 2019)*

ulate or change them. If I have emotional intelligence, I know when the right time is to talk to my boss. I know that my new clients had a terrible flight and lost their luggage and won't be so receptive to my planned presentation, so I comfort them first to calm them down. Or I know that, if I take them to this particular restaurant or I book tickets to this spa, I can shift their emotional state to one in which they are feeling more gratitude towards me and are more likely to listen to me.

Now, this may sound at first like cynical manipulation, but in fact it is simply a way of trying to alleviate an emotional situation that is not conducive to the business at hand, and an attempt to counter the effects of things that have already happened that have nothing to do with that business yet which might easily derail it. Unrelated yet important events that happened prior to a business meeting might cause one of the participants to be far less receptive to ideas which that person might ordinarily be excited about. What Runde is talking about is recognizing this and acting accordingly. He is, in the last analysis, talking about Emotional Intelligence and how to actually apply its principles.

In the decades since Goleman first put forward his theory, experimental evidence strongly suggests that his theory is accurate. For example, across two experiments, researchers have demonstrated that emotional states influence how receptive people are to advice (Gino and Schweitzer, 2008). The focus of these experiments is on incidental emotions, emotions triggered by a prior experience that is irrelevant to the current situation – exactly the kind of scenario Runde speaks of. The authors demonstrate that people who feel incidental gratitude are more trusting and more receptive to advice than people in a neutral emotional state, and people in a neutral state are more trusting and more receptive to advice than people who feel incidental anger. In these experiments, greater receptivity to advice increased accuracy of judgment. People who felt incidental gratitude were more accurate than people in a neutral state, and people in a neutral state were more accurate than people who felt incidental anger. These results offer insight into how people receive advice, and the authors identify conditions under which leaders, policy makers, and advisors might be particularly influential.[62]

> *My intuition was that we often base complicated decisions on how we feel. If I ask you something complicated like, 'Should we hire this person or should we buy this house?' you have to consider a lot of attributes and compare a lot of complex things. So we often use a simple summary statistic, which is how we feel about the job candidate or the house. When we do that, we open ourselves up to the possibility of making a mistake based on emotion.*

In other words, the primary role of emotions in decisions of all kinds needs to be acknowledged and factored into our vision of how people operate in the real world. Rationality isn't everything, and in many cases it may not even be primary. Emotional Intelligence, as Goleman sees it, either works with us or against us in all areas of life. We can either understand ourselves and others better, to foster good relationships of all kinds, or we can flounder in a sea of misunderstood emotionality. The choice is ours.

---

62  Gino, Francesca and Schweitzer, Maurice E., *Blinded by Anger or Feeling the Love: How Emotions Influence Advice Taking*, Journal of Applied Psychology 93, no. 5 (September 2008): 1165–1173.

## Subject-Subject Relationships

Ultimately, emotional intimacy, the goal of this kind of intelligence, rests on relationships with no preexisting definition of who is "in charge." It is a play of equals in a realm of possibilities that are dictated by neither party, but by both as the situation unfolds. The conditions for emotional intimacy are based primarily on the fact that neither party is the object or subject, but that the subjectivity of the self or the other can vary, as each subject relates to the uniqueness of the other(s). This strengthens the perception that the other matters and makes a difference. The precondition is that each is attuned to and in tune with the embodied subjectivity of the other. It involves caring for the other (Bologh 1990).

This kind of thinking goes back at least as far as the thinking of Existentialist philosopher Jean-Paul Sartre. In his *Being and Nothingness* Sartre speaks of the self as free and constantly changing, and about the Other as another self, which can be seen as another transcending subject.[63] Thus, in interaction between self and the Other we can find a constant learning process in either consensus or conflict. Any reaction which originates in the free, responsible, and deciding center of the person is influenced by their feelings, their emotions and their observations of the outer world, creating a kind of inherent bias based on these inner states and perceptions. When we interact with objects, every reaction is determined by the action producing it, by the nature of the object acted upon, and by the universal context within which the action occurs. But in encounters with sentient beings, it's crucial to realize that they are not fully determined because they are essentially subjects, not objects. Since every individual is free to

---

63  Jean-Paul Sartre, *Being and Nothingness* (New York: WSP, 1956).

decide what he or she will do, that person's reaction is only partly calculable, and ultimately undetermined. This creates the living reciprocity of a subject-to-subject relationship. We act or speak, but we never know with certainty beforehand how we will react to the action of the other, or vice versa. Every moment of a living relationship is characterized by an element of indeterminacy. My own continual transcendence means that, by necessity, I cannot know now what I will be in the next moment. And I certainly cannot know the full reality of another person at any moment.

Seeing the uniqueness and constant change in another person creates, almost automatically, a genuine care for that person, and sometimes a feeling of being one with him or her. If that other person is not separated from me, it is impossible *not* to bring love and care towards that person, which creates emotional intimacy and underlies the importance of the other in one's own transcendence, in one's own being. Every interaction is an interchange of feelings, impressions, imaginations and projections between two or more interrelated selves, and this creates an intersubjective field which can have its own texture or taste. When this aspect of inter-subjectivity is observed and named, it becomes another tangible factor in the transcendence of the individuals involved.

## Can You Feel It?

When speaking about emotions I find it important to differentiate between the somatic process, or what happens in the physical body, and feelings, which are more abstract than tangible, and which cannot be measured. Strictly speaking, emotions are instinctive stimulus-response patterns which can be observed by others and objectively registered through measurements of Galvanic Skin Response (GSR), Blood Flow, Facial Expression, Body Language and Brain EEG Patterns. Feelings, on the other hand, can be explained by every individual differently. Two people can have the same basic feeling but label it with different names. Of course, typically when we speak of the emotions, we mean both emotions and feelings – the full scope of the inner life. But it's important to take the time to tease out these differences, if we are to really understand how to work with these forces within us.

Interestingly, in managerial discourse we often use bodily metaphors having to do with physical reactions and emotions. We speak of such things as "gut reactions," or of becoming aware that there's "tension in the air," or of people being "abrasive," or of problems starting to "rub" or "grate" on oneself, or of feelings of "heaviness" when things go badly. And sometimes we name feelings directly as sadness, fear, joy, anger, or shame (which can be difficult for people, when starting to strengthen our social-emotional competencies). When we are in the grips of an emotion, often we cannot do anything other than go through it. We can do this in a conscious way, rather than just blindly "pushing through it," if we have done some training before. In the moment we sense a feeling we can look at it, name it, give it a color, a texture or temperature, or we can even delve deeply into it and observe how it changes in the process.

However, as researcher Joe Shirley points out, we are far from being able to map such things, objectively:

> *In the current state of affairs in psychology we have no such observational method with which to observe the actual, felt experience of feeling, mood, or*

*emotion. We do have tools by which to derive im-*
*ages of the brain in action, but these are limited in*
*their usefulness by our inability to correlate what*
*we observe with precise descriptions of the actual,*
*conscious experience that accompanies these im-*
*ages. We have no way of comparing the experience*
*of one feeling state to another in the same person,*
*let alone between one person and another.*[64]

I think Shirley's point here is an absolutely crucial one. We have developed machines that can show us patterns of electrical or chemical activity in the brain, but how those patterns correspond to felt experience is a frontier that has yet to be explored, one which may not be understood in our lifetimes. We can see a map of what is happening inside the brain, so to speak, but this is not the same thing as what is happening in the mind, in the inner being. Many people in the field of consciousness studies consider these snapshots of brain activity to be of something "external," since they do not get at the inward, lived nature of the subjective experiences happening while that snapshot is being taken. Ultimately, when we look at a brain scan, we are not looking at anything having to do with emotions or feelings but something happening in the brain itself *while* we are having those emotions or feelings.

To try to get at the inner states that brain scans cannot access, Shirley has developed a method called *Feeling Path Mapping*, designed to align one's felt state to the ideal state of wholeness which the body is trying to achieve by having such feelings. This, in turn, allows people to integrate their feelings into their daily lives. In situations where one feels powerless, imbalanced or dis-

---

64  Joe Shirley, *The Feeling Path - Restoring the Natural Wisdom of the Feeling Mind (Preview Edition)*, Oct 2011.

tressed, his three steps of mapping, moving and living are extremely useful.

> *Mapping allows you to tease apart the various feeling states that drive your pattern. Moving reconnects each feeling to the experience of wholeness it was originally trying to achieve. Once feelings have been shifted, they are able to function once again as accurate feedback about the state of balance in your life.*
>
> *When you systematically run the entire set of feeling states which drive any challenging pattern through the three steps of The Feeling Path, you will experience a wonderful liberation. The pattern will no longer own you. You will be free, and you will find yourself spontaneously making new choices, taking new paths, closing some old doors and opening new ones.*

Shirley's approach (which is a technology, in the original and fullest sense of the word) offers one way to utilize feelings as they come up in the way the body originally intended them to be used, all in the service of greater wholeness. It is that greater wholeness that we all should be looking for, and we should strive to find it in the way we interact with each other in all walks of life, including the workplace.

Chapter 9

# The Power of Collaboration

........................................................................

*Why is collaboration so important and what does it require to even transform it into a co-creation? How can the mental and emotional proximity be a force to support better collaboration?*

I believe nobody ever achieved any great projects alone. Of course, to design and manufacture some jewelry from gems and sell them at the local craft market, or to bring some other art or craft to the market – perhaps you might not need anybody else to do that. But if you want to build a bigger business and sell your creations on a larger scale, especially if it is a national or global one, you need plenty of other people to help you organize the whole supply and distribution chain. Whether you see your stakeholders as your subjects or as allies on the path to success strongly influences how you will be received in the market, not to mention your health, relationships, and your personal image. If you treat your fellow human beings as gold you will become gold yourself – that's a simple universal formula.

A study carried out by Cornerstone on Demand (2013) found that, among 1,029 American working adults, 38 percent felt that there was not enough collaboration in the workplace.[65] To try to understand the significance of this number, one might imagine having this percentage in a single organization, with almost 40 percent of the employees unhappy with the way collaboration happens (or doesn't happen) in their work environment. This is far too great a percentage! Moreover, participants of this study also named factors that would encourage collaboration, including positive recognition of input (50%), encouragement from senior staff (41%), and the ability to easily share input with different departments (33%). This study clearly shows that individuals who are unhappy with the nature of the collaborative aspect of their workplaces are already thinking about how to improve it. But it's possible their voices aren't being heard precisely because of the lack of collaboration they complain of. Perhaps it's time to for someone to listen.

Though a big part of modern collaboration is based on technology, personal interaction is still needed for creativity to flow. Now, I am aware that even in virtual communication, in video conferences or even in writing, sexual feelings can sometimes emerge, whether or not the participants have met each other before in person. In other words, even supposedly "impersonal" forms of communication are not necessarily free of sexual aspects. However, rather than tackle this topic in detail here, I would like to focus on the interpersonal form of collaboration that happens when people are together in the same room, at least from time to time. In such settings, if we allow feelings and emotions to arise, if we make them visible and share them with

---

65 Cornerstone On Demand, State of the Workplace Productivity Report 2013, https://www.cornerstoneondemand.com

others in the room, it can build a safe space where a collaboration based on trust can be created. Let me explain.

To begin with, collaborating means working alongside someone to achieve something together and have a shared ownership of the outcome. It is one step closer than cooperation, where the partners enable each other to do something, like providing information or resources they wouldn't otherwise have. So collaboration needs a more proactive participation and can be very messy in the beginning, especially when the various stakeholders have diverse cultural backgrounds or radically different kinds of experience. Working together like this requires respect for other people's roles, thoughts and skills, and it requires at least some vulnerability, and the will to give up control and be open to new perspectives. With broad diversity the likelihood for tensions is higher, but the probability of greater inventions and bolder ideas increases as well.

With this said, I will now look at some of the underlying factors involved in face-to-face collaboration and see what we can learn from looking closely at such factors.

## Growing Together

Even though there is a rising separatism and nationalism in politics, we can also see increasing collaboration in many other areas all over the world: co-working, co-learning, co-branding, co-sourcing, co-housing, co-gardening, co-parenting. People like to share knowledge, resources, technology and power with each other, some because they see greater potential in working together, some to save money, some out of a longing for community, and some simply because these days it's considered cool.

*"Humans can unfold their potential only in community,"* says German brain researcher Gerald Hüther. And he points out that therefore *"they need to meet as subjects, and this is only possible in non-hierarchical structures."*[66] He thinks one cannot unfold one's potential in communities with a culture of all-against-all, ruled by merciless competition. Competition, after all, tends to be about extrinsic rewards, about winning or losing something, with the winner at the top of a kind of built-in hierarchical structure. There are, after all, many other ways people can interact with each other besides competition: they can collaborate, of course, or play, or fall in love. Many if not most of these involve intrinsic rewards, which is to say they are done for the sake of participating in the activity.

From early childhood, when we are first told how to do things (for example, how to build a proper tower from play blocks), we begin to lose our intrinsic motivation for top performance. As soon as the motivation becomes one of doing a thing the way we are told by our superiors, as soon as the motivation is extrinsic, coming down from above, we are more concerned with doing it right than doing it well. But we are born with the urge to achieve higher goals, as that's the Eros in all of us, but it gets lost when we are treated like objects by our parents or in school, and when we are treated as if we were all the same. Most communities we grow up in are based on fear, misery, need and the preservation of vested rights, and the question is whether or not we can manage to build communities where people can grow, both with and towards each other.

Imagine if each of us would be able to evolve into an integral human being, beginning in our early years, and when we would

---

66 *Interview with Gerald Hüther for Deutschlandradio Kutur, Nur gemeinsam sind wir stark, Februar 21, 2017, http://www.deutschlandradiokultur.de/hirnforscher-gerald-huether-nur-gemeinsam-sind-wir-stark.1008.de.html?dram:article_id=379479_1487836132 (accessed April 2, 2019)*

reach that age where were going to step into the professional world we could bundle up all our individual potentials and turn it into some kind of powerful innovative machinery or technology. Imagine if we could bring together our most evolved selves and compassionate souls to solve today's world challenges, and if everybody could have the opportunity to become an independent kind of leader, even those who were never inspired during public education or were born in poverty. According to Hüther, such a scenario requires the conditions which awaken the intrinsic enthusiasm to grow beyond ourselves. Mutual encouragement and inspiration can help us to explore all the great possibilities in this world. Growing together in communities makes us happy and independent beings, no longer so susceptible to negativity and fear.[67]

With all this intrinsic growth energy and need for knowledge and novelty, *"what matters is the intention with which we hunger after it."* The kind of responsiveness and adaptability the world demands from us right now has to be generated from within. *"It requires a shift from acquisition of something out there to a developmental mindset that seeks feedback and learning in order to drive self-development."* The enthusiasm and freshness through which we can perceive solutions gets lost when instead we spend our time taking on too many facts and relying on models from books or from top-down leadership. Our inner knowing might be, as Rebecca Colwell puts it

> *held back from sensing what is emerging in the moment from the whole subtle field in which we are participating with a question much bigger than any one of us can possibly answer. Otto Scharmer*

67 Gerald Hüther, *Nur mit Begeisterung lernen wir wirklich gut*, April 30, 2011, https://www.welt.de/debatte/article13309602/Nur-mit-Begeisterung-lernen-wir-wirklich-gut.html (accessed April 2, 2019)

*calls this a type of listening which 'originates out-side the world of our preconceived notions.' The shift we are living today is from a world where in-dividuals had answers to one where the collective, collaborative process holds the answer. Through emergent collaboration, we create new space for productivity and generativity.*[68]

Somehow, the problem seems to be that we can't really listen to each other, and that we treat each other as means towards ends, while the solution is collaboration, real collaboration that encourages individuals to explore their own unique ways towards goals that are possible only when working intimately with equally-empowered colleagues.

## Co-Creation Requires the Willingness to Learn

Of course, many if not most of the challenges we, as individuals, are facing every day don't really need much collaboration: they can be solved individually or under supervision. The messy process of real collaboration can be a challenge in itself for most people, so they tend to reduce it to a minimum in their life. It needs strong enthusiasm and commitment to the task to be really open and ready for a constructive collaboration. The more emotionally engaged all the stakeholders are, the more transformational power the collaboration has and the more it can become a true co-creation, in the best sense.

---

68  Rebecca Colwell, *The mindset of collaboration, Ten Directions*, July 3, 2014, https://tendirections.com/mindset-collaboration-one-thing-cant-fit-wagon/ (accessed April 2, 2019)

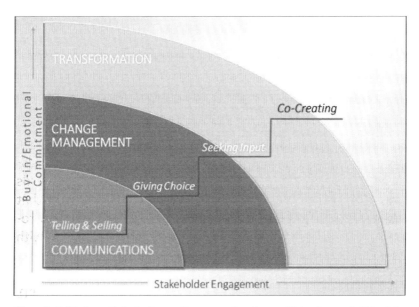

*Figure 3: Fall in love with the problems – the more emotionally committed and engaged all the stake-holders are, the more transformational is the collaboration. (Source: collaborateup.com)*

The more adaptive and transformative potential the mission we are on has, the more substantial the collaboration of a committed group will be. An adaptive challenge has *"multiple possible causes and therefore multiple possible solutions and solving them involves enrolling multiple stakeholders without the ease and benefit of pure power-and-authority relationships."*[69] Too often it happens that we fall in love with our own solution instead of the challenge we are facing. *"We can create a space for true co-creation by stepping back, really understanding the problem, and investing our egos in solving it – and not in pushing for our pre-conceived solution."*

To really understand a task, it can help to look at it from different perspectives, as suggested in a previous chapter. And per-

---

69  *Collaboration Tip #2: Fall in love with the problem, http://collaborateup.com/collaboration-nation/ collaboration-tip-2-fall-in-love-with-problems (accessed April 2, 2019)*

haps the simplest way to gain understanding is to look at things from both an inner and outer perspective, and from an individual and collective vantage point. For an individual, it can be difficult to take these various perspectives, but when people with a diversity of attitudes and viewpoints collaborate, the bandwidth of solutions becomes bigger and it is difficult not to look at things from various perspectives. Someone in the group will see a part of the solution that no one else has seen, and, once this has been seen by that one set of eyes, the others cannot help but see it as well.

When we take principles from dialogue and apply them to collaboration, then we can become communities dedicated to growth and development. We can use principles like active listening, being interested in and recognizing other worldviews, acknowledging and validating the insights of individual members and building on these, being more interested in co-creating a positive vision for the future rather than coping with the mistakes of the past. The possibilities are basically limitless.

## Collaborators in Dialogue

In writing about dialogue, I want to begin by saying that I am not limiting my ideas to a literal dialogue, a talk between two individuals. As I have suggested in the previous paragraphs, I am interested in theories about dialogue that apply to larger groups as well, ideas that have to do with the interplay of speaking and listening that honors however many speakers are present in an exchange. Specifically, in thinking about dialogue, I have in mind the management style called Dialogic Leadership, developed in the 1990's at the Hardenberg Institute for Cultural Science in Heidelberg, Germany. This approach is now practiced in many companies and NGOs, and it works with the question, *"how can as many people as possible in an organisation reach an individual entrepreneurial disposition, and how can they have a fruitful collaboration from there?"* Autonomous personalities are taken seriously and supported, in a way that is not dependent on their position and role in the organization. They shape their own tasks with regard for the whole, without predefined job descriptions. It's not about technical or social skills, but it's about encouraging an approach in which creativity and originality are highly valued, just like the dignity of the individual, and the responsibility for joint action.[70]

In an article titled "Leadership Is a Conversation" (HBR, June 2012), Karl-Martin Dietz and Friedrich von Hardenberg have identified four elements of organizational dialogue which reflect *"the essential attributes of interpersonal conversation: intimacy, interactivity, inclusion, and intentionality."*[71] Their advocacy of a dialogic method that is highly inclusive is perfectly in line with the general approach I am taking throughout this book. Indeed, their article is about intimacy in collaboration, and it points to my original idea, that *"personal conversation flourishes to the degree that the participants stay close to each other, figuratively as well as literally."* As globalization, new technologies, and changes in value creation have sharply reduced the efficacy of a purely directive, top-down model of leadership, the authors suggest that the old command-and-control approach to management must give way to a corporate communication that is more dynamic and more sophisticated.

> *Where conversational intimacy prevails, those with decision-making authority seek and earn the trust (and hence the careful attention) of those who*

---

70  Karl-Martin Dietz, Dialogische Führung, Friedrich von Hardenberg Institut for Cultural Science, Heidelberg, Germany, http://www.hardenberginstitut.de/de/dialogische-fuehrung-dialogische-kultur.html (accessed April 2, 2019)

71  Boris Groysberg and Michael Slind, Leadership is a Conversation, Harvard Business Review, June 2012, https://hbr.org/2012/06/leadership-is-a-conversation (accessed April 2, 2019)

166

> *work under that authority. They do so by cultivat-
> ing the art of listening to people at all levels of the
> organization and by learning to speak with em-
> ployees directly and authentically. Physical prox-
> imity between leaders and employees isn't always
> feasible. Nor is it essential. What is essential is
> mental or emotional proximity.*[72]

Mental and emotional proximity is key for a collaboration to become true co-creation. Not just the ideas of the individual participants come together, but, through the closeness and openness they have with each other, a kind of "third" entity or intelligence emerges, a group intelligence, itself informing and fertilizing the process. It is actually a little like having a child together, but in this case the child will be the great new vision the collaborators will give birth to.

What is most important in creating this mental and emotional proximity is a willingness to really show up, and to be transparent with one's ideas, feelings and doubts. This builds up a trusting safe space, as long the openness and transparency are mutual. Naturally, when people are not used to doing that, it can help to begin by setting aside certain times to self-consciously practice what it is to genuinely share whatever comes up while working openly in pairs or groups. And, of course, training in how to do this would be useful. Later in the process of collaboration it will become totally normal to be in that sharing mode, even during a meeting about a task, or when there are tensions between the collaborators.

To reach a point where such collaboration is natural, it needs to be nurtured carefully, and to do that, it needs to be understood

---

72 *Boris Groysberg and Michael Slind, 2012.*

consciously. These, I think, are goals that all businesses should have as we move forward into an uncertain, exciting future.

Chapter 10

# From Purpose to Co-Creation

*The Why is not about making money—that's a result. The Why is a purpose, cause or belief. Your Why is the very reason you exist.*

- Simon Sinek

To build up enthusiasm for co-creating something with others requires a strong Why. As in: Why am I doing what I am doing?

Even if you don't clearly know the answer, just asking yourself the question can help to connect you to your purpose. This purpose could be something small, or it could be the general purpose of your work or even of your life. When you know the Why, this inspires others around you – those who have the same cause for doing what they do – to connect with you and to work with you to make it happen. As Simon Sinek points out, employees of companies who know the company's Why *"are more productive and innovative, and the feeling they bring to work attracts other peo-*

---

73  Simon Sinek, Start With the Why, 2009

*ple eager to work there as well.*"[73] Having a clear purpose helps to create clarity, which in turn helps people work together in a collaborative environment. If the purpose itself is shared, this will empower all stakeholders to follow the path to fulfill it, and it helps to create a collaborative process that includes fewer discussions that are basically just about finding consensus or resolving hidden tensions. All of that is, in a sense, already done, because of the shared purpose everyone has right from the get-go.

In groups it might be hard to find this shared purpose, as sometimes people with different worldviews and ideas come together who seem to share very little. Often it is one person who has a vision and brings people together to collaborate in order to achieve whatever the aim of the vision is. As long this person can let go of claiming ownership of the vision, the vision can flourish within the group. In other words, the role of the leader is to create an environment in which great ideas can happen, not to supply those ideas, exclusively, and then delegate responsibility for carrying them out. When the people in the crew are allowed to do the needed tasks and take over responsibility and leadership in their own areas, real co-creation can happen. Co-creation is not a leader-follower process.

## Purpose as a Higher Calling

Finding your purpose can either be an active process, like asking questions in meditative self-inquiry, going on a vision quest, or doing one of these retreats where you spend some days in darkness, to connect with your inner knowing. Or some people just embrace gratefully one life challenge after the next and discover over time that there is a pattern underneath it all which might lead them to discover their life's purpose. Whichever way you go, accepting your purpose is the same thing as following a higher calling, and it can even be seen as a spiritual journey.

Of course, talking about spirituality at the workplace is very similar to talking about intimacy, or sexuality — it is often a taboo. Having a purpose can really be something spiritual, when you feel an inner calling and you cannot explain why you are doing what you are doing. It just feels good, and your heart is burning for it, and you feel drawn to it and you just do what is necessary to follow the path, fulfilling your purpose. In truth, this is very much an example of something driven by Eros – in the fullest sense of that word, rather than the more limited sense implied by the modern use of "erotic." It is a deeply passionate enterprise, and it is truly driven by forces within us that we might call spiritual. It is described in exactly this way by Sergio Rodriguez-Castillo, summed up neatly in the following passage:

> *Spirituality has been called the last corporate taboo (Kendall, 2012). Many businesses are still hesitant to use spirituality related terminology, instead going for more neutral terms like "value-based", "value-driven" when referring to higher (aka spiritual) values. Notwithstanding such reluctance, corporations have evolved and —terminology aside— we can observe a clear progression: From hiring "hands" for the production line a hundred years ago to hiring also "heads," as companies became more dependent on creativity and innovation. Nowadays, as emotional intelligence has become more appreciated, companies are also hiring*

> *"hearts" (motivation, meaning, alignment), allowing —even encouraging— people to discuss and express their feelings at work (Hatala, 2004). As this tendency to invite more and more aspects of employees into their workplace continues, it is only natural that the next step is to bring in spirituality to properly address all the needs of a healthy human being.*[74]

In other words, we can see that what we can call Spiritual Intelligence (SQ) has become more important in recent years, as companies are hiring people based on such qualities.

It is no surprise, then, that over the last twenty years or so people have begun to research this phenomenon. Following Daniel Goleman, whose groundbreaking book made Emotional Intelligence (EQ) popular in 1995, two years later Danah Zonar coined the term Spiritual Intelligence in his publication *ReWiring the Corporate Brain*. More recently, Cindy Wiggelsworth used it in the title of her book *SQ21: The Twenty-One Skills of Spiritual Intelligence*, and Ken O'Donnell used the term prominently in his book *Endoquality: The Emotional and Spiritual Dimensions of the Human Being in Organizations*. Even Stephen Covey has said that spiritual intelligence is *"the central and most fundamental of all the intelligences, because it becomes the source of guidance for the others."* Clearly, then, this is not a phenomenon that only people on the fringe of the business world are concerned with. In one way or another, whether it is called spirituality or something else, the spiritual dimension is becoming increasingly important in the corporate sphere.

Indeed, an important recent study, *The Impact of Spiritual Intelligence on Organizational Performance*, revealed that spiritual

---

[74] Sergio Rodriguez-Castillo, *Spirituality in the Workplace, CIIS Public Program*, January 25, 2018, https://www.ciispod.com/#/sergio-rodriguez-castillo/ (accesses April 2, 2019)

intelligence plays a positive and significant role in the quality of work.[75] Based on the results of this study we can see that spiritual intelligence increases organizational performance, while age, gender, education and organizational culture act as moderators on their relationship. This research might motivate managers to try to find ways to enhance the spiritual intelligence of their employees to increase efficiency and effectiveness.

With higher spiritual Intelligence one has the ability to

- comprehend bigger contexts intuitively
- foster hopes and visions for a desired future
- recognize windows of opportunity rapidly and use them for a personal and professional benefit
- activate the senses for contexts in inner and outer nature
- reflect on one's own thoughts and the meaning of one's actions, to explore new solutions for the survival of oneself and others
- create ecological niches and fill them completely.[76]

According to Wigglesworth, Spiritual Intelligence is *"the ability to behave with wisdom and compassion while maintaining inner and outer peace regardless of the situation."* In her book, she advocates both a faith-friendly and faith-neutral model to develop one's own SQ. She refers to it the way a physical therapist might refer to weightlifting and training different muscles, as a kind of exercise. In this case, the exercise is designed to shift our focus away from the ego and towards a more loving and peaceful Higher Self. Wigglesworth even offers an assessment to find out

75  Muhammad Shaukat Malik, Sana Tariq, Impact of Spiritual Intelligence on Organizational Performance, International Review of Management and Marketing, 2016, 6(2), 289-297
76  Mathias Schüz, Warum Topmanager «spirituelle Intelligenz» nötig haben, HR-Today, November 25, 2015, http://www.hrtoday.ch/de/article/warum-topmanager-spirituelle-intelligenz-notig-haben (accessed April 2, 2019)
77  Cindy Wigglesworth, SQ21-The Twenty One Skills of Spiritual Intellogence, 2012, https://deepchange.com/

where on the spiritual line of development one stands and what is needed to support the training.[77]

## Co-Creation of Higher Selves

If you have a good connection with your inner calling and Higher Self, the commitment to co-creation with others will become stronger. Wanting to collaborate with others is one of the truest, most organic results of having an increased inner awareness. When your thoughts become more world-centric, when you begin to really envision and comprehend more of the complexity of this world, and when you open up further, to a cosmic (or cosmos-centric) perspective, then you will invite and recognize the intuitive force and collective consciousness that inspires other stakeholders in the ventures you are involved in even more deeply.

Many authors see a natural development towards collaborative economies, participatory leadership and co-creation in the future. Marx-Hubbard, for example, has been speaking about it for almost 20 years. Jeremiah Owyang, founder of Silicon Valley-based Crowd Companies, spoke in a talk at Google about the collaborative economy, seeing it as *"an economic model where creation, ownership, and access are shared between people and corporations."* Fredrik Laloux writes of it in his book Reinventing Organisations:

> *It's conceivable that in the future the evolutionary purpose, rather than the organization, will become the entity around which people gather. A specific purpose will attract people and organizations in*

---

*78 Frederic Laloux, Reinventing Organisations, 2014, p. 719 e-book fluid and changing constellations, according to the need of the moment.*[78]

The top-down hierarchical structure of corporations as we know them will have to change, so that we can organize ourselves around shared ideas and shared purposes. This makes a lot of sense, once we realize that co-creation is a process that can increase the innovative potential of a team or an organization.

What's more, this process can involve any number of stakeholders, whether it's just your team members or the whole organization, or your business colleagues in other organizations, or even customers and potential clients in the greater community. It's a fluid process which can include a fluid number of participants. It can be a process in a workshop where, within a certain time frame, you invite other people outside your team, or it can be a continuing commitment of long duration. Every participant is free to stay, and every participant is equally free to leave, if the commitment is not so strong for a given time. The clearer the shared purpose and the stronger the commitment, the more connection and trust can flow between the stakeholders, and the more power the collaboration will have. As envisioned by the people at Noomap:

*In a co-creative eco-system, there is a shift away from linear, disconnected forms of organisation towards interconnected network-based approaches. Co-creators synchronise around synergised intentions, dreams, goals, skills, needs, resources and passions for a window in time to share their gifts and then fluidly reorganise once they have realised their visions. This creates an infinite and dynamic*

> *loop of self-rewarding action, resource-sharing and gifting, where the creator is free to explore unlimited possibilities. Our currency becomes one of trust rather than material exchange.*[79]

I can see this kind of co-creation as a form of surrendering to something greater than myself, but in a way where I get to keep my values and make a real contribution to the whole; it is not surrendering in the old way, where I simply become an instrument of the organization in exchange for a salary, it is surrendering to a shared vision that is greater than any single individual involved.

It's important, at this point, to acknowledge the fact that receiving and acting on intuitive insights from a higher or collective intelligence is only possible if the Ego steps back a bit. Manifesting this insight and taking action on it can only come out of a more inclusive position, one where all stakeholders have space, not just the leaders, and where the work is done without exploiting or thwarting anyone involved. Admittedly, sometimes bringing everybody into the discussion and finding consensus can be tiring, but as long as a majority of the team is burning with the desire to create a prototype, the others can still support them and be constructive sparring partners.

79  *Noomap, Synergistic Co-Creation, http://noomap.info/synergistic-co-creation/ (accessed April 2, 2019)*

Chapter 11

# Toolbox and Practical Exercises

........................................

In the previous chapters I mentioned a few methods which might be helpful to bring more intimacy, sincerity, integrity and trust into the workplace. A daylong or multi-day workshop can be a good start to ignite such a process, but in my experience it is better to make it a practice, to exercise whatever method or tool one is using regularly, and as often as possible, in order to create the space where transformation can happen.

## Dialogue

For organizations that would like to change their internal communication style, I suggest, to begin the process, that the entire team should go to a good communications workshop for at least a whole day. If that isn't possible and only the team leaders can go, hopefully they can transmit the knowledge to their colleagues. However, if the goal is better communication for all, perhaps all of the team should be involved right from the get-go.

178

I think it's important that, if at all possible, the entire team has the experience first-hand.

Dialogue, as a self-conscious practice, is based primarily on the art of deep listening. But in common practice they do most of the talking and not a great deal of listening. That is, traditional leaders are often experts in a certain field, and so they know the field better than the others and are therefore the ones being listened to rather than doing the listening. They talk, and talk, and talk, and the others do very little talking. But for mutual understanding and more intimacy in collaboration to happen, leaders need to have open minds and hearts, and this can be developed through listening, not just to the words spoken, but also to what is being transmitted between the lines, so to speak. The space between the people in conversation, the dynamics and energy in the room — these kinds of things gain greater significance in an environment where the leaders listen as well as speak. Over time, if the participants in dialogue are practicing self-conscious dialogue skills, the words themselves come more and more from the heart, instead of just the brain, and the practitioners can also become increasingly aware of what is happening below or beyond the words themselves.

There are different forms of dialogue used in the field of organizational development. One of the most popular is based on the work of David Bohm, a form which encourages *"a freely flowing group conversation in which participants attempt to reach a common understanding, experiencing everyone's point of view fully, equally and nonjudgementally."*[80] This "Bohmian dialogue" is not about reaching a certain goal or decision, but rather a simple way of exploring and learning. Using Bohmian dialogue, an organization can have

---

80  https://en.m.wikipedia.org/wiki/Bohm_Dialogue

meetings that don't have an agenda or a fixed objective, to create a "free space" for something new to happen. In this method, a "talking stick" (or sometimes a stone) is often put in the center of the circle, and every participant picks up this stick when he or she intends to speak. This way nobody talks over another person, and each person is clearly a speaker at one time and a listener at other times. After having spoken, the speaker puts the talking stick back in the center, and the next speaker begins only after he or she has taken up the stick. This causes the conversation to slow down and makes space for short pauses between comments.

Peter Senge, dialogue specialist, renowned author and senior lecturer at MIT, recommends a type of dialogue based on Bohm's principles that is a key part of his strategy to help groups become *"learning organizations"*.[81] Together with William Isaacs, another MIT lecturer, Senge has developed "Generative Dialogue," a special "creative" dialogue where new ideas and thoughts are generated by building on the statements of the speakers across four distinct stages of dialgue. These four stages are: 1. Shared Monologue, 2. Skillful Discussion, 3. Reflective Dialogue (which is approximately Bohm's idea of dialogue), and 4. Generative Dialogue, which builds on the three others and tries to emphasize the creative aspect of deep dialogue. This approach is also used by Otto Scharmer and others at the Presencing Institute.

## Transparent Communication and Non-Violent Communication (NVC)

Another useful kind of dialogue is Non-Violent Communication (NVC), which was developed by psychologist Marshall Rosenberg. NVC teaches people to suspend projections, and not

---

81  Peter Senge, *The Fifth Discipline*, 1990

to blame others when strong emotions are triggered. If, for example, I am upset by something another person says, I begin to express my anger by really recognizing that it's my anger. It may be that what was said would not anger another person, and the fact that it did anger me may have more to do with me than it has to do with what was said. Recognizing and honoring this "owning" of one's own experience is one of the hallmarks of NVC. Followers of NVC always try to realize that the responsibility for one's feeling is always one's own, and they try to express their feelings and state their needs in a respectful and peaceful way.

Another extremely useful kind of dialogue is Transparent Communication, which was developed by Thomas Huebl. Transparent Communication is an empathic form of communication based on NVC, but includes an additional level, the transpersonal perspective. Transparent Communication recognizes that the point of view is always shifting, and it always strives to include an awareness not just of the individual people involved but also of the space that surrounds them. Without this transpersonal aspect one can be completely bound to one's own perspective, and the view through one's own eyes doesn't necessarily change. Huebl's model tries to frame dialogue so that change is possible and to open new doors to a more comprehensive perspective about our lives.

For example, according to this theory our focus on our individual needs and goals has been strongly ingrained into us by our conditioning, our preferences, our habits, and even our most basic assumptions about the world. We experience the world through the lens of our inner conditioning – a conditioning that didn't necessarily arise from our own needs but from the family and culture we were born into. This lens focuses our attention and limits our view of reality. If we strip ourselves of this lens, we will perceive more of the dynamics of life that exist beyond our own habits of thought, and this allows us to see into other people's worlds and to increasingly experience others as if from the inside. We recognize that we don't meet people themselves so much as the realities in which these people live, and this creates a deep compassion and a new kind of comprehension.

Transparent Communication is a way of life, ultimately, one in which different levels of consciousness are included and given equal attention, as various levels of development and intelligence. It requires us to engage in an experiential investigation of life and to see the world as a form of interchange. We relate directly to each other instead of dealing with the symptoms of our increasingly outmoded ways of dealing with each other. This creates a high degree of clarity and fosters authentic expression and a higher collective intelligence.

There are four key factors that characterize Transparent Communication:

**First, there is the recognition of inner spaces of experience**, that each person lives in her own individually colored world. Our experience of the world is filtered by our belief systems, our conditioning, and even energies and potentials that we have chosen to deny in ourselves. They influence the perception of the present moment.

**Another key factor is the open relational space.** Whenever we contract or narrow the shared space of communication, we reduce the potential of the present moment and our mutual creativity. In such moments we often feel separated from the other person. Here we want to open up this space, to inhabit an increasingly expanding space where we meet each other.

**And this brings us to the next key factor, the expansion of our subtle energetic awareness.** The more that all available information happening within the current moment is visible to us, the more transparent other people become to us, and the deeper our sympathy and compassion is for them.

**Finally, there is what Huebl calls the authentic answer to the Now.** Transparent Communication needs authentic expression, all the impulses which emerge in the current moment. Each kind of energy and power in us which cannot come to life and find expression will filter our awareness. When we manage to allow the free, authentic expression in connection with the whole, no vital energy will accumulate in us, but instead it will come forward into the conversation.

## Circling (Authentic Relating)

Another practice that encourages a deeper kind of listening and relating to others is Circling. Sometimes known as Authentic Relating, this practice has become quite popular in the US and Europe during the last few years. It's a process where the participants go into a kind of collective mindfulness meditation, starting by sharing what's present in the current moment and trying to stay as rooted as possible in what is happening in the present. Sharing what sensations are noticed right now and what one's personal experience is right now, on the emotional and the physical level can connect the participants strongly.

Circling can be done in a one-on-one setting or in groups of various sizes sitting together in a circle. There is no goal, and nothing has to be achieved, which can be very liberating, especially for people who often feel lots of pressure to be doing something, or to behave in certain prescribed ways. In this process people show up as they are, that's why it is also called authentic relating. This can be frightening at first, for some people, as we are so often used to playing a role for other people.

I experienced Circling for the first time at a conference in Denver and I liked it from the beginning, so I brought it to Switzerland, where until today more than 250 people have done an introduction workshop or came to our immersion weekends. Some of them did an intensive training together and are now experimenting with bringing this practice into their professional environments.

Circling can be used for team building as well for meetings to check how certain topics are impacting the people in the group. If someone says, for example, "that doesn't feel good to me," somebody else can ask to hear more about this feeling. A felt tension about a decision, once it is acknowledged and explored, can help in finding a better way to implement the decision. If a decision does not feel good for the stakeholders, why should it be implemented? Feelings are sometimes good metrics for finding a solution, and they have to be considered, as if they were just like empirical data.

When I do Circling the way I learned it from the leaders of Circling Europe, I always bring the following five principles to the awareness of the participants. These principles are guidelines to keep in mind when doing this practice.

1. **Commitment to connection** - This principle is an invitation to increase the level of commitment you

have to staying in connection with whatever is arising between you and other people. This does not
mean you have to stay in difficult situations at all
cost, but with more commitment than usual you can
stay longer and even be able to share your disagreement or dissatisfaction in relation with others. This
might connect everyone more, and people who do it
can leave with less disappointment, because they
have resolved things, or tried to, in connection with
the others.

2. **Owning your experience** - This principle is about
communicating your most truthful experience in the
moment. It is about recognizing that the experience
I have is my own experience, and my reaction to
what someone else says is precisely my reaction,
and it is not totally dependent on what that other
person said.

Some simple linguistic examples will help to illustrate this:

> "You're being aggressive" puts the focus on the
> other, whereas "I'm feeling fear" keeps the focus
> on the person feeling the feeling.

> We can also see this if we compare a statement
> like "You betrayed me" with "I feel alone." Again,
> the first statement puts all the agency in the other
> person and the latter places the agency within the
> individual making the statement.

> A statement like "I hate how the room feels," like-
> wise, puts the agency in the others in the room,

whereas "I feel tension sitting here" puts it squarely on the person feeling the tension.

Owning one's experience is not, of course, simply a matter the way a person expresses him- or herself; it's about really recognizing that the experience is, precisely, one's own.

3. **Trusting one's experience** - This principle points to having a fundamental trust in the embodied experience of ourselves and others and in the natural flow of attention. If you fully trust in whatever is arising in your awareness, it might feel easier to own your experience and express what is present for you. It is often an invitation to trust the unknown, to include non-rational experiences, and it can even point to something beyond our individual consciousness.

4. **Staying on the level of sensation** - For those with a strong meditation practice, staying at the level of sensation will be familiar, but this is also about ensuring that when speaking you are in resonance with what you are feeling, physically. It means bringing attention to and staying with the sensations and subtle feelings in your body while being in connection with others.

5. **Being with others in their worlds** - Walking in someone else's shoes is taken to the next level in Circling. It involves a radical curiosity which assumes nothing but explores whatever distinctions may be available for understanding a given situation. For example, it is possible to have many assumptions about what sadness is and what it is like to feel it. Common as-

sumptions include that it is difficult or lonely, that the person needs sympathy and that it feels awkward. When making finer distinctions the reality of sadness in the moment can be explored in many ways, such as: "Is the sadness difficult?" or "What kind of sadness do you feel?" or even "Do you want us to come closer to you?"

In the beginning, of course, it's easier to focus on just one or two of these principles, but after diving deeper into the practice all of them can be guidelines for most interactions in daily life.

What the five principles all have in common is a radical exploration of what is actually happening in the present in communion with other people. For that reason, I think Circling is a practice that would be very useful in organizations of any kind.

## Active Listening

These days it is often said that active listening is the most effective leadership tool. This might feel like a sharp contrast to the styles of leadership we know from our experience of bosses we've had in the past. But the truth is that leadership is in transition, from a top-down, demanding approach to one where supervisors meet their employees at the eye level and consider their ideas and concerns as guidelines for their leadership.

In his book *Active Listening: Improve Your Ability to Listen and Lead*, Michael Hoppe brings our attention to six skills which leaders need if they are to become better listeners.

> *No. 1: Pay attention. One goal of active listening is to set a comfortable tone and allow time*

*and opportunity for the other person to think and speak. Pay attention to your frame of mind as well as your body language. Be focused on the moment and operate from a place of respect.*

**No. 2: Withhold judgment.** *Active listening requires an open mind. As a listener and a leader, you need to be open to new ideas, new perspectives and new possibilities. Even when good listeners have strong views, they suspend judgment, hold their criticism and avoid arguing or selling their point right away.*

**No. 3: Reflect.** *Learn to mirror the other person's information and emotions by paraphrasing key points. Don't assume that you understand correctly or that the other person knows you've heard him. Reflecting is a way to indicate that you and your counterpart are on the same page.*

**No. 4: Clarify.** *Don't be shy to ask questions about any issue that is ambiguous or unclear. Open-ended, clarifying and probing questions are important tools. They draw people out and encourage them to expand their ideas, while inviting reflection and thoughtful response.*

**No. 5: Summarize.** *Restating key themes as the conversation proceeds confirms and solidifies your grasp of the other person's point of view. It also helps both parties to be clear on mutual responsibilities and follow-up. Briefly summarize*

188

> *what you have understood as you listened, and ask the other person to do the same.*
>
> ***No. 6: Share.*** *Active listening is first about understanding the other person, then about being understood. As you gain a clearer understanding of the other person's perspective, you can then introduce your ideas, feelings and suggestions. You might talk about a similar experience you had or share an idea that was triggered by a comment made previously in the conversation.*[82]

Listening is a key part of our emotional intelligence, because only if we listen carefully can we begin to grasp the wholeness of the other person and be truly empathic. *"Leaders who listen are able to create trustworthy relationships that are transparent and breed loyalty. You know the leaders who have their employees' best interests at heart because they truly listen to them."*[83]

Otto Scharmer says listening is the most underrated among the various leadership skills, and a lack of this skill leads inevitably to a disconnect between leaders and the people they are leading. He focuses on four levels or kinds of listening in his work:

1. **Downloading:** listening from the assumption that you already know what is being said, therefore you listen only to confirm habitual judgments.

2. **Factual Listening:** when you pay attention to what is different, novel, or disquieting from what you already know – only those things that are somehow novel, or disquieting.

82  Center for Creative Leadership, *The Big 6: An Active Listening Skill Set*, https://www.ccl.org/multimedia/podcast/the-big-6-an-active-listening-skill-set/ (accessed April 2, 2019)
83  Glen Llopis, *6 Ways Effective Listening Can Make You A Better Leader*, May 20, 2013, https://www.forbes.com/sites/glennllopis/2013/05/20/6-effective-ways-listening-can-make-you-a-better-leader/#271f12461756 (accessed April 2, 2019)

3. **Empathic Listening:** when the speaker pays attention to the feelings of the speaker. It opens the listener and allows an experience of "standing in the other's shoes" to take place. Attention shifts from the listener to the speaker, allowing for deep connection on multiple levels.

4. **Generative listening:** This deeper level of listening is difficult to express in linear language. It is a state of being in which everything slows down and inner wisdom is accessed. In group dynamics, it is called synergy. In interpersonal communication, it is described as oneness and flow. At this level a conversation becomes a co-creative process from which new ideas and innovations can be generated.

## Social Presencing Theater

Developed under the leadership of Arawana Hayashi at Scharmer's Presencing Institute, Social Presencing Theater (SPT) is another practice that can help leaders become better listeners. STP is a methodology for understanding current reality and exploring emerging future possibilities. It can be applied at an individual level, in groups, or in organizations or larger social systems, and it brings an embodied, experiential learning to the participants. It's not a *"theater"* in the conventional sense, but a communication practice that *"uses simple body postures and movements to dissolve limiting concepts, to communicate directly, to access intuition, and to make visible both current reality, and the deeper – often invisible – leverage points for creating profound change."*[84]

SPT offers a practical approach to open up a space in which people can practice new ways to be beneficial to each other. It is

190

a way to experience the fact that all human beings have unique and rich wisdom, and a method to co-create situations in which this wisdom can emerge naturally and crystalize into insights, innovations and fresh Ideas. It can support an individual or group process, in order to show hidden issues and dynamics, and it helps create an open stage where issues can be "played out." In this theater the participants take roles but do not know the "script" beforehand. The "story" is created in the moment, and each role uses body-intelligence to form a "character" who investigates the social field operating among the participants, bringing out the creative potential of the moment. *"It quickly generates information about patterns and relationships that are 'stuck' in a system and offers methods for prototyping emerging futures that promote the wellbeing of all stakeholders in a system."*

Some of the exercises like the Stuck excercise or the 4D Mapping are quite simple, deeper explanation can be found online.[85]

## Mindfulness Sessions

Mindfulness Mindfulness has become very popular in the last few years, even if it is just another name for meditation. It is a translation of the Pali word sati and an essential part of Buddhist practice. In mindfulness, one recognizes the phenomena of reality through a process of bringing one's attention to experiences occurring in the present moment. Mindfulness is a practice one can do in daily life, and it does not need to be practiced in the same strict way that it is in Buddhist insight meditation and/or its application within clinical psychology. It may be seen as a mode of being and can be practiced outside any particular formal setting.

84  Presencing Institute, Social Presencing Theater, https://www.presencing.org/aboutus/spt (accessed April 2, 2019)
85  Here are some links for more information about the source of Social Presencing Theater: www.presencing.com; arawanahayashi.com

One famous application is the Mindfulness-Based Stress Reduction (MBSR) program founded by Jon Kabat-Zinn at the University of Massachusetts. This technique was developed for the treatment of a variety of conditions occurring in both healthy and unhealthy people. MBSR and similar programs are now widely applied in schools, prisons, hospitals, veteran centers, and other environments. One of MBSR's techniques — the *"body scan"* — was derived from a meditation practice ("sweeping") from the Burmese *U Ba Khin* tradition, as taught by S. N. Goenka in his Vipassana retreats. It has since been widely adapted in secular settings, independent of religious or cultural contexts.

Traditionally, mindfulness meditation is practiced while sitting with the eyes closed, cross-legged on a cushion, or on a chair, with the back straight. Attention is put on the movement of the abdomen when breathing in and out, or on the awareness of the breath as it goes in and out the nostrils. If one becomes distracted from the breath, one passively notices one's mind has wandered and returns to focusing on breathing. It's important to recognize that, especially at first, one will inevitably become distracted from this focus, and the whole point is simply to notice this when it happens, in an accepting, non-judgmental way, rather than to try to make sure it doesn't happen – which would be next to impossible. A famous exercise, introduced by Kabat-Zinn in his MBSR program, is the mindful tasting of a raisin, in which a raisin is being tasted and eaten mindfully.

Meditators start with short periods of 10 minutes or so of meditation practice per day. As one practices regularly, it becomes easier to keep the attention focused on breathing. Eventually awareness of the breath can be extended into awareness of thoughts, feelings and actions.[86] This, in turn, helps the meditator to become more aware of the thoughts, feelings and actions of others.

## Radical Collaboration

This work has its roots at the State of California's Public Employment Relations Board (PERB), where it was developed by Jim Tamm, a senior Administrative Law Judge and former Regional Director. The Radical Collaboration approach has been utilized in a wide range of applications in both public and private sectors, in such diverse areas as healthcare, heavy industry, the military and higher education.

It assumes that organizations live or die in terms of the relationships they foster, or which happen within them. Our ability to create successful collaborative relationships can make or break our careers. Effective executives have one skill in common: collaborative influence, which is the ability to get things done by getting people to collaborate and by building strong collaborative networks.

According to this model, to develop a higher collaborative influence one needs to have five skills:

> *1. **Collaborative Intention:*** *Maintaining a non-defensive presence and making a conscious personal commitment to seeking mutual gains in your relationships.*

> *2. **Truthfulness:*** *Committing to both speak and listen to the truth, and the ability to create an atmosphere where it feels safe enough to raise difficult issues.*

---

86  https://en.m.wikipedia.org/wiki/Mindfulness#Jon_Kabat-Zinn_and_MBSR

**3. Self-Accountability:** *Taking responsibility for the full range of choices we make, either through action or inaction, and taking responsibility for both the intended and unintended or unforeseen consequences of those choices.*

**4. Self-Awareness and Awareness of Others:** *Committing to know yourself deeply and showing a willingness to deal with difficult interpersonal issues. Whether you want to improve a single relationship or change the culture of an entire organization, the first step is to increase people's self-awareness.*

**5. Solving Problems and Negotiating:** *Skillfully negotiating your way through the conflict that is inevitable in any long-term relationship.*

Clearly, according to this model, true collaboration begins inside the individual and works its way out into organizations. By concentrating on these five skills, people can not only become personally more effective, they can have a big influence on the effectiveness of their company or organization.

What's more, Radical Collaboration distinguishes between two basic kinds of organizational cultures, called Red Zone and Green Zone environments. The Red Zone is a more adversarial, conflicted and un-collaborative environment, and the Green Zone is a more collaborative, supportive one. We rarely see an organization that is pure Red Zone or pure Green Zone; most are a unique combination of both, to varying degrees.

The two approaches might be broken down into various different components.

**What follows are components that characterize the Red Zone approach to potentially conflicted situations:**

- Low trust/high blame
- Threats and fear
- Guardedness
- Hostility
- Withholding energy
- Risk avoidance
- Attitude of entitlement
- Cynicism and suspicion
- Work is painful
- External motivation

**And here is the Green Zone approach:**

- High trust/low blame
- Mutual support
- Dialogue and shared vision
- Honesty and openness
- Cooperation
- Risk taking
- Sense of contribution
- Sincerity and optimism
- Work is pleasurable
- Internal motivation

As this breakdown clearly shows, for each bullet point the two approaches are at opposite ends of a spectrum. While a pure

Green Zone approach may not be possible at present, the idea is to steer things in that direction.

Ultimately, Radical Collaboration explores the range of attitudes people bring to the task of collaboration and relationship building, and not just the nature of each side of the various polarities. The defensive, adversarial Red Zone attitude is contrasted with a more effective and collaborative Green Zone attitude, but the full range in between is taken into account. Maintaining a Green Zone attitude wherever possible is the single most important thing one can do to increase his or her effectiveness when working to turn conflict into collaboration.

With this approach one can create a personal "early warning system" and "defensiveness action plan" to increase one's effectiveness in stressful situations. Radical Collaboration provides tools for being open and honest in an accountable way, and for being a more effective listener. One becomes more aware of the choices one makes and becomes more accountable for the consequences of those choices.[87]

## Playshop (Work Party)

Sometimes we become so serious during work that we forget that we have been kids and still have access to a playful aspect of our being. And this disconnection from our playful side often leads, for one thing, to a loss of resiliency that can be detrimental to our more serious purposes. In this section, I would like to look at the importance of finding some time for play in the workplace – particularly a kind of playful activity called a Work Party.

---

87  http://www.radicalcollaboration.com

196

But before I go into the specifics of this activity, I first want to say a few words about what recent research has said about the benefits of "play." As Daniel Goleman points out:

> *Time spent playing pays off in neuronal and synaptic growth; all that practice strengthens brain pathways. Beyond that, playfulness throws off a kind of charisma: adults, children, and even lab rats are drawn to spend more time with those who have had abundant practice playing.*[88]

Relearning how to play and to have fun can shift our focus away from our need to be productive and busy all the time. Immersed in a silly and playful activity, we forget all the trouble around us and get to the core of our creative life-force. Then that life force, in all its fullness, becomes available as part of the problem-solving process when we are busy with the serious matters at hand.

Play can be included even in short sessions during the working hours, as Manfred Kets de Vries, a business school professor who has worked with thousands of executives, states in the following passage:

> *Short periods of "play" – experimentation with ideas and feelings – in a group setting can yield more insights than hours of presentations. Play unleashes the opportunity to start conversations that contribute to change. Taking the form of various "ice breakers" touching on deeply felt emotional issues, these "play sessions" create a transitional*

---

88  *Daniel Goleman, Social Intelligence, 2006, ch. 12, p. 321.*

> *space where participants become willing to discuss*
> *the things that really matter.*[89]

In these play sessions people can explore things they would not normally do during working hours. Studies have found, that *"people communicate from a more profound level in play."*[90] During playful moments, it seems to be easier to collaborate and be open. Play creates special moments, where new understandings can occur. With play we can create a unique space in an organization and a safe place for individuals and groups to experiment and reflect. As long as play is done freely, people experience moments of trust, honesty and empathy, and they feel more present and joyful. This produces energy and opens creative and dynamic processes, freed from rational bonds and functional pressure.

Instead of a workshop, for example, an organization might offer a Playshop, which is like a workshop but much more centered on having fun. It can be a weekly experiential activity lasting 60–90 minutes, or a monthly half-day session in a supportive, collaborative and creative environment. It might help the participants, and even the whole organization, to become more creative, more mindful and more resilient.

By the same token, an organization can easily arrange frequent work parties, which is to say office parties, but ones that aren't about holidays like Christmas or company anniversaries. They can be a great opportunity to develop workplace relationships and strengthen bonds. They also give the opportunity for employees to meet, mingle and get to know each other. They could happen, perhaps, on Friday afternoons, or, better still, to start the working week on Monday mornings. You can prepare the space with some party decoration, play music and have some fun.

89 Manfred Kets de Vries, *Corporate Heaven: The 'Authentizotic' Organisation,* INSEAD Knowledge, December 12, 2017, *https://knowledge.insead.edu/blog/insead-blog/corporate-heaven-the-authentizotic-organisation-7911 (accessed April 2, 2019)*
90 Ann Charlotte Thorsted, *Play in Organizations,* 2010, *http://vbn.aau.dk/files/75648365/olkc_paper.pdf (accessed April 2, 2019)*

## Moderated Sharing Circles, for Tensions and Hot Topics

When difficult, tense situations arise at work, sometimes it's important to use something like the strategies I have outlined above to swiftly respond to the issues at hand. Whether you have employees who are good listeners and moderators, or you yourself are a supervisor with such skills, or you invite external moderators to facilitate meetings about hot topics, it is always good to get to it as soon as these topics appear, instead of brushing them under the carpet. Of course, to bring major tensions to the table and discuss them can be frightening. But having a focused and clarifying approach in a relaxed setting, with somebody acting as observer and moderator, can help to make that task a bit simpler.

As colleagues are often biased in their various ways, an internal moderator is often not the best choice. An external one can listen without knowing the story behind it and thus be able to observe what is going on between the participants right in the present moment. What is the dynamic between them, how charged are they, how attached or detached are they to their own perspectives, how connected are they to themselves, and how open are they to understand the inner world of the other people involved? An outside moderator, not caught up in the politics of the office in general of the histories of the conflicts between individuals, can see these dynamics as they unfold in the present discussion.

It does not have to be a circle — sometimes it might be only a conversation between two people. But whether it's done as a dialogue or in a group, the first principle should always be "what happens in the circle stays in the circle." And after the conversation it is good for all participants to have some time to integrate and digest what has happened. A time limit, perhaps a minimum of 24 hours, during which the participants do not talk about it again, should be respected.

## Concluding Remarks

I have called this chapter a "Toolbox" because it is precisely that: it is a set of tools, or rather a description of a set of tools, any one of which might be the right tool for bringing deeper collaboration into a given business setting. Perhaps one or more of these tools might be chosen because it seems like the right one to fix a certain problem. Or perhaps one might be chosen not because of any particular problem but because it resonates with the reader more than any of the others. But as I look back over the various tools offered here, I notice one thing that seems to be at the core of all of these ideas: the notion that wisdom is innate to all people and groups, not just the official leaders, and that it may be that a deeper kind of wisdom arises when individuals and groups take the time to listen to and work with each other in newer or better ways – perhaps some of the ways suggested here.

Chapter 12

# A Vision for the Future

Y ou may remember the questions I asked in the prologue and at the beginning of each chapter, and you might have found some answers to them in the ensuing paragraphs. What is more important to me, rather than having answers, is being able to ask the right questions, and creating a space where we can ask more questions, as a process of constant learning. Listening to each other seems more constructive to me than having strong opinions and fixed answers to every problem. What I want to present here are some wishes and longings I have, all of them in some way questioning the current system, in order to help provoke the construction of a new one that's suitable for our grandchildren and for future societies.

## Safe Spaces for Potential

In future workplaces I would like to see people, regardless of sex and gender, be acknowledged for what they are, in situations where everybody can unfold their full potential and be able to fulfill their life's purpose. I would like to see this in an environment where feelings and emotions are valued the same way as numbers and facts.

For this vision to become reality, starting from where we are right now, perhaps we don't need to change as much as we might think. The most important thing is the willingness and openness to make some key changes in our corporate structures, which are often still organized like they were in the 20th century, or even the 19th century. So many people are ready for the leap forward, and individuals at the management level are feeling the need for new kinds of collaboration, but they all still feel bound to the company's structure, and they fear to lose the standard of living that they have worked so hard for. The status quo stays in place not because people aren't interested in new ways of doing things but because they're afraid of losing old certainties. One needs a strong mind and the ability to operate without a safety net. But anyone who has experienced what's on the other side would not want to go back to the way things have always been done.

However, as progressive and post-modern ideas are perceived as a threat to the old paradigm, most companies have their own security nets to block off all attempts at changing the system. This is a great pity, because people with experience in new business practices, and whose eyes have been opened to new possibilities, could contribute so much to the transformation of organizations that are still structured in old and outdated ways. And it's clear that corporations which do not adapt to the needs of employees or potential employees that are part of generations X, Y and the coming Z's — who are often not willing to be subordinate to traditional hierarchies and to 9-to-5 working hours — might be stuck, strongly resistant to change, and unable to attract people from the up-and-coming generations. Some managers and board members think change means going back to a practice that worked in the past, though what the organization needs most is a leap into the unknown, into a future that's emerging right now. With all its uncertainty and its countless opportunities alike, the future needs to be met with appropriate organizational structures.

## Wholeness and Mindfulness

I would like to see workplaces where people are not just seen as resources, where they are seen in terms of their potentials, which still need to be developed. Because we spend so much of our life working, the environment where we work should be supportive of that development. Supportive rooms and spaces, supportive colleagues and supportive supervisors, supportive organizational structures — this is what we need as we move forward into the future. A curiosity about the world of the other, an interest in where they come from, where they are standing in life and where they want to go from here — these are important parts of the working environment we need as we move forward. Only together with others we can define ourselves, and so others depend on us just like we depend on them.

> *The more you know about another person's journey, the less possible it is to distrust or dislike that person. Want to know how to build relational trust? Learn more about each other. Learn it through simple questions that can be tucked into the doing of work, creating workplaces that not only employ people but honor the soul in the process.* [91]

The emphasis should be on wholeness, on acknowledging and developing the entirety of one's own being: the body, the

91  Parker Palmer, *On the Edge: Have the Courage to Lead with Soul*, Journal for Staff Development, National Staff Development Council, Spring 2008.

mind, the emotions and the spirit. It is also about seeing the bigger picture, by acknowledging and comprehending the outer world, other people, the stakeholders in a process, the dynamics between them, and the long-term perspective.

It seems important to me to envision a world where the leaders have a comprehensive perspective on what's going on in and around them, and act according to that knowledge. Not making decisions biased by a certain ideology or political view, but on objective empirical data as well as subjective experience, based on feelings and intuitive insights. An integral consciousness is emerging slowly, but the development is also threatened by increased confusion, much of it the result of the "alternative facts" and other disinformation floating around on the internet. Traditional news sources and media outlets cannot be trusted anymore, and many alternative sources are running their own propaganda efforts with different goals. In times like these, a trust in our own gut feeling and inner authority becomes more important, as well as our own responsibility to check any information given to us. This trust can grow — to give one example — through the practice of mindfulness, or other forms of meditation, where we can open to a broader intelligence, or a collective field of higher knowledge.

## Safe Harbor for Emotional Days

Everybody can have a bad day from time to time, whether it's caused by hormonal fluctuations or a situation in one's life which occupies one's attention. When we are working at a company where we don't have the freedom to just skip a day, it's often hard to stay focused on the work at hand and to be productive. On such days it might be good to have a buddy around to share these worries or be able to share them in a morning check-in round. This isn't so that someone can be maudlin, it's so that colleagues can know what's occupying their colleagues, to help them understand why the work might be going less smoothly than it normally does.

Naturally, the workplace should not be a replacement for therapy or loving friends. But, still, since most of us spend so much time in that environment, it seems important to me to have it be a safe space to fully feel and express emotions. We know from many studies that holding back emotions can cause health issues, and I believe that what doctors call burnout might come in large part from suppressed emotions, or from having little room for honest expression of who we really are while in the workplace.

## Digitalisation of Intimacy

In our work-life, and obviously in our life outside of the workplace, we are more and more connected through digital and virtual communication. Facebook, WhatsApp, etc. help us to stay up to date with what's going on in the lives of friends all around the world. Many teams already work with virtual communication and collaboration tools like Slack, Basecamp, Trello, Google-Docs, Hangouts, Skype, Zoom, WebEx, Dropbox, TeamViewer – you name it. The more we do our work from a distance, be it in our home office or at the beach, the more we need spaces where we balance our Oxytocin level through human connection, by eye gazing, touch or words of encouragement in a support group, or by doing voluntary work for other people, or, if possible, by using the time when we are in the office to really come together in person and create spaces where we can bond with our colleagues.

With the rise of Artificial Intelligence, and with so much of physical work done by machines, we will find more time to reconnect with real people in our surroundings. We should use this opportunity and look out for the emerging possibilities to have more in-person meetings. We can prepare for this by learning and practicing new modalities of deeper connection, by using new ways of authentically relating with each other. When robots are doing our jobs, we will hang out in cafés and on beaches, spend the Universal Basic Income generated by the machines, and find new ways to express our inherent creativity.

Sure, this sounds like Utopia, I know. Still, digitalization and automatization are developing exponentially, and if we are not prepared for it, AI might find us unnecessary and we might find ourselves in a dystopian rather than a utopian world, as seen in so many science fiction movies. Right now is the time to decide which path we want to go down. With the focus on a more human and conscious business environment, on loving and caring workplaces, and on more wholeness in the process of collaboration, we can create a better society, one where the next upgrade for humanity also includes an updated version of the Co-Creation-App.

## Let the Energy Flow

Energy flows through connections. When people are connected with themselves and others, creative energy can flow. In many jobs, like bookkeeping, creativity isn't always thought of as important, but a healthy level of creativity, joy and freedom can, I think, help to keep the accounts in balance and the machinery running. To keep the level of creativity high in a "dry" job would require an environment where the energy of life can freely flow in any direction, be it through playful interactions between co-workers, or regular breaks to boost the creativity. Practices which encourage this could easily be inserted into the regular schedule at any organization

So that executives can benefit from being connected with themselves, corporate Mindfulness sessions have become popular in recent years. To gain more awareness of one's inner space, and to have various perspectives on one's surroundings, a meditative approach can really help. It can support, for example, keeping a healthy connection with one's feelings, which is necessary for today's demands, and for what the future will bring, whether it is in daily life or in the highest leadership positions. A greater self-awareness often brings with it a need for more authentic relations and meaningful conversations, and consequently a deeper and stronger connection to others. Future leaders will need strong emotional intelligence, to listen to what their employees need and what the current situation needs. There has to be a connection between the different levels of a company's hierarchy. Not all companies can be led in a grassroots approach, and some hierarchies will still be needed in the future, but the vertical links between the levels are as important as the horizontal links between the people on any given level.

## Pro Eros is Pro Life

Eros is the evolutionary force in this universe, it keeps all sentient beings reproducing, evolving and adapting to ever-changing life conditions. If we choose to let Eros freely flow, we organically choose to allow life to be able to unfold, and we allow to emerge what will emerge. This doesn't need much thinking, controlling or steering. When Eros is alive in you, you will feel sensations in your body that will clearly show you the next step you need to take, in whatever situation. In business, you might find yourself doing your work with joy, making decisions and finding solutions that feel perfectly natural, and finding that others trust you when making such decisions, as they come out of a true and grounded self-confidence and inner knowing.

Choosing life is not about just having fun and creating a superficial kind of happiness, it's about fostering an individual attitude and corporate culture rich in life-enhancing and sustainable processes and products. Evolution from simple to the more complex and conscious forms how we evolved in the first place; it is constructive, positive and fundamentally good. With this in mind, we can support a culture in our organizations that is truly life-affirming, where we can stimulate each other's creativity and evolve together.

If we listen carefully, our deepest longings will show us the next steps on our personal and common evolution. We can listen to longings that come from deep within us, from the soul, or even from a higher universal source (which is significantly different from our egoistic and physical desires). This deeper longing has its source in a primary incompleteness, and a desire for fullness in all things. When Eros, the evolutionary and transformational force, can flow freely, then full human creativity can unfold, and more complex forms of thinking, or even more complex life forms, can emerge.

## Vibrant Collaboration Continues

Collaboration is a continuing process. To keep it alive and vibrant, we need a strong commitment from everybody involved, and for everything that arises on the common journey. The path might not be an easy one but, still, as you might also have experienced, perhaps even many times, the journey itself is often fun and rewarding, not just the outcome. Indeed, the fun will come with your personal engagement. The more you involve yourself, the more you can be proud of the results you've achieved, and the more you can be happy that you are part of something big. "Stay hungry, stay foolish," Steve Jobs said in his famous speech at Stanford, and this might be great advice for collaboration, too. I would add this as well: stay honest, stay erotic, stay vibrant, show up as your unique and authentic self, because that might deepen the collaboration and make it a true co-creation.

With all of this in mind, I now turn to some interviews I have conducted with people on the vanguard of moving into new kinds of organizations, ones with a better balance of Yin/Yang, ones that honor both the masculine and feminine principles that are so basic to the human experience.

# Experiences from the Field

..........................................

(Essays and Interviews from Different Perspectives)

1.  Interview with a Transgender CEO,
    by Sascha Hümbeli

2.  Kaouthar Darmoni, Feminine Capital

3.  Nilima Bhat, Turning *eros* to Eros

4.  Jeff Hearn,  Seven Challenges for Sexualities,
    Intimacy and Non-sexualities at Work:
    What (and What Not) to Do?

# Interview with a Transgender CEO

................................................................

*"Personal growth takes place where you leave your comfort zone. For example, if you accept a task and do your best even if you are uncertain of the outcome. As long as you only move where you already know everything, you do not learn anything new."*

**Interview conducted by Sascha Hümbeli**

**Karen Hill** (name changed) grew up as a man and made a career in a global corporation. After taking over the role of CEO as a man, she changed the gender and has since passed on the company as a woman. This unique constellation enables her to look at the corporate world from both perspectives as a man and as a woman.

\*\*\*

Sascha: Karen, you changed your sex three years ago. Are you a different person today?

*Karen: I've always been the same person. But people see two different individuals from the outside. At first, they saw me as a man, and later as a woman. But my inner values have not changed.*

In the course of your career, you had always been asked to take on new, more responsible positions. Do you think your career would have developed differently if you had been a woman then?

*I would say rather no. I was recently asked for a leadership assignment in a male-dominated area, even though I am a woman, and even though I am a transgender person. I think they got me because of this, and they approached me as a unique human being. I am more likely to ask myself if I would be where I am today, if I had been born as a woman, or if I had changed my sex at an early age. I think I would not have gone down the same path in either case.*

Why not?

*The women's roles in my family were rather traditional. When I look at what has become of my cousins, I would probably have learned a profession, married, had children, and would have been a stay-at-home mom, who will later return to the professional world.*

How did you deal with your passion at a young age?

*When I was 17, I spoke about it for the first time with my parents about it. That led to treatment from a psychiatrist. This was a very painful process for me because my par-*

*ents could not accept it. They were afraid for my future. After half a year everything was too much for me and I took it all back, and I said it had been just a phase. I did not have the strength to fight for myself and my identity, because I had the same fears in me.*

*After finishing schooling at 19, I moved out to be on my own. The experience of the half-year during which I shared my real feelings, and the fears that it would not be socially accepted if I shared them again, and that I would be marginalized — all of this caused me to repress it completely. I did that by throwing myself into the work. I worked a lot and I had good times, and my superiors were drawn to me. So I became the youngest head of an agency at 23. Four years later, I became department head, and at 30 I became the youngest director in the company's history. All this has to do with the fact that I used the work as compensation for what I had to repress in my private life.*

**So, the work became your life?**

*Yes, it did. If I could have changed my gender at 17, my life would probably have taken a very different direction. As it was, I didn't pay much attention to my private life. I had some friends, but I did not really live fully. Therefore, at 30, there was a certain frustration. Although I was successful in my job, I was not at all successful in my private life: no relationships and only a small circle of friends. At that time, I blamed my repressed transgender identity.*

*Then I went back to a psychiatrist. During the next year and a half she helped me to come to terms with myself. That is, to accept that I have these feelings inside me, and that I must not be ashamed because of it. And, above all, I also let my feminine facets flow into my life, so that I could show this in my role as a manager. I started to live this part more consciously.*

**Was this noticed in your environment?**

*In the course of my career, I often did things that were then regarded as more feminine. For example, I was already very "inclusive" by involving the employees in management decisions. I did not make decisions alone but arrived at them together with the people I worked with. That was 1999. At that time, the typical management style was still somewhat different.*

*Once, for example, a boss demanded something from me, and I told him that I would need a week to implement it. He said, "Why do you need a week? You can just tell the people in your department what to do, and it will get done." But I said: "No, this works differently in my area. I would first like to discuss with my employees how we would implement it together."*

*My style of leadership also affected how we understood what we were doing. I always had discussions because I asked why, rather than just take the orders blindly. I always asked what the purpose was and why I was doing something.*

*On the one hand, this behavior helped me to be successful with my people. That's why new opportunities were often offered to me. On the other hand, this behavior sometimes hindered me because I didn't always fit into the scheme. Certain bosses could not deal with my style.*

**In general, management style has changed since the 90s. Did this cultural change support your approach?**

*Yes. For example, I was entrusted with the task of dealing with "behavioral values," as part of a major strategy project. This was because my superiors noticed that I strongly represented and lived the "new" values.*

**After working with the psychologist, when you came to terms with yourself, could you show your true face in your private life?**

*It had led me to get to know a woman. That was my first relationship. I told her from the beginning about the trans identity was part of me. She was able to accept it, but there was no place for it in the relationship. For she had fallen in love with a man and wanted to have a relationship with a man.*

*Although I was closer to her, very intimate, when it was about cuddling, which she enjoyed very much, my female side had no place in the relationship. But when it came to real sex, I played a role, in which I never felt comfortable. She could feel it and it led to separation after three and a half years.*

**Did you primarily look for a man or a woman?**

*At that time, I was still dominated by the thinking that is regarded as "normal" — that I should be with a woman. The realization that I am interested in men came only later when I began to live as Karen. Before my transition in the summer of 2014, I had even expected that I would still have a relationship with a woman.*

*Some experiences as Karen changed this, when in certain encounters with men my heart began to pound, and it became warm. Then I realized that men did not leave me completely cold. I then understood this about myself and realized that I had suppressed it and had not allowed any of it to come forward.*

**How was it with you as a teenager: Do you look at boys or girls at the time?**

*I was indifferent. At that time I had two school friends whom I loved, both girls, because it was "normal". But there were also boys, which I loved. I imagined then how beautiful it would be if I were a girl, because I could be with them.*

**How did you feel like you wanted to make the transition?**

*When the relationship with my girlfriend dissolved, I went back to my psychiatrist to process this. Because I knew it was my issue. At that time I had the desire to learn what it would be like to go out into the public as a woman, and not just stay at home within my four walls. I flew to New York, where I met a few women from a trans-organization. I went there for the first time with women's clothes in the public.*

**So you consciously changed your environment to show yourself what you wanted?**

*Yes, at that time I was still afraid to be discovered, that someone in my immediate environment could find out. It was such a great experience, an incredible feeling of freedom, to be a woman with people outside, even if it was anonymous. That's why I began to make more and more weekend trips, not only to New York, but also to other cities, to spend a weekend as Karen there.*

*In the beginning I was very nervous every time I left the hotel room. I was also afraid that someone might really appeal to me, and then I would have to talk to that person, all the while thinking about the chance that he would notice my true nature. However, I soon realized that this risk is low, and that I was accepted as a woman. Later, I began to involve my acquaintances abroad. I made plans with these people, and I told them about my trans-identity and that I am Karen when I am in one of their cities.*

**So you broadened your boundaries little by little, right?**

*Yes, exactly. I kept going out of my comfort zone and stayed there until I finally felt comfortable. So, I broadened my boundaries step by step. When my best friend wanted to come to New York, I had to introduce her into my secret world there. I told her that while she was allowed to come, she had to deal with something she did not know about yet.*

*Later, a time came when I felt more and more secure as Karen. My public personality and self-confidence as a woman had been able to develop, because I could live out a few times a month as a woman. Karen became so strong that, well, on Monday mornings it was difficult for me to return to my other role. Then I had the conviction that I simply had to go all the way, to take the final steps.*

*Still, because of my fear of losing my job, I started attending the university, so that I could re-train myself and have another option. This training then became a catalyst for me. The training included some modules, in which we were very much concerned with ourselves, and they helped me get more clarity.*

*During this time, I took the job I have today and came to this subsidiary. In this environment I was quickly successful, and I won the trust of my employees. It was the right time for me to make the transformation, in the environment of a smaller company. So, all the puzzle pieces fit together, and I could take the step.*

**During this step, did you get help, either by coaching or therapy?**

*Yes, I had a psychotherapist who accompanied me, but rather in a coaching role. I went there once a month, and we discussed the individual steps. For example, we prepared certain important talks. The therapist was very happy with me, because each time we met I had already, most of the time, achieved more than we'd ever planned.*

**This is part of your nature, that you are purposeful and know what you want, right?**

*It also has to do with the way I wanted to be with my environment, to be appreciative of others, wether that involves a deep conversation in the earliest stages, or plenty of time to process and/or ask questions. This certainly contributed to my being accepted. Now, other people in similar situations often have to overcome great resistance in their job or family. This was not the case with me, because I had this openness myself, and I was sensitive to other people as well. Today, I often do not know whether people are aware that I am a trans. I don't care about it. But I always have very good conversations and encounters. I take people as they are. This is what people realize about me.*

When I saw you for the first time as Karen, I noticed how self-assured you are, and how you seem to feel really good about yourself. I had the feeling that you have a greater self-understanding than before. How were things just before the time when you made your transition publicly known? How long did this preparation take?

*I decided in December 2013 to tell the world. At that time, I contacted the transgender network, which the psychotherapist told me about. Through the network I got three contacts with trans-women, and I was able to learn from their experiences.*

*In the following February I then asked for appointments with certain superiors in the company. I wrote to them that I had to discuss something personal that was unknown to them so far, and that it was very important to me. I prepared these conversations with my psychotherapist. I also discussed the procedure within my study group where I received great feedback.*

*One important bit of feedback I got from the group referred to talks with superiors. They pointed out that people in leadership functions are usually careful not to show any weaknesses. They believe that they must have an answer to all questions. If you come up with a topic that is completely unknown to them and that they have never learned in management training, then it can be that they feel helpless. There is a danger when they cannot deal with this helplessness, and the result will likely be that they will not accept you so. That's why it is important, when you recall yourself to them, you also tell these people how they can help you, at the same time. That is, I told them that I planned my transition for the second half of that year, and that I would like to draft the announcement of this change together with them. And I told them I needed their support.*

**Apparently, the talk came out well. Otherwise you would not still have your job.**

*The people I spoke to were all very positive. As it turned out, I was even over-prepared. Not all preparation I did was necessary. But for me it was good, because it helped me to give me me a feeling of confidence when I went into these meetings.*

*In such a conversation, it's important to tell people what your reality is, and what will happen — and that you'll do it with or without their support. In the meantime, I've met many transgender people who have been living in their new world for a long time, but some of them are still ashamed of being trans. If you feel like a victim around your superiors, then you will be treated as a victim.*

**Yes, that depends very much on you. You can influence it yourself.**

*That's why it's important that you don't say you are helpless, that you need help from them, but instead you tell them what your intention is, and how they can support you. You take them on your journey.*

*If you are helpless, then they will take action themselves. Then you give them all the control. But when you tell them what you want them to do, you yourself are in control of the process.*

When you informed us about your transition, you wrote that it was very well received by your workforce, that certain women, for example, spontaneously embraced you. Were there negative experiences?

*Not with the workforce here. I know that for some it was a bigger step to accept it. But there were never any negative statements. So far, I have not had any really negative experiences.*

This probably depends on you being self-confident.

*Yes, and I have often had very touching experiences. For example, people came to me, who I only knew from passing them in the hallways and things like that, and they congratulated me on my decision. I also received a lot of positive emails, from people saying that they were proud to work in a company where this was possible. I forwarded such emails to our communications department, in order to say thank you, on the one hand, and to pass on this appreciation on the other hand. I also did this so the next person to make the transition would get the same appreciation — someone who may need more support than me.*

How do you deal with people before and after your transition? Are there differences between the role of man and woman?

*My perception is that I could continue my relationship with the people in the company as before, regardless of whether I appear as a man or a woman. Because people accept me and accept what I say and do.*

*To the outside, of course, there is a bias because I am CEO. When I act as a CEO in the role of a woman, men also listen to me, more than if I were a clerk or team leader. So far, nobody ever asked me if I would get coffee for him.*

**Yes, that's because everyone knows what role you have.**

*That's why it's difficult to say how much respect I would get anyway as a woman, and how much I get from my role as CEO. The respect I get from my function is probably more important than what I get because of my gender.*

**In the company environment, it is therefore difficult to distinguish your appearance as a man or woman from your CEO role. Could we talk about your private environment? There you're just a woman. How do you experience the difference, in situations where people do not know you or your leadership role?**

*I often have chance meetings in which great conversations develop. For example, I had an encounter with a man last week when I came out of my hotel. The taxi driver was just loading my suitcase, and a man came by and saw my other bag, which had the logo from my university on it. After passing by at first, he turned around, came to me and asked me if I had studied at this university. After I said that I had, we had a short conversation, and he asked me if we could meet again later and we exchanged business cards. Then he wrote to me, and we agreed to have lunch together.*

*This was just a spontaneous encounter. It would not have happened to me if I had been a man. The man probably used the university bag as an excuse to speak to me. I have also similar encounters on the train. These show me that I am accepted as a woman.*

**I notice that you have a higher voice today than before, in addition to the changed external appearance. Do you do that on purpose, or has this voice developed naturally?**

*This was already happening during the times when I was just being Karen in other cities. In the beginning I was still a bit awkward, but later it went better and better. In the summer of 2014, I went to a speech therapist. After five sessions, she told me that all was well. I no longer needed to practice. Women not only speak in a different voice than men, but they have a different way of speaking. That is, the words they use, and the body language are quite different.*

**What is different in the language of men and women?**

*There are certain stresses and the use of certain words, which is different in men and women. My speech therapist told me that she only saw a woman in my body language and my voice. My voice has probably evolved over time.*

*Often you notice that you don't like your own voice when you hear it on a recording. For me it was the same. But today, with my female voice, I feel very comfortable. After I became comfortable with my female voice, one time in the car, I tried again to speak with my old male voice, but it really bothered me. I didn't want to hear it anymore.*

So, for you, now, the women's voice has become the normal mode. How would you personally describe typically male and typically female behavioral patterns?

*The provocative answer to this is that they do not exist. But the truth is that these patterns are embodied and stylized by society and by our socialization process. Of course, many people live up to these patterns, so they feel like they are part of nature. But there are also people who do not live up to them.*

*In society, of course, being male is associated with being more aggressive, more specific, harder, and being female is associated with being softer and more emotional. When a man struggles and hits the table with his fist, he is regarded as strong. If a woman does this, she no longer has control of her feelings.*

This is a projection that our society gives to things.

*Yes, exactly the same behavior can be regarded as a problem for a woman and a strong point for a man. There is a double standard, which still makes it difficult today for men and women to have equal opportunities. This is not only bad for women and good for men. It can also be reversed. For example, if men want to work in a field like nursing, they will likely have more difficulties because they are less trusted.*

So you are of the opinion that there are no stereotypical behavioral patterns by nature, but that they are produced by the society, so that people are unconsciously absorbing them. Would you consider the economy and business world, as you know it, as more masculine or neutral? It is often said that this is a male world.

> *If I go to events in the corporate world, then it is clearly male. If I count the number of men and women there is a huge difference. At an event with, say, 50 top managers, usually only three or four of the participants are women. In our company, there are many different committees that are purely male. The climate in these teams is often typically masculine — how they talk about others, how they use humor. Such committees also try to protect themselves when a woman wants to join, because they could no longer behave like this.*

> *I am not a fan of quotas myself, but I think that right now we probably need them to promote diversity. Until it's normal that top management teams consist of men AND women.*

**Do you think that a mixed organization works better than when it is made up of both men and women?**

> *Yes, mixed teams work better. I think diversity is always better for a company.*

**So you say that men and women ARE after all different?**

> *(Karen laughs). Yes, they are it today because of their socialization. Just as a man who grew up in southern Italy tends to be a different kind of man than one who grew up in Denmark. They are both men, but they are different in behavior in many respects.*

**Is it unpleasant for you when you go as a woman to an event where almost everyone else is a man?**

*It's an advantage for me that I had already lived in the "men's world" I've just described. And now I am living as Karen in the same world, and I feel quite normal.*

**It's often claimed that the culture of companies is masculine due to the fact that there are mainly men in management positions. Do you think so too?**

*Yes. That is why I also say that quotas don't make sense for supervisory boards. Supervisory boards have almost no influence on the culture of a company. Because of this, the quotas must be introduced at the management level in the operating environment. Then the cultural shift can also be felt in the rest of the company.*

**In a study at Google, it was found that the performance of teams doesn't depend on the composition of the team but on how they work within the teams, and wether or not people can sometimes show emotions or speak about their private lives. What observations and experiences have you made as a leader in this regard?**

*I had to let go of a team leader because of sexual harassment. But otherwise I have had positive experiences. There are plenty of women in the middle management positions in our company. That means that the culture is oriented towards what we might call "human" qualities, and we are very all-inclusive. The company, under my leadership, is very familiar. There's room for private conversations.*

**What do you do as a leader to promote this inclusive culture?**

*I have used working methods that invite inclusiveness. For example, we have already organized three open-space workshops, where all employees were invited to help shape the company's future.*

*Next week, I will be holding a two-team workshop on the topic of personal value contributions, where I will work with the participants on what their role is in the company, and what their contribution to its success is. The goal is that they understand this by themselves, and that they get the appreciation from others for what they are doing. We want them to understand how they could increase their contributions through entrepreneurial thinking.*

*One could say, in summary, that you promote this culture by your behavior as a model, and that you also demand this from the employees.*

*Demanding is a hard "male" word. It sounds like exerting pressure. I would say "invite": I invite people to participate. I do not want to exert pressure, but I want to make it so that people can speak up when they want to contribute something.*

**We had previously talked about the fact that the corporate world is still strongly male-dominated. What tips would you give women so they can survive in this world?**

*They should not hold back, they should say what they think. They should not adapt themselves to their male colleagues. For example, I have a female colleague who is wearing only gray trousers at work. She adapts to the men. She says she does not want to exploit her femininity, and she does not want to be reduced to it.*

**Aha. By doing so, she hides her femininity and becomes neutral or even male.**

*Yes, unlike her, I wear colored figurative dresses in the summer. I don't do as men do, nor hide my femininity. But I am delighted that I am a woman and can live as a woman. And I show that too. I do not want to be defined by it, but by what I am doing.*

**This means you encourage women to act as a women?**

*Yes, they are to remain a woman and not to adapt to the rules of the men so that they can better fit.*

**Is there not the danger that women, in the eyes of the men, are regarded as something less valuable when they are so feminine?**

*That depends on a person's self-worth. You can only be less valuable when you consider yourself less valuable. The value is inside you. And if you have self-worth, but are treated poorly by someone else, then you have to make that clear. But if you just get up and get the coffee when men ask you, then you accept that role.*

**This means that women should be on the one hand feminine and, on the other, self-confident and not be pushed into a particular pattern by others.**

*Yes, if someone says you should get coffee, then you answer neutrally that this is a good idea to have coffee, but it is not your role to bring it. For example, everyone could go together, or someone else could go. There is also a risk if you react like this, namely that the double-standard impression can emerge, and that the woman is regarded as a bitch. But she must be able to handle it.*

**And the other danger could be, if she is very feminine, that sexist behavior comes out.**

*Yes, here too, a woman has to set clear limits and do not tolerate such a behavior.*

*I had an interesting experience where this came into play. I was at lunch with another manager and two business customers, who were our guests. When it came time to pay I first asked if anyone still wanted coffee, otherwise I would ask for the bill. My colleague then said I did not have to pay, because I am here with three men, and that in this case the woman does not have to pay. I answered, "Really? But I'm the CEO and these are our guests. Then it's clear to me that I will pay."*

*The next morning, I clarified the incident with him by saying that it's important to me that the CEO role is not related to my gender. Even after changing my identity, I will continue to pay the bills as CEO, not as a woman. I should point out that in general I do not want to be emancipated. I am glad when a man opens the door for me. But they are two different things, and I don't want to lose my function as a host just because i am a woman. There is a line between gallant and degrading.*

**Karen, thank you very much for the interesting conversation!**

# Interview with Kaouthar Darmoni

Dr. Kaouthar Darmoni was born in Tunisia, and grew up on the Mediterranean coast, where, as a young person, she turned naturally to music and dancing. From a very young age she concerned herself with women's emancipation. She is an independent scholar and expert in Gender Studies. After an extensive academic career as Assistant Professor in Gender & Media (University of Amsterdam, Netherlands), she decided to combine her academic talents with her passion for dance and body awareness.

Kaouthar unchains and unleashes the inner strength within women by using a kind of "Sacred Dance" (*"Raqsat al Ilahat,"* or "The Dance of Goddesses"). She has thoroughly investigated the many aspects of this ancient art. By traveling to various Middle Eastern and North African countries, and through her gender studies research, observation and practice, she has developed her own concept, "Feminine Capital & Goddess Dance," a unique women's empowerment method based on brain/gender theories and body/Arab dances. She also focuses on training women at work — "Corporate Goddesses," — to become ambassadors of conscious business and FeMale leadership. kaouthar.com

*\*\**

**Heinz: Kaouthar, when I hear of "Feminine Capital," I immediately associate this with capitalistic thinking, like taking resources out of something.**

*Kaouthar: Not necessarily. When I refer to capital I'm thinking of the way the French sociologist Pierre Bourdieu used the term. In the '90s he said that every human being has three kinds of capital. We have cultural capital, which is what we have studied, our diplomas, our knowledge about art or philosophy—everything that has to do with culture, including our education. It's our personal value in terms of culture. Then we have economic capital, which is our value in terms of the economy—our finances, how much we earn, whether or not we own a house, how much we have in the bank. And then there is social capital, which is basically a network: the people we know, the people who are really in our network, how many people these are, and the power of these people. It also includes the value of the people you know. These are three kinds of capital, in terms of actual value.*

*Catherine Hakim, at Oxford, started to use the term "erotic capital" in 2010, because, especially in the visual culture in which we live, the elements of erotic capital also have value. Hakim uses the idea of erotic capital as a data base, as Esther Perel uses the concept of erotic intelligence. But Perel uses it in the private sphere and Hakim in the professional one. Erotic capital is based on beauty. Not necessarily* beauty as in "You look beautiful," but more as the Latin languages use it, as in the French "La Belle Laide." That's number one. Then we have the concept of sex-appeal, which is everything related to charisma. This criteria applies to both men and women—it is gender-neutral.

Erotic capital is also about liveliness or vibrancy, about how alive you are in your body. It mostly involves physical and emotional elements. Aliveness, sexual attractiveness, sex-appeal, charisma, and social skills like humor, the ability to interact easily, and even a little bit of flirting. It also includes physical fitness, how you use your body, and how you represent yourself socially, which is very much related to how you dress, your makeup, your jewelry, and everything else through which you present yourself in your social surroundings. And there are also two additional elements: sexuality and fertility.

These last two elements, depending on which culture you are in, are only to be dealt with in private, never in the workplace. I stress these elements strongly in my work. Sexuality means how skilled you are in your sexual performance. And, depending on the culture in which you are living, fertility can be added to your erotic capital as well. In the Mediterranean and in many Arab cultures, being a sexy mother can also add extra value to your feminine capital. But, again, the last two elements, sexuality and fertility, belong more to the private sphere, even though the first one can sometimes be found in the professional world as well

People who use their erotic capital, whether women or men, earn 3 to 13 percent more than those who don't. Iron-

*ically, men who use erotic capital earn much more than women. The erotic capital of men, when it comes to earning money, has more value than that of women.*

*Now we come to the next phase of the argument, which is that women's erotic capital has been excluded from power within the patriarchy and confined to the arena of sexuality, in order to serve men, especially in prostitution and pornography—what we call the culture of pornification. In gender studies analysis you can see that porn-culture is currently everywhere—even in normal, seemingly non-pornographic situations. For example, there is research in Australia and in the US that shows that in any normal magazine you will find younger and younger girls, maybe 14 or 15, posing in a way that is very pornographic. The result of this culture of pornification is that the erotic capital of women is so pornified in the mass media that it makes women very scared to use it in the working place, because they don't want to be associated with that image.*

*Throughout centuries of patriarchy, erotic capital has consistently been devalued and associated with the sex industry. I absolutely believe in this concept of Hakim's, and I love how it allows us to talk about something which is very provocative. It is funny because I come from an Arab Muslim culture, and in Islam, which is 1,500 years old, they have always spoken about this concept. In Islam, talking about erotic matters is normal, by the way. The only rule is that erotic matters always have to occur in the field of marriage, not outside. But in Islam the erotic, and sexuality, are seen as a sacred gift from God to human beings. This is why* celibacy in Islam is forbidden, and it is why both widows and widowers are expected to remarry immediately—because of these sexual needs. Sexual needs are acknowledged, they are written about, and there are a lot of discussions of sexuality in the scriptures of the prophet Mohammad

During the early days of Islam, on Friday afternoons, after prayers, there were always discussions about sexuality with the prophet. Women and men both attended these discussions, though separately. The believers would ask all kinds of questions. In Islam, it is amazing what you can find out about sexual practices—such as what kind of positions are allowed, or if anal or oral sex are allowed. Islam is diverse and very open here, with frank discussions about different aspects of sexuality, and how it should be practiced. But, in the end, sexuality is sacred and must be practiced as a way of reaching the divine.

In Islam, the sexuality of the woman is superior to the sexuality of the man. Women are erotically stronger than men, because men always place more demands on female sexuality. And because men demand this energy so fervently, they are the dependent ones, "the weak ones," as they say in Arabic. Men cannot resist. This makes women more independent, because men are so dependent on them.

In order to deal with this problem, the Muslims cover and isolate women in order to control this energy. This "solution," however, has more to do with patriarchy than with Islam itself.

This is different from what happens in western culture, where attitudes towards female sexuality come from Freud *and psychoanalysis, and female sexuality is seen as hysterical, inferior, and passive. In Islam it is just the reverse: the women are the ones who are active, and the men are seen as passive, because the men react to the actions of women. Women don't have to take action, in terms of being provocative—they just have to show up. They just have to be, and that's all.*

*Hakim describes it a bit differently, because she talks about the male sex deficit. Men, because they don't get enough sex, are more demanding of it. Women have the upper hand, because, based on scientific research, the sexual libido of men and women is more or less equal until the age of 35, or until women have children. When women have children, their libido shifts to their children. Perel also talks about this shift in her book Mating in Captivity, where she claims that the reason a lot of couples do not have sex as much after they have kids is that the women are sharing their erotic space with the baby. It is like an erotic fusion, and this is very normal—but after 18 months or two years you have to shift back to the relationship with the spouse.*

*Instead, a lot of women stay erotically connected to the baby, and then they are too tired, too busy. Men don't have babies, they don't give birth, so the libido of the men stays the same, whereas the libido of the women declines. When the kids grow up and leave the house, they are not dependent on the women anymore, and around the age of 45 or 50 women's libido starts to go up again. At this age, however, the men's libido has declined, and they start to use Viagra. In short, there is no balance in male and female erotic evolution, and this makes men frustrated, because they want more sex than they are getting from their women. Thus, sexual frustration starts to play a role in the interplay between the genders: there is an erotic gap in the way female and male sexuality progresses.*

*In Muslim culture men try to get around this problem by covering the women and controlling them, or by having access to more women. In western culture, men and the patriarchy—which also includes masculine women, not only men—devalue the erotic capital of women and make it literally ordinary, vulgar, bad, pornographic, dirty, and cheap. Prostitution, for example, is very cheap. In Amsterdam prostitution is legal and they have their display windows in the red-light district, in which the women sit and display themselves openly. There are laws around this business and the women are very well protected. There is a kind of price agreement: the ladies charge between 30 and 50 Euros for 15 minutes, which is very inexpensive for a rich country. Patriarchy has made the value of erotic capital drop, because of the male sex deficit—they want a lot of sex and they want it for cheap/free, or at least for as little money as possible.*

*Women, especially at work, don't want to be associated with anything that has to do with prostitution, because there is so much pain and abuse in this area. Thus, the last thing they want to have is erotic capital. They shut down. But by doing so, they shut themselves off from their source of creativity, from their source of power, as if they are castrating themselves. The work that they need to do is to heal that part and to put it back into perspective.*

*You asked me before the interview whether I have ever had sex with a colleague, and I told you this is a no-go area for me. It is out of the question, and this is what I also say to women. If you cannot master that skill don't even start. The Number One rule is that sexuality needs to stay out of the professional game, and you never ever get into sexual activity at work. And this is something that I learned from my grandmother, when I was little girl.*

*In Arab culture we have spaces that are only for women, where men have absolutely no access. We have spaces that are free from any male eyes, any male energy, and there we explore, completely freely (you cannot imagine how free it is), our sexuality. From when you are one year old until you are eighty—there is no age limit. But one of the first rules we learn is that you keep it inside. And, second, it is for you and only for you, and you don't go out with it, you don't manipulate men with it, and you don't do anything to anyone else with it, because then it's bad karma. You just don't do that. And, third, there are three categories of men with whom you never exploit this energy—your neighbors, your family members, and your colleagues. Because if you start playing with this energy with them and it doesn't work, you have to be very careful. These are people you see every day, so if something goes wrong it might become a disaster. I see it also at my work. People who engage in sexual activity, when they cross the line between erotic capital and get into sex itself—most of the time it's a disaster. It's a drama. It's just a no-go area. But the problem is how to master that energy. How do we keep it pure? How can we be the master of it? And this is what people have not learned—especially* women, but also men. They have not learned how to recycle that energy in social creativity rather than in the sexual act itself. Because we live in a culture which is fucked up, sexualized and pornified.

**That brings me to my second question. When you do your work with women, they get more attractive. For me it is also important that men should take responsibility for their actions and behavior, and not exploit this sexual energy which exists between them and their female colleagues. What would be your suggestion for men for how to keep it together, and not abuse this energy?**

*Here I would go back to my Arab Muslim culture. It's not up to men, it's up to us women—it's agency. I cannot control the men of the world; I cannot influence them. I can influence my child, because I raise him, and I can influence the men around me, but I can't control the men in the streets or at my work. But I can have agency, I can do it myself. Esther Perel interestingly addresses this in her work, when she talks about liveliness and all that it brings into gender relations. At a certain point, you first need to be able to have that in you, before going to look for that energy in somebody else. I work only with women and my work is only about women. This is why I work with the goddesses archetypes, because it is up to you as a woman to put up the boundaries. It is you who has to have clarity.*

*In Arab Muslim culture, boys are with the women until the age of 8-10. They go with us to dancing events and see us dancing sensually, erotically, wildly. They go with us to the Hamam, the Turkish bath, where we are naked and do dances and have massages—it's very sensual. A more erotic* culture than this doesn't exist, but it's a hidden world. You don't see it from the outside. When I was six years old, we were reading The 1001 Nights, while in Europe the kids read Cinderella and Snow White. Snow White is lying in a coffin, eyes closed, waiting for a prince to kiss her. This is such a bullshit story, pure romance. In The 1001 Nights, there is also a woman in a coffin, but she was imprisoned by a man. She starts to seduce him—to use her erotic capital— and he thinks he's going to have sex with her. She gets up, starts to dance for him, and after that she takes a knife and kills him. This is what we learned when we were six years old. Agency and the erotic capital, not laying down on your back, closing your eyes, and waiting for the prince to kiss you on your mouth to wake you up, to bring you back from death and to make you alive again. This is very passive. So we grew up with this kind of imagination, and stories in which the women are proactive, have agency, and have to master their destiny, erotically, and not be dependent on a man to come save them.

If we now come back to agency, we will step back to the dance, to all these elements that we talk about in discussing erotic capital, liveliness and such things. But then, what does that mean, to be alive? How does that feel, to be alive in your body? This can also be just a concept. I feel alive, I feel attractive, I feel sensual—how does that work, how does it look, how does it feel, how do you know you feel sensual? This is also one of the limitations of western culture—everything is mental; it's just concepts, ideas. But what is very important to be able to do is to really know how something feels in your body. This is how I started to use my method. I took all these intellectual academic concepts that I was teaching at the university, and I started to practice them when I was dancing outside of the campus.

In that sense I use an Arab ritual which we learn at home, which is 5,000 years old, and it is called in Arabic "Raqsat al Ilahat," or, literally, "The Dance of Goddesses." It's a pre-Islamic ritual and in the pre-Islamic era, the culture was matriarchal, not patriarchal. And there were goddesses, not gods. Men in that period worshipped women as goddesses. The dance, or at least what is now the modern version of it, technically, is what the people here call belly dance. Sometimes I also use this term, because it is easy, but in Arabic it is called Raqsat al Ilahat, and it was always among the practices of the goddess Ishtar, in Mesopotamia. Ishtar's temples were closed, and men were not allowed in them, and the high priestesses were actually teaching erotic intelligence through dance. It had to be kept amongst women because it's about tapping into your life force as a woman, to be alive, to be creative, to be vibrant, to be attractive. And one of the elements is sexuality and fertility, but these form only a small part of it. Most of the rituals were made for women among women, to develop this agency.

So, the Raqsat al Ilahat is about enhancing the spirit of the goddesses in women. The movements I use with women go back to that era, and one concept from that era is what we call in Arabic "Cabasa," which means a grip, and has to do with dancing literally with the pelvic floor muscles. All the movements come from that source. I developed this method myself by working with physiotherapists and gyne-

*cologists. I combined gender studies, the goddesses dance (as I learned it from my great-grandmother, my grandmother and my mother—because we pass this on from generation to generation of girls), and pelvic physiotherapy, which is a modern form of this 5,000 years old Cabasa. With this grip you are literally activating sexual energy all the time, and there is one rule, which is, you don't fuck with that energy. It's not meant to have sex with.*

*The original purpose is to empower yourself as a woman, to be in your body and to create intimacy and sisterhood among women. This is to avoid jealousy, disloyalty among women, competition, bitchiness—which is what you see in the workplace: women who are such bitches together, it's horrible. It's better to be with men than with such women. But when women can become intimate by using their sexual energy to bond together, then they are completely free, they don't sabotage each other, and they are not busy manipulating men with that energy, because they keep it clean, as they remind each other, "Ohh, ohh, we don't do that!"*

**That means also, when I think about a company, that there should be bonding between the women, the female colleagues.**

*Absolutely! If you want to work with sexual energy you have to develop that energy among women. Women start first of all to experience the purity of it, because when women are among each other, you don't have this tension as you do when you are with a man. Because with the men it might go in another direction. The sexual tension that exists between men and women completely disappears when you are among women, because the sexual energy which you feel among women is of another kind. This is the energy of Demeter and Persephone, who are the mother and the child. You go into this melting feeling, like a mother with a baby— you go into a dimension where you feel safe. Women start feeling safe together with that sensual energy, and they feel for the first time in their body how this energy is de-sexual- ized. The sensual erotic energy is often sexualized, and is often associated with sexual action, but it doesn't have to be.*

*Women understand intellectually that this is not about the sexual act, but they don't know how sensuality feels. When they are among women, they feel it for their first time, because they dance sensually with other women, they dance erotically with other women, they explore that space with other women, they go wild with other women, ex- tremely wild—you have no clue. And then, all of a sudden, they realize, "Oh, this the life force, it has nothing to do with sex." That gives them self-confidence, so that when they go back to the men, they have natural boundaries around sex- ual interaction, because they know. Before that they know mentally but they don't know in their bodies what it means, they don't know how this energy is when it's completely awakened and on fire, and yet still within boundaries. They didn't know that, they hadn't learned that. This is the foun- dation of my work.*

**Is this independent from being, say, a more feminine woman or a masculine woman? Because when we speak about that binary feminine/masculine, or even when there are les- bians among one's colleagues, is there a difference? Because**

**then it could also become sexual? Or, in this case, could it still happen without being sexual?**

*I work a lot with lesbian women, and they are very, very good at that. I work with the goddess archetypes. In my method I call it the divine nine. I have nine movements, which are the foundation of the Raqsat al Ilahat movements, like water movements and fire movements and earth movements. Nine movements and nine archetypes of goddesses. Here we have the feminine archetypes, the masculine archetypes, and the great goddess, who masters them all. The masculine archetypes, for example, Artemis or Athena, are excellent for dealing with boundaries, because they keep the "three brains" aligned—the intelligence, which is the brain in the head, the heart brain, and the belly brain. These three have to be in alignment. Even if I feel my sexual energy in my belly brain—this is my Aphrodite—when I do the cabasa with women, then I feel it strongly all throughout me; it is not just located in the belly.*

*In my work I use something I developed with physiotherapists that I call "goddess balls." In China they have jade eggs, but in Mesopotamia, 5,000 years ago, they also had vaginal eggs, and using them is an ancient practice. If women start using them, they feel a lot of excitement and lots of energy. It feels like the Pavlov reaction, a conditioning process which was first studied by Ivan Pavlov, with his dog. He rang a bell and gave his dog food. After a while the dog thought he would get food every time the bell rang, but sometimes there was none.*

*With our sexuality, women and men, especially men, we have a kind of Pavlov reaction: it is very instinctive. If I awaken that energy, then I am going to have sex. The women too: in the beginning I use these movements very intensively, and at the end of the day the only thing they want is...to just fuck. But I have an agreement with them: for 30 days, minimum, no sex. For those who want to go into another leadership level: for 60 days, no sex. Nothing, nada. You have to feel the rush in your body and still do nothing with it. But, because you have the movements, this is a way to channel the energy when you feel the rush. When you are dancing, for example, doing snake-like movements, it gets transformed. Then the energy starts to flow, and it doesn't get stuck down in your pelvis.*

*This is in your body, this is the Aphrodite, or the Arab goddess Ishtar, and you feel it down here. This you have to relate to your brain, the Athena part of you, who puts up the boundaries, the structures. Athena says, we are at work and we are not going to fuck at work. So, she gives the message to Aphrodite down there to say, uh-uh. Athena is the general. Also, just as in the army you have a commandant who goes on the field and fights, here we have Artemis: she is the warrior, the one who protects the boundaries. When a man crosses the boundaries. immediately you have to hit back with a fierce energy, an energy these men can understand. Don't try to be nice.*

## For that you need to know your boundaries

*I work a lot with lesbian women, and they are very, very good at that. I work with the goddess archetypes. In my method I call it the divine nine. I have nine movements, which are the foundation of the Raqsat al Ilahat movements, like water movements and fire movements and earth movements. Nine movements and nine archetypes of goddesses. Here we have the feminine archetypes, the masculine archetypes, and the great goddess, who masters them all. The masculine archetypes, for example, Artemis or Athena, are excellent for dealing with boundaries, because they keep the "three brains" aligned—the intelligence, which is the brain in the head, the heart brain, and the belly brain. These three have to be in alignment. Even if I feel my sexual energy in my belly brain—this is my Aphrodite—when I do the cabasa with women, then I feel it strongly all throughout me; it is not just located in the belly.*

*In my work I use something I developed with physiotherapists that I call "goddess balls." In China they have jade eggs, but in Mesopotamia, 5,000 years ago, they also had vaginal eggs, and using them is an ancient practice. If women start using them, they feel a lot of excitement and lots of energy. It feels like the Pavlov reaction, a conditioning process which was first studied by Ivan Pavlov, with his dog. He rang a bell and gave his dog food. After a while the dog thought he would get food every time the bell rang, but sometimes there was none.*

*With our sexuality, women and men, especially men, we have a kind of Pavlov reaction: it is very instinctive. If I awaken that energy, then I am going to have sex.The women too: in the beginning I use these movements very intensively, and at the end of the day the only thing they want is...to just fuck. But I have an agreement with them: for 30 days, minimum, no sex. For those who want to go into another leadership level: for 60 days, no sex. Nothing, nada. You have to feel the rush in your body and still do nothing with it. But, because you have the movements, this is a way to channel the energy when you feel the rush. When you are dancing, for example, doing snake-like movements, it gets transformed. Then the energy starts to flow, and it doesn't get stuck down in your pelvis.*

*This is in your body, this is the Aphrodite, or the Arab goddess Ishtar, and you feel it down here. This you have to relate to your brain, the Athena part of you, who puts up the boundaries, the structures. Athena says, we are at work and we are not going to fuck at work. So, she gives the message to Aphrodite down there to say, uh-uh. Athena is the general. Also, just as in the army you have a commandant who goes on the field and fights, here we have Artemis: she is the warrior, the one who protects the boundaries. When a man crosses the boundaries. immediately you have to hit back with a fierce energy, an energy these men can understand. Don't try to be nice.*

**What I hear in this is that it's also about bringing these masculine and feminine qualities together in yourself.**

*Yes, because if you are only in your feminine part, you won't make it, especially not at work and in leadership. If you are only in your masculine side, it's no fun either. Women suffer a lot at work. Because what we see there now is that the only women who are allowed to function at work are the masculine women, especially in leadership. In lead-*

ership there are mostly masculine women, because these are the ones who can hold their ground with men, as they are non-sexual, a-sensual, a-feminine. This is the price they must pay, and it doesn't make them happy. I have many women in leadership roles as my clients for personal coaching, and they are usually 45 to 50 years old, and they have spent most of their lives in this masculine energy. They have made it almost to the top, they have their reputation and everything, and now they want to climb the last step to the top, but they are exhausted, and they want to do it differently. They want to explore their feminine side, but they have no clue how that works.

**Is this the way a female leader needs to go, to push through in their masculine energy and then explore the feminine side more later?**

Not all of them, because many stay in the masculine parts of themselves—they don't have the need for the feminine. But some of them reach the age of 45 or 50 and realize they are missing something. Me too: I had this system, I was a kind of "schizophrenic" in my work/private balance. I worked at the university in a more masculine mindset, and when I went out I changed to the feminine through the dance. It was only in 2010 that I finally brought these two worlds together. How I lived before that was very schizophrenic. But after being so masculine your whole work life, in your private life you also start behaving that way. It doesn't make you happy. Many women continue like this. They behave the same at work and at home. Usually they start to have problems in their private relationships, private life; then they realize they want to function in a more femi-

*nine way, but they don't know how this works anymore. When they come to me, I say, I won't help you to bring out your feminine side in your private life, but I will help you to do it in your work life. Because if you can bring out your feminine side there, you can bring it out anywhere. In private it is very easy, but how to transfer it from the private sphere to the workplace? That's the question.*

**In my own work in the last few years I have integrated a more inclusive way of leadership, which I consider to be more feminine. I get inspiration from different concepts, like the Conscious Capitalism movement started by John Mackey, Fred Kofman's Conscious Business, flat hierarchies, Holacracy and Sociocracy 3.0. What's your perspective on that?**

*The problem is, the patriarchy feels threatened by the feminine. Only masculine values are allowed in business in general. So, as a woman or a man, when you want to enter that arena, especially the arena of leadership, you must have mostly masculine qualities. The feminine ones are nice to have, but they are not the core values in business.*

**They are often called the "soft skills."**

*Yes, exactly. Which means, you have mostly masculine men and women playing in the arena of power, and the feminine doesn't have a voice in that field because it's a "soft skill."*

**And this has also been changing a bit, especially in the last three to five years.**

*Right. The idea of the work I do—and I go back to the work of Hakim, because she pushes it into hardcore business arenas—is, that erotic capital should not be the most important capital. Erotic capital is always something that you add. The most important thing, as a woman, is to have your cultural capital developed as much as possible, your knowledge. You should also have your economic capital, as you have to be financially independent. And you have to develop your social capital as well. Women are often very bad at networking. Men are very efficient at networking, but somehow women haven't learned the skills yet to network well in business. It is very important to build relationships, but also to make very clear and visible to men what you want from them. Women have the tendency not to say what they want; they are a little bit too humble. So, social capital is very important.*

*Erotic capital is like extra capital, which brings certain values and qualities. Here is a difference between my work and Hakim's. Hakim likes to use erotic capital as a strategy. For me it has to be an internal strategy, a compass. I think if you develop erotic capital first of all in the external world and as a strategy, it makes you too fragile and weak as a woman. Because, for example, if to develop the concept of beauty and sexual fitness, liveliness and all of these things, you invest in them only as exterior elements, you are too dependent on the outside. There comes a moment when the beauty will go down with age, or sexual fitness, or liveliness—all of these things. So, if it's too much on the outside, it makes you insecure as a woman. What you need to do is to bring it to the inside, which I do in the work with the goddesses. You have to feel beautiful from the inside—you have to feel attractive from inside. It all has to go on inside, inside your body and your system—otherwise it's just a perfor-*

mance. This is why it's essential to experience it only among women.

One of the challenges I often experience, working in companies, is that there is always a point where I want to have the women alone. And usually they say, "we cannot separate women and men," and I say, "find something for the men to do among themselves, it's also good for them." There are certain things I do only with women, with no men around. Because that is the only space I know where I feel I can take them inside. If there are men around, they are too busy worrying about other things.

When women are able to integrate erotic capital from the inside, then they can master it according to wherever they are on the learning curve. The first stage is "unconscious incompetence," or, "we don't know that we cannot do something." When I learned Dutch, for example, I thought it would be very easy, as I already spoke four languages. I didn't know that I would not easily be able to deal with Germanic grammar, as I was used to Latin and Semitic languages, like Arabic and Hebrew, where the system is totally different. I didn't know that I wouldn't be able to slide right into the Germanic system, so I was unconsciously incompetent, "I didn't know that I couldn't learn Germanic languages." Once you do learn that, you go into the "conscious incompetence" phase which comes with lots of frustrations. For example, when I teach women the movements with the pelvic floor muscles, even when they know ballet, salsa, or other dances, they freak out, because all kinds of insecurities rise up. Then I tell them, you are in the consciously incompetent stage, because you know you cannot do it and you get frustrated. If you keep on exercising you will get to the third stage of the learning curve, which is the consciously competent stage, where you know how to do it and you can do it. Finally, we reach the fourth stage, unconsciously competent, where you can do it without even thinking about it.

The way Hakim elaborates her theory, it stays very much in the consciously competent. It's like something that I am going do in a certain way. I dress up nicely, put on makeup, I go to a salsa course, I go to a belly dance course, I learn things and then do them. I will learn all these things, then I will master them and then I will use them. But then you are at the level of consciously competent, you are still thinking, and using, and manipulating, and creating a strategy for how to get somewhere. It's exhausting, and you feel like an "imposter." But when you keep on practicing and internalize the knowledge, you reach the stage of unconsciously competent: it becomes a natural skill, and then you're safe, because it has become a part of your personality. This is also why the work I do takes a lot of time. I say to women, it will take you at least two to three years. They usually freak out. Sure, even the first time they do it, they will gain at least some benefit, but to master it, for it to become natural, it will take at least one year, even if you are a fast learner.

When I work with women, I work with Artemis, the warrior of the heart. Then I say, for example, you have to use your breasts. I learned this from my grandmother, who grew up in a harem. When she was pissed off at the men, she *stood in front of them, raised her chest and said, "This won't happen anymore"—then they were all silent. But western women, because this posture is so sexualized, keep their chest small, more inward. I always say, if you don't agree, don't raise your voice, raise your boobs. But it's not something that you use like a trick. You have to practice it as much as possible, so it comes out naturally, which means you have to practice it first with your children and your dog. When you practice it with animals or children, you are not into being sexual or manipulative—you are in a completely neutral and erotically innocent environment. From there you can go on to use the erotic capital, but not before; otherwise you are busy with strategy and manipulation. This is one of the things with erotic capital: it too can be capitalized..*

**Speaking about capitalizing: There is a big discussion about equality for women, also regarding salaries. When I hear your idea of women showing up in their full feminine qualities, I think it might also make them more valuable in a financial way. Right now, we speak about quotas and equal remuneration as top-down decisions, as if we should have this from one day to the next—but this would not change our culture. How would you deal with that: how to build up an equality, or equity, of women and men in a company?**

*My opinion about quotas is this: you can wait until it grows organically, but when you look 100 years further, or at least 50, do you want to wait that long? We actually have an emergency, a crisis—there's something that needs to change, and so we need to accelerate. I am personally in favor of quotas, and I can tell you why with an example from Tunisia. Tunisian women are seen as the most emancipated in the Arab Muslim world. Tunisia became independent in 1956. I am part of the first generation who grew up with a certain freedom, in an independent country. We women were lucky, because the first president of Tunisia, Habib Bourguiba, grew up in a harem, only with women, as he was very sick. He did not go out to play with the boys; he always stayed inside and he was very much influenced by women. But he also became angry about how women were treated like second- or third-class citizens in the existing patriarchal system. As he was always with the women, he was always treated as they were, and he felt for himself how unfair that was. Then he promised himself that if one day he came into power and he had the possibility, he would do everything he could to help women. So, once Tunisia became independent, he decided, from the top down, that the government would make a law forbidding polygamy and other practices that were unfair to women. And he had a huge clash with the theological university.*

*Tunisian women could vote before Swiss women could, and Tunisian women had the right to have abortions before French women, and there was obligatory education for girls already in the '50s. Parents who didn't bring their children to school, especially girls, went to jail. Bourguiba introduced positive discrimination. If you had a job available, you got subsidies from the government if you hired a woman. He put a whole new system in place in Tunisia in the '50s and '60s. All that I know in terms of emancipation and feminine power I learned in Tunisia; I never learned this in Europe. When I came here, I thought they were retarded. I saw all the means they had, and the democracy and money, and yet* the women were like slaves. In Tunisia, we were emancipated through this one man's vision, and it worked. I believe in that system even today, after the "failure" of the Arab spring movement. Tunisia is, until now, the only "success story" to come out of the Arab spring, and it's because of the women and the men supporting the women. Women continue to participate in all aspects of life; they kicked the Islamists out of power. They are very active. Why? Because we have a quota and a law which protects us.

There is still a gap, and it will take another generation to narrow it, but then you can catch up very quickly because you are protected by law. Otherwise you would have to wait. We will get there, but do we want to wait 50 or 100 years?—that is the question. I don't want to wait.

On the other hand, to answer your question, if quotas work, I would say they don't necessarily work so well. Why? A study about leadership and women in leadership was done in the Netherlands by a colleague of mine, and this study suggests that if you want to bring change into an organization—and it doesn't matter what kind of change—if you want to have a change in mentality, you need to create more diversity, and then you integrate minorities into the structure. Let's say you want to support a minority like homosexuals, Arabs or Blacks, or we want to have more women— well, if the minority is less than 30 percent it won't work. If they are only 10 percent, they will adapt to the rules of the majority. It only works if more than 30 percent of the whole group is formed of this minority, so people feel safe enough to stand up for their identity and their values. That's why *quotas can be so important. So, if you want to promote feminine values, you need 30 percent of decision-making positions to be filled by women, in order to create a change in the mentality of management. A quota under 30 percent won't do the job. Quotas themselves don't automatically work.*

*By the way, in 2017 the EU tried to push the women's quota to 40 percent on the boards, but Germany, the Netherlands and Great Britain blocked the attempt. There were companies in Holland which had already reached the 30 percent mark, but when we started to study what kind of change was happening, it was almost zero. Why? Because the criteria and processes of selection and promotion were based on masculine values. This is another real problem. It is masculine men, or women, who are hiring masculine women, because they move like them (I call it an "incest intent" group). They are hiring only their "own blood," those who are like them, with strong masculine qualities. In the end women with feminine values weren't getting a chance. And if you hire masculine women it is even worse than hiring a man—it's a disaster; it doesn't work. So, we not only need a quota, we need feminine values, otherwise it simply doesn't work.*

**How can you really measure feminine values? The feminine qualities are often called soft skills and can't be pinned down with a number. How can you integrate this in terms of scientific evidence?**

*There have been these kinds of studies, looking into what exactly feminine values are. For example, inclusiveness is strongly feminine. We have to study the management styles of both women and men, and integrate more of these feminine qualities. Ironically, in leadership positions there are more men who integrate the feminine than women. Men often go more into their feminine side than women do. These qualities include, for example, this inclusiveness, along with empathy, collaboration, compromises, emotional intelligence. In terms of emotional intelligence, the last study of this was done by a university in the US—I don't remember which—and it was about leadership styles and the different skills you need to have in order to be a good leader. Women scored as high as men or higher on all the skills except two: self-confidence and emotional control.*

*It seems women have a lack of self-confidence, which I also see in my work, and it might be because they have been kept small for thousands of years by patriarchal systems. But, on the other hand, what are the criteria for self-confidence, what is the norm? The norm is the behavior of men. Yet many men in leadership positions are narcissistic and egocentric. They pretend to be able to do a lot, and in the end it's nothing. That's how they are—they behave macho and think that's enough. On the other hand, men are also very bold, and they cannot say No to certain tasks. Even though they cannot do it now, men will say "I can do it, or I will learn while I am doing it." I think this is a good attitude. A woman would say "I don't know if I can do this job, because I'm missing this and that." But, also, a lot of men lie, and they make something seem more beautiful than it is. My grandmother said, it's a pity that their egos are bigger than their penises. So, if criteria for self-confidence are based on the behavior of men, who have bigger egos than women, it is a self-centered self-confidence—it's based on air. Narcissists are very insecure and they have little self-confidence, but they cover it with flamboyance, like Donald Trump. So if you're going to use this as a norm, it's a "dysfunctional" masculine norm.*

*In terms of emotional intelligence women score much, much higher in leadership than men, but they might score lower in emotional control, because men control their emotions better. Yet many men are also "emotionally autistic." So, what is the norm? This is something else that I see in my work: women have a lot of difficulties expressing their emotions in a healthy way. When they get angry they become bitchy, when they get frustrated they start to cry, and when they cry they cannot function anymore because they haven't learned to cry and function at the same time—to feel, cry, think and be in alignment, and to move on from there. Often, they collapse, and everything becomes a drama, and when a man sees that he hates it, and he doesn't know what to do with it. When women start to behave like dramatic little girls, going into shaming and blaming, that is terrible. So, there is a problem of emotional control when things go wrong. In relation to the goddesses I call it the light and the shadow. When the women enter their shadow sides, they can't master their emotions anymore, they can't go into the light, and they stay in the shadow and start to go down, down, down. In that sense there is an issue about emotional control for women, but the issue is also that the norm is masculine, and the norm is emotional autism. So, these two are the only two aspects in that study where women didn't score as well as men, while all the other skills they master just as well as men do nowadays.*

**What would you say is the right way to express feelings and emotions in the business world? Often in this world emotions are not really valued. What would be the best way to express emotions, so that we could even think of emotional capital?**

*Emotions have to become healthy first. Expressing unhealthy emotions in general, and especially at work, is a no-go area:—it is not professional, it does not work, and it sabotages the whole thing. The question is, how can we as individuals, or as a company, make sure that our emotions are healthy? When I work with the goddess archetypes I refer to the concept of shadow, which was developed by Carl Jung, and also by Sufism, the mystical branch of Islam. In Sufism there is no difference between light and shadow. In western culture everything is good or bad, hell or paradise—always this polarity. In Sufism it is not good/bad. It's one: they say, "the shadow is the place where the light enters you." The only question is how to transform it into light. The shadow has the potential to become light; it is one and the same with it, ultimately. The thing is, you can't erase the shadow, but you can increase the light, so the shadow comes into the light. If we talk about the archetypes, women have the most difficulties in terms of emotions in what we call the feminine archetypes, or the vulnerable ones.*

*The masculine ones are in control, not very emotional. Athena, Artemis, they are not very emotional. Persephone, the child, Demeter, the mother—these are very emotional. These are the archetypes that we miss—the ones that are about vulnerability, empathy, caring, about nurturing—but the shadow of these is victimhood, helplessness, powerless- ness, suppressed anger, weak boundaries, defeatism, worth- lessness, etc. All of these, where we feel we don't deserve things, that we are small: these are the shadows.*

*I use the movements for that, but I always work first on the shadow, and from there I move to the light. The move- ment is a tool. You cannot say to a person who is emotional, "So, and now go into the light," because they don't know how to do that. They are into their drama. I use the body-work with my Divine Nine method to get into the shadow first, and after that to release the shadow—for example, with vi- brations, which I call shimmies. I have different shimmies for different functions, for different archetypes. We go into shaking from low to high and from there we go into the snake and water movements. First, we start with the fire movement, to take the tensions out of the shadow. Before it can go into the light it has tension, it has drama, and this drama has to exit. With the vibration it can go out. If we lit- erally talk about vibrancy in erotic capital, it is really there in these movements, where you shake your energy to be- come alive. From there, once you have cleansed it with the fire, you can go into the water, which includes a lot of sen- sual snake movements.*

*Once you have these tools and know how to manage them, you have more self-confidence to explore your emo- tions, and you also know how to transform them. I say to my women, at the beginning, that I also get regularly very over- whelmed by negative emotions. When I'm in a meeting, for example, and I get overwhelmed, and I feel like I'm going to cry or scream, I shift into anger, or sadness, or into collapse. Then I go to the toilet, I lock myself in, and for five minutes I do the movements. All the women who do the work with me do the same thing. They can do these movement anywhere. Women need to have tools—physical tools, not just mental ones, as the emotions are in the body as well. You can try to channel emotions through the mind by understanding what is going on, but this is a long, long route. Sometimes you don't have time; sometimes you need to act immediately. I always say to my women, the mental analysis, you can do that later, but first do the bodywork, quickly, to get back on track. If your body relaxes, especially from the pelvic floor muscles on up, you can channel stress. If you feel stress, you squeeze and release the pelvic floor muscles very fast, so the energy can come down. When your head is running hot, you bring your energy down to your pelvis. Once you bring it down, you can channel it back up again. Afterwards, you can analyze it with your mind, but first you need to become calm, not by suppressing the emotions, or by denying them, but by transforming them.*

**And this could even be important for men as well. In my ideal world, a person who is overwhelmed, or getting emotional, doesn't have to go to the toilet to do this exercise, but could do it even in the boardroom.**

*Yes, but it is difficult, it takes time. You can go to the toilet for five minutes, and it's not the end of the world. But to a certain degree, this is what I teach, because I work a lot with women who are in politics, in parliament, where they are debating. They cannot say, "Stop debating, please, I have to go to the toilet." When they are standing there, and they have 300 people shouting at them, they have to hold their ground. Later they use the bodywork, but it's all based in the pelvis. I sometimes say this to women: "In situations where you need self-confidence, you wear your balls and you go to work with them." That's why they should not have sex, because that way they recycle that energy into sexual practice. And then they freak out and think, "What, I have to go to work with the Goddess Balls inside?" And I say, yes.*

*Once you master your sexual energy, it is so powerful, you can master everything. Sometimes you might even get scared of yourself. Women, especially, don't dare to be alive and vibrant, to play with that erotic intelligence and capital at work, because they are afraid of getting shut down, or that they won't be able to control themselves. I ask sometimes "What is your biggest fear?" and they answer that it's that they might fall in love with a colleague or with the boss. But if you control your energy you won't go there. When you feel it start you can hold it back, you can manage it—but for that you need tools. This is all about control in the body, in the system.*

*In the beginning, when I started to practice this with the balls, I thought I could fuck the whole city of Amsterdam. I became restless. Women who come to me the first time are on level zero and after the first session they are on 150, it goes very fast. You have to come down again and recycle, with snake-like and water movements, and use this to explore your emotions, to explore depression, worthlessness, or pain. While you are feeling pain, you do these sen-*

sual movements. The sexual energy doesn't make a distinction between depression and happiness, between feeling depressed or feeling ecstasy. No, it's just energy, it's just flow. The moment you start using this energy, you start to feel alive, because depression, feeling worthless and all these other things are also part of your emotional baggage. So, use your sexual energy to get in touch with these things in an intensive way. The sexual energy intensifies all emotions. Also, depression, negativity and pain get intensified.

People ask me, how do you do that? I don't do that. When I am in my groups I also cry with the women because, like we say in Africa, "Ubuntu"—we are one, your pain is my pain. I don't place myself outside of the group; I am one of the group. I can also switch immediately—it's not a problem. But I get women into these emotions quite fast, because I use the sexual energy as a shortcut, a quick access to emotions, especially to the shadows. This is the biggest part, which women are not used to, because this sexual energy is for ecstasy, and for joy, to feel good, to feel on top of the world. But no, you also feel good down in the seventh hell in the underworld. That's also sexual, because in the end everything is sexual, everything is about vitality. This is why people are so afraid of emotions, because the so-called negative emotions, the shadow, are things we don't want to feel because we don't know how to manage them.

Erotic capital helps you to manage these emotions. The sexual energy helps you to manage the shadows, but you have to know how to have access to this energy and to activate it all the time. I call it the erotic bank, La Banque Ero-

*tique, as sometimes I am a capitalist, too. I am an Arab, so I don't have a problem with capitalism—as long it helps people and the planet it's okay. Whenever you go to the bank and you borrow money because you need it, and especially when you explore your shadows—all of that is okay. When you take out a loan from the bank to explore these shadows, these low vibrations, then afterwards it increases your capital. When you go back to your light you grow stronger, so it's an investment, your capital grows, it gets higher. But first you have to take it out, and afterwards it comes back, ten times as much. It's a win-win.*

**That's a good wrap up for our conversation.**

*This is why I like the word capital, but it depends on what kind of meaning you give to it. Capital as a value—yes, in Pierre Bourdieu's terms, it is just a value.*

**Thank you very much.**

*Merci!*

Nilima Bhat

# Turning *eros* to Eros

**Nilima Bhat** is co-author of the book Shakti Leadership, together with Raj Sisodia, she is a facilitator of personal transformation, coaching individuals and organizations in their quest for conscious evolution. She is an international speaker and trainer on organizational culture, conscious business, women in leadership, and self-awareness for work-life balance, as well as Indian wisdom and wellness traditions.

Her integral approach synthesizes best practices and paths from around the world, and is customized to meet audience needs. Her particular expertise is in developing Body Intelligence and Spiritual Intelligence (BQ & SQ).

She has delivered leadership training and facilitation for Microsoft, Whole Foods Market, Tata, Societe Generale Bank, Vodafone, and YPO, as well as academic institutions and developmental organisations such as Indus International School and SKS Microfinance. She is an active supporter of the Conscious Capitalism movement and Women's International Networking (WIN) and serves on the advisory board of MixR, 20-first and Peace through Commerce.

Nilima is currently building the Shakti Fellowship, jointly certified with the University of San Diego and WIN, with a mission to create 100,000 women changemakers by 2030, and as well the Truth & Reconciliation movement for healing collective trauma and leading harmonious interdependence at a planetary level.

shaktileadership.com

\*\*\*

# The great artistic work of our time

*eros* is the unconscious sexual drive / instinct. It arouses lust in us; and left unchecked, it turns to aggression, *thanatos*.

Yet, it is the Vital, the life-force and needed to perpetuate Life.

Instead of being suppressed (through vows of Poverty, Chastity and Obedience) as in the many male spiritual traditions, perhaps Female Spirituality, which is based on embodiment rather than simply enlightenment, has the key and therefore the responsibility to make conscious the drive.

When expressed as Eros, it is what lends the RASA to Life. Making Life juicy and joyful. And expressed not just through lovemaking of a couple, but as the heightened taste and textures of good food, Art, Relationship, Beauty, Nature. All creative expressions of Shiva-Shakti saamrasya. The experience of the elixir that flows when Shiva and Shakti are in holy embrace.

When the god *eros* marries the girl *psyche* who has come-of-age, the offspring is called Delight. We are invited to call that Delight, Eros. It will bring the sweetness to Life that will fulfil our Human birth. Quenching our longing for the Beloved, through all Human acts, interactions and experience. Giving it Purpose.

A yogini can begin the process when she channels her eros towards such heightened and deepened expressions. She can initiate her partner in the act of sacred love making. She can turn her cooking, her art, her dance, her song, her leadership into Eros. By adding her soul shakti to her life-force, as she expresses and embodies both, together.

Modelling and transmitting Rasa-anubhav, the inner experience, as Rasaanubhaav its outer expression. Being and sharing the REAL TASTE OF LIFE. DIVINE LIFE.

We know the Shakti who enables this process as the Mahavidya, Lalita. Let us invoke Her to bless us on this great and most necessary quest. If we are to stop the battle of the sexes and become fully and truly Human.

## Turning *logos* to Logos

### The great scientific work of our time

What would be the other great work of our time then? Turning logos to Logos. The parallel journey needed to achieve Embodiment, is that of Enlightenment. The quest to embrace mythos by making the magical, creative invisible possibilities visible. Holding them in the Light of Awareness, in a playful childlike way; letting each Word reveal its greater, more complete Truth. As whole-brain thinking.

This seems to be an adventure that would call the curious thinkers, the open rationalists. We need many good men and women with a well-honed scientific temper, to answer that call. It will bring the Awe to Life that will quench our thirst for Meaning.

When *eros* and *thanatos* are integrated consciously, they become Eros.

When *logos* and *mythos* are similarly integrated, they become Logos.

Together they meet our quest for Purpose and Meaning.

We cannot successfully complete one journey without also undertaking the other.

And, to make these journeys with least suffering to self and others, the invitation is to undertake both consciously, i.e. from Presence.

When all sexes can integrate Eros and Logos, we become the Whole Man, Whole Woman, Whole Human.

Savouring the ANANDA, the innate DELIGHT of EXISTENCE itself.

As the symphony of resonant Song and Dance it seems to have been playfully and joyfully created for!

What a grand design.

Wishing us rapture and awe through each Holy Season.

# Interview with Nilima Bhat

*Notice: the use of upper- and lower-case letters in this text, for example, logos will sometimes be spelled Logos to reflect a larger, more integrated version of logos.*

**Heinz:** I want to talk to you about the article that you wrote, "Turning *eros* to Eros," going from eros with a small letter to Eros with a capital letter. And it's really touching for me, this idea that Eros is nothing sexual but is more really like an expression of life energy. I'm wondering how, and maybe you can share it, how you are seeing it.

*Nilima Bhat: I began with the short article that you read; and after that I have a longer article explaining it in very mythic terms which I'm also going to share with you. But, in a nutshell, my journey to understanding these drives began when there were these horrific rapes in India in December 2012 and shortly after that. And it was as if every woman was "raped awake," not just in India, but around the world. There was a young girl who was brutally gang raped and mu-*

*tilated on a bus in the capital of India. Some events are kind of archetypal and go beyond the personal. This was one such event. The girl was called Nirbhaya, which basically means the fearless one. That wasn't her real name. It's a name that has since been given to her. And that's how the country remembers how she died of her injuries a few days later.*

*Men have been raping women; this has been going on for Millennia. And yet there was something about the way this happened that just woke people up. And this was December 2012, when I was in Peru leading a journey, a spiritual journey called the Divine Marriage of the Himalayas and the Andes, and creating a very sacred ceremony where I was taking waters from the Ganga, all the different tributaries, and from Kailash, which represents Shiva, the divine masculine, and I was taking water from all those great bodies and I was going to offer it to Lake Titicaca, which represented the feminine pole. The Andes are very beautiful and feminine. And so, seeing Lake Titicaca as the great womb of the planet, we were inseminating the waters with the waters from the Himalayas.*

*And around this time, that's when this rape happened here in India. So for me, all these things were very live, and I was trying to understand the polarities inside. Again, this was in 2012, well before the book Shakti Leadership came out. I entered into a very deep quest or search for what it is in the human condition that makes us capable of such brutal behavior towards another human being. And what is it about men wanting to overpower women, who are weaker than them? What is it about, what do they get out of that? And* when I was searching for the root of violence and destruction in human nature, I came across this book called Terror, Violence and the Impulse to Destroy. Have you heard of it?

*It was brought about at a Jungian conference right after 9/11, as America was doing a lot of soul searching, thinking about what makes another country want to, you know, destroy us in this terrible way, to actually bomb our buildings, and what is it about. Where does this terror and the violence and the impulse to destroy come from? They wanted to understand this issue from the full perspective of human psychology and depth psychology. So many Jungians came together and offered papers, and those papers were put together for this book. It's available online. I bought it on kindle, and I read it and I came across a very important piece by Dr. Brian Skea, who is a Jungian, and who talks about the fourfold self. And this comes from Freud, originally, and was then taken up by Jung. The idea is that inside us, at a somatic level, we have these two drives. We have eros, which is the sexual instinct to procreate, and we have thanatos, which is the survival instinct of fight and flight, to basically save one's life. If a lion is coming at you and you're a deer, you need to run away; or if you're the lion, you need thanatos in order to be aggressive and kill; otherwise you don't eat. So the death drive and the life drive, thanatos and eros, are actually two sides of the same coin. It's a somatic drive that's hardwired into our animal bodies, part of our evolutionary heritage. It's needed for survival, to either kill or be killed, as well as to procreate.*

What happened is, as we became humans, yet another faculty opened in our animal nature, where we are no longer just somatic beings, we also became psychological beings. So *Mind* appears. Psyche appears on the evolutionary scene. And this too has two sides, the logos and the mythos. The logos is our rational self, our ability to make meaning. But we also have an imaginative, intuitive, creative side to our mind, to our psyche, and that's called mythos. In many ways it parallels the split between the right brain and the left brain.

Of course, if we were just mental creatures and we didn't have anything below the neck, we may have become balanced, integrated mental beings by now. But what has happened is that humanity right now, as a species, is not yet fully evolved into its evolutionary niche. We are still struggling out of our animal nature and we haven't yet fully entered into our full psychological wholeness. So right now, psyche and soma are not harmonized in the human body-mind. And so at any given time, any of these drives is seeking to lead us. And sometimes one gets the better of us and sometimes the other.

Now, in the grand scheme of things, we're actually meant to be thoughtful creatures, we're meant to be discerning creatures, we're meant to be conscious creatures, we're meant to have a sense of ethics and responsibility. Just because we have the capacity to kill and rape, it doesn't mean we should, every time that impulse takes hold of us. It may be okay in the animal kingdom, to always act on impulse, but as humans we have a choice, because we have a mind that understands the consequences of our actions. So, *there has always been this, the logos in us, which is in a way the human mind in its fullness, and this logos has always been on its own heroic journey to come of age and to claim its sovereign place over this bodymind. Am I worthy of leading, and not being led, by the erotic and the destructive instincts? That's the question we all have to ask ourselves.*

*Eros and thanatos, logos and mythos – these forces are not going to just give themselves over. These are very powerful instincts that are part of nature.*

*So, our yoga, our self-conscious evolution, requires that we discern these four drives inside ourselves and learn to harmonize them around what we call Presence. You can't only be logos because life would be a very boring place. It's from eros, it's from that somatic self, that you experience the Rasa, the juice of life that makes life worth tasting and being in, and also this is what keeps alive the juices that create life. So, eros with a small e has to go to Eros with the capital E, which is what I have written about.*

*But it cannot go from small e to big E by itself. This is an important missing piece in some of the perspectives I have encountered so far. What they're missing is the idea that small eros can't become big Eros without small logos going to big Logos. Without this, we're still stuck in dualistic thinking, saying it's all about Eros, just Eros, and there we go again. We're stuck in one side of the polarity and we've neglected the other, even though these are interdependent polarities and you can't have one without also having the other. This is very, very important.*

*Now, what has happened is that in order to control these impulses in an age of science and thought and spirituality, an age that denies these urges, we have overvalued the mind and logos, and, in the process, we've lost touch with the feeling of the connection between the two poles of these polarities. If you understand this from the perspective of Yin and Yang, Logos is more masculine, more Yang, and Eros is more feminine, more Yin. Both are needed for wholeness and balance.*

*As we were saying, in our cultures it has too often been only about logos, neglecting eros almost completely. We just became dry, desiccated creatures. And, what's worse, if you don't express your eros consciously, you're doomed to experience it unconsciously. And so it comes out anyway, and it comes out as unhealthy, inappropriate sexuality and aggression and violence, etc. So for me, the big thing is: don't glorify Eros if you cannot, in the same conversation, understand the role of Logos. Because I fear we will go back to eros with the small e, and this is the reason why all the masculine-led spiritual traditions have basically said, don't touch eros. Just don't touch it. Don't go there, because it is archetypal, it is way beyond what this little ego self can handle. So it's like a salt doll going to measure the depth of the ocean.*

*If we go to such a deep place, we are just going to get consumed by it, dissolved in it. So it's better not to touch it at all, until you have sufficiently developed your Logos, your discernment, your Presence, in a more holistic way; when you've taken your intuitive, imaginative, mythic self along with you. From this place, it's okay now to understand eros and enter the waters of eros, so to speak.*

*So coming back to what you were saying, let me just close the loop on Terror, Violence and the Impulse to Destroy. It becomes obvious that, as a species, we haven't yet come of age. And so, of course, we have a great capacity for death and destruction, which is coming from this somatic aspect of thanatos, at a time when our logos isn't fully grown and matured.*

*So, if you understand that evolution follows a certain arc, there is a kind of heroic journey and process, and there is an unfolding and it doesn't all happen at one time. On one hand, while you may feel sad when you go to work and see that everyone is so structured and constricted, that they are kind of missing the juice of life, well, that's not the whole story. Yes, if I were to simply accept the reality that this is the way evolution seems to be flowing (and you can't argue with the way it has happened so far), I would only be looking at part of a larger cycle. Indeed, it seems to me that our journey to individuation and our coming into wholeness happens over three cycles. (I understood this when I came across Penelope Lively's book The Mythical Quest: In Search of Adventure, Romance & Enlightenment. I was struck by Lively's Introduction of this idea.)*

*The first journey is the quest for adventure, which is your ego-self looking to integrate your shadow-self. That is a very masculine journey. Your ego is basically your mind, which is saying that this is good, that is not good, it's okay to do this, it's not okay to do that. And so, in the process, as we develop this very parental version of the self, we lose touch with parts of our child-self, our inner child and that remains undeveloped around a fortification of defense mechanisms. A big and important part of us becomes lost to our rational self, as an undeveloped part of our child-self, and therefore every time it gets triggered, it comes out in a disproportionate, exaggerated way. And so we experience a "shadow attack." Whereas, if we know how to, from a place of Presence, we can stop judging the shadow behavior and, with great compassion, go towards it, much like a parent would go towards a child. By approaching this undeveloped part of the self in this way, we can dismantle the defense mechanisms that surround it and go to the heart of the lost part of us, where the libido is stuck and locked away. It is a part of our inner child, and we are better off when we're in touch with it.*

*If you can find that part of yourself, you'll also find some shame or guilt or fear or sorrow. It's your part of your own child-self that got split away at some time, when you were growing up. And if you can reclaim that inner child, that split self, and if you can integrate that back with the other parts of yourself, and bring it into the light, then this logos/mythos healing takes place. The parent child healing takes place, right? The child is your curious self that lives in the mythic world, so to speak. It's the more feminine Yin energy, compared to the more masculine Yang energy of a parent, so to speak.*

*So this is the first journey, our journey to meet our fears, and therefore it's called an adventure, which I think is a masculine journey of the mind coming into its wholeness, where logos and mythos can get integrated.*

*Once that kind of psychological wholeness has been achieved, now the soul starts questing for romantic wholeness, for putting together the wholeness of love and meeting the other "half." The animus in us seeks the anima, the anima in us seeks the animus. And so Jung would call this embracing the shadow, as the apprentice part of the individuation process, as it were, and embracing the anima/animus as the masterpiece of individuation. And I believe Jung's view was still incomplete. There's still one more piece left, and now we'll come to that.*

*So if we have done the ego/shadow integration, the logos/mythos integration, now we are sufficiently psychologically mature to enter into the somatic realm of the body and experience this force, which is at once love that's coming from the sacred heart center and the sexual force that's coming from your second Chakra, the procreative center.*

*All these are part of the same id, the libido. So, if you are sufficiently mature, now it is okay to enter into getting in touch with your own sexuality. But from a place of presence and acceptance, of true self-acceptance, of getting in touch with your own aggression and your capacity to be a really forceful creature. Maybe even fight and kill, if necessary, in an act of self-defense. That's a very important energy we need to honor and hold in ourselves.*

*Each person has both the anima and the animus within. And in many ways the sexual force is the deep yearning towards finding the lost half, the other self that lies within us. If you're male you have another self in you which is female, and if you're female you have another self inside you which is male, and in both cases there is this id part of the personality that contains both sides, and which has the capacity to bring you to the fulfillment of that yearning you have – that we all have.*

*Coming from a place of psychological maturity, we will not be overtaken by our sexuality. We will know how to contain it and how to channel it. How to supplement it, how to transform it and not to just react to it or from it. It's as if we could say, "Oh, because I'm feeling an impulse, I'm feeling an urge, this doesn't mean I've got to go have sex with someone, or I have to go masturbate or, you know, I've got to rape someone."*

*This ties into what we were saying about eros and Eros. This Eros with the big E, this is what is called Kundalini in Yoga; Life's evolutionary force itself, which lies coiled in the base of our spine until awakened by Life's desire for itself, the desire to move on in creative ways. As it happens to rise up from the Mooladhara (the root chakra), it hits the Swadhisthan (the sexual chakra, located just above the root chakra), it activates the sexual impulse, eros with a small e. So the sexual impulse itself is animated by Eros with the capital E. And we have to remain in touch with the capital E and not get hijacked by the small e.*

*Now, when we say that ideally you should have first integrated your logos and mythos, it's as if there has been a descent of consciousness from the upper chakras down into your lower chakras. So that NOW when this Eros of Life is seeking to rise in you (it's called spandana or spanda, the 'Shakti wave'), it rises within the contained safe space of your Logos, and it's not going to get hijacked by other impulses, and it won't find other ways to disappear into what's called the "vital" planes, which are present at that second chakra level, and so it can rise up all the way to your solar plexus and your heart. There, it can now be expressed in harmonized and life-affirming ways.*

*As I see it, when we achieve this kind of synthesis, we are invited to in the sacred heart traditions of Christianity. The whole concept of divine, unconditional love and forgiveness is that same eros, now transmuted and expressed as this incredible ability for compassion and unconditional love, and forgiveness, and the ability to be in divine, holy, sacred relationship with other human beings and with oneself – and even with source itself, called God. So, the actual erotic energy is needed to do all this great work, and it should not be hijacked, expressed solely in a sexual act, and dissipated. This is why in Yoga this energy is considered sacred. Sexual energy is considered sacred.*

*You're not meant to just dissipate it and lose it. You're supposed to honor it and then express it in a way that is truly bringing in the divine, the holiness and sacredness to life, as it should be in all your actions. And, yes, that would include the act of making love with your partner. It's no longer an animal expression of a lustful act, it becomes a very beautiful, sacred ritual that you participate in together, offering your bodies to be the ground in which these great forces of Logos and Eros can harmonize and come together. And in the process, you get to savor it and bathe in it and be blessed by it. So it's a totally different way of understanding* these impulses, and then of channeling them in a way that doesn't suppress them but actually elevates them, expressing them in a way that is appropriate for us as human beings.

Just because we can express ourselves as animals doesn't mean we should, and just because we don't have to be animal doesn't mean we should disregard the "lower" side of our nature. Once we go through the process of coming into the fullness of our mind, in order to then engage in the fullness of our body, we are now ready for yet another quest, which is the third! The first quest is for adventure, the second is the quest for romance. The third is the quest for enlightenment.

We come to realize, after successfully completing the first two journeys, that there's yet another journey and another polarity, which is the polarity of the personal self and the divine self; my ego self, and the higher self. And how do I merge those two together, so that I experience my divine, my fully human divinity, which hasn't yet been attained even with the bringing together of the inner masculine and the inner feminine selves (Anima and Animus)? Because we are more than that as well.

So the third prod that we will feel during this big journey is the one that takes us, finally, on the quest for enlightenment. It's beautiful.

And we may have the time to savor this whole process. We may live a hundred years old, the way science is going today, the way medicine is going today. Why would we want to rush it all? Let it unfold. Let the journey unfold. Let us achieve levels of wholeness in stages of wholeness, let us go *from one level to the next. And let's do this in a way in which we can pace ourselves, not expend ourselves too soon, before we are physically and psychologically and spiritually ready. To do otherwise, that would end up being an animal existence. And then we will miss out on the gift of having a full and complete human experience.*

That's touching many points that I'm also writing about in my book, which is also largely about the Anima/Animus. The four aspects – these are new to me, the interplay of logos, eros, mythos and tanathos. I mean, I'm aware of these concepts, but I've never thought about their interplay in this way, and I find it extremely interesting.

Thinking about all of this, I have three questions in mind. The first is, because you also said Eros is more a feminine and energy ...

*... as compared to Logos. Every time ... when something is Yin, it is in respect to something else that is Yang. By itself it may not be Yin, but when it's in polarity with something else, then one of those things takes on the receptive aspect and one takes on an active aspect. From my understanding, eros seems more feminine because it's hardwired into the body. It is a somatic drive. I would call logos more masculine because it's more mental, having more to do with mind. And because, in Nature, the body has been given to the woman to give birth, it's as if the feminine woman's body has to learn to master this drive of procreation and sexuality.*

I was just wondering, because you also mentioned *eros* in the context of Christianity, and there, for example, it's seen as a more masculine principle, in opposition to agape. Eros is more the ascending love from humanity to God and agape is more the descending love from God to humanity.

> *For me, the realization, after so many years trying to really understand polar energies, is, frankly, that it doesn't matter what you call it, masculine or feminine. Because, as we see in the Yin Yang symbol, Yang contains Yin and Yin contains Yang. There can't be Shiva without Shakti, there can't be Shakti without Shiva. We only create separation in order to be able to work with each, and enjoy the differences within each, but actually they're just different aspects of the same underlying wholeness. And so, for me, instead of asking what is masculine and what is feminine, I would simply say, make sure you have covered both poles in whatever it is you're working with. Because when you engage in one to the neglect of the other, you'll break into a schism and you'll lose wholeness. You'll lose energy. When you're not whole, you lose contact with the Shakti of it all.*

That is another thing that you just touched on before, by integrating logos. I wrote about it especially in the chapter "The Response-ability of Men." For me, especially when it comes to men, they have to become better able to respond in a certain way when *eros* is triggered in them.

> *And that is the logos. If they haven't taken the time to really mature their Logos, which is done by integrating their mythos, then they will try to control, to "parent," the inner child within them rather than try to develop it, and they will therefor fail to realize an integral part of their self.*

> *If they haven't done that work and become aware adults, they won't to be able to manage their eros.*

**And the third question which came up: how do you relate that to leadership, or especially to leadership in business?**

*I begin with my understanding of the fourfold self and how that relates to good leadership.*

*To begin with, this also maps out in yoga. For example, in the way Sri Aurobindo talks about the four great powers of Shakti that are here to facilitate the evolution, and how they become wisdom, strength, harmony and perfection. If you look at logos, thanatos, eros, mythos, when they flip and become conscious, they basically become wisdom, strength, harmony and perfection, and all four are needed, regardless of gender, for us to become individuated. And therefore, I say it's time to become the 'WISE FOOL of TOUGH LOVE'. That is the leadership quest.*

*Do I have access to my wisdom? Have I cultivated my logos? Do I have access to my fool, which is an aspect of my child-self, do I have my curiosity, my willingness to fail? And have I learned from that, accepted that; my foolishness, taking risks... have I mastered my inner "fool"? Have I mastered my "tough," which is my inner man, who knows how to draw boundaries and say no and fight the good fight? And have I mastered my "love," which is my inner woman, the feminine side that knows how to hold and nurture and care and take everyone along, to gather as I go. So in leadership, the answer isn't from eros to Eros, or logos to Logos, but both. And the best way to sum it up in leadership and in business and to make it very practical for ourselves is to say that we have to make sure we have access to the wise fool of tough love within us all at all times. And the game is then the dance* among these four selves and to know how to be flexible and agile and present in each situation, and to ask, does this situation require my wise self or my foolish self, my tough self or my loving self?

If I can do this, I'm now coming from psychological wholeness, and from what I'm calling "the holy family reunion." My parent, my child, my inner man and my inner woman. When I express wisdom and foolishness and toughness and love.

When we lose contact with any one of these four, we are at risk of falling into dysfunction. And not succeeding in what we need. We will either lose sight of harmony and relationships because we're so focused on the task or we will be so focused on loving and caring for everybody that will not get work done. Or worse, we just end up being tough with everybody and being stupid along the way. So when you look at leaders today, we'll see which of these four archetypes they are ruled by and how well they have integrated the other three as they lead.

One of these is our core self, and that's a good thing, not a limitation. That's how we differentiate ourselves. You choose the one that is your deepest essence, but you make sure you are also backed up by the other three. When we were looking at Donald Trump, Raj was joking and saying, oh, he's a tough fool, has no love, has no wisdom – the perfect tough fool. With him, we kind of have the worst of both worlds. And yet we know there is a time when toughness is needed, and there are times when the fool is needed. But if you're only stuck on being tough and being the fool to the *neglect of your wisdom and your love, that's when problems arise.*

I was just now very touched before when you spoke, and it makes so much sense to me.

*The reason I'm always careful about people out there who are kind of holding the flag for Eros these days is they are not telling the full story. And that's dangerous, because when we haven't really come from a wise and tough self we can get caught up in the fool and the love parts of the self and we can lose ourselves.*

That's why it's so important to me to bring in different perspectives into my book. Like your model of the fourfold self, my book is also a collaboration of many voices. So it's not just my perspective in it, and maybe my foolish love. Even what I heard so far, like the toughness part, I like to hear this, especially from women. Also, when I hear you, there is a certain direction you give in your words, but it's like there is some toughness in you, but it's coming through very sweet, touching words.

*It's the stength. The fourfold self, in Integral Yoga, these become the divine powers. They're basically Maheshwari for wisdom, Mahakali for strength, etc. My own core archetype is Kali, the tough one. And yet, when it's coming from that fullness of Shakti the strength is offered in an integral way. So it comes with love and wisdom, it comes with all the rest. Maha Saraswati would be the perfection, the child, the inner child energy on getting everything diligently done. Then Lakshmi, Mahalakshmi, would be the whole energy of harmony and love. These together make up the fourfold self. I've touched on it in the book, towards the end – you would look for a page where it says, "Turning our Drives into Our Power Bases" ... on page 144. Hmm, page 144, how perfect! 144 is a very sacred number. So you can also have a look at that. And it's the Jungian archetypes of the warrior, magician, lover and the king, or queen. Again, it's coming from those same four core selves, the four archetypes.*

*Two more things. First, I will share with you my understanding of where the collective consciousness of men, in general, is located, which is still at a very infantile level. And the collective consciousness of women, this is at an adolescent level. Both still need to make the journey to adulthood. So women have one step up to go, and the men have two.*

*Therefore, in a funny way, it's the responsibility of the more awakened women to lead the way. Instead of being victims of the patriarchy, we are the ones who hold the key to showing the way out of the patriarchy. So even though we were the disempowered ones, stifled by the patriarchy, subordinated in the patriarchy, we hold the key to healing and showing the way out of this false situation, to a more equal society. We can't expect the men who have the power in the Patriarchy to actually show us the way out.*

*Finally, I'll suggest to you that the whole myth of baby Zeus, this is the very infantile level of the psyche; and the myth of Persephone, this is the more adolescent level of the psyche. So it's like baby Zeus is running men but Persephone is running women, and both still need to grow up.*

**How can men support that development, when they're in their childhood?**

*How can they support?*

**Is there a possibility. When you say women have the key, is there of possibility for men to support that?**

*It takes a kind of mature, secure man to be able to truly support a woman. And if he's not there yet, his biggest contribution can be to not stop the woman. He must not hold her back and must do work on himself, on maturing himself psychologically, and in that to take the support the woman is more than willing to give. A woman is more than willing to support a man to grow up. If he would let her, if he would let her lead the relationship in that, and not be insecure in it, a lot of progress could be made. So in a way, if he can do it, he can be a conscious child and let her, in a way, consciously parent him towards his own adulthood, and then he can move into his own wholeness in his time.*

*We can't do the work for each other. Each one has to do their own work. And the first task for both is to find their own inner center, their own presence. Become their own parents, their own children, before they can seek to be lovers. Otherwise we are going to be juvenile and infantile in our sexuality and our relationships.*

**There was something you had mentioned before, the two more things.**

*So the other thing is one way is to actually just look at these drives and say, "Oh my God, our work is to make them conscious." But if we are doing this from our little ego self, these drives are way bigger than us, they are archetypical forces, they take us over. So a far better way was the way of the great geniuses, The Mother and Sri Aurobindo, as expressed in their Integral Yoga and The Mother's symbol. The Mother talks about these 12 qualities that we are required to cultivate in ourselves. It goes from Sincerity, Humility, Gratitude, Perseverance, Aspiration towards the Divine, Receptivity to receive Grace. Then Progress, to want to move to the next level of our being. Courage, to have the heroic capacity in us. Also Goodness towards others, Generosity towards others, Equanimity within ourselves, and Peace within. If we actually take up each of these qualities instead of trying to master our drives, these qualities once developed in us, very naturally flip these four drives into the four powers.*

*You could say it's a judo way of waking up, growing up and showing up. You know, you don't try and take on the fallen forces. You make yourself with your own Sadhana, your own practice, your own self perfection. You're working on yourself to cultivate these qualities and capacities, which we all can cultivate as humans. These are very human qualities. We should not go for wisdom, strength, harmony and perfection. Those are divine qualities. We can go for sincerity, humility, gratitude.*

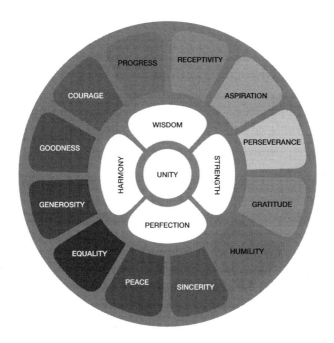

Creating A World That Works For All (inspired by The Mother's Symbol)
Developing 12 Conscious Leadership Qualities to awaken the Four-Fold Shakti
and reclaiming power from our unconscious drives

*When we can cultivate these 12 human qualities, then very naturally our own unconscious drives become the gods that they are, which is to say that they become wisdom in us, strength in us, harmony in us and perfection in us. These four drives are actually mythic deities; Eros, Logos, Mythos, Thanathos – they are deities. But when they are in the unconscious, they are expressed by people as very inappropriate, or incomplete behaviors. They are expressed unconsciously. But when we become more capable as human beings, in our values and our behaviors, then those* same gods are no longer in the unconscious. They can show up in our consciousness, they can show up in our conscious expressions, as wisdom, strength, harmony and perfection, and we will very naturally be moved to express them in appropriate ways.

In the Sadhana we do therefore, we don't go out and teach people to take on their sexuality. Whoa! Be careful, because we may not be in charge there, right? So what we can teach the world is this: let's practice sincerity, let's practice humility, let's practice gratitude. Let's go for aspiration, which is that intense yearning and longing to be a higher version of ourselves. So, when we actually work on those aspects, then the creative juices start flowing in these very beautiful ways, which are safe. For us and for those around us.

**This might be for everybody, a different Sadhana.**

Yes. Therefore, one of the things that I've run (I've just started one with my Shakti Fellowship group yesterday), it's called the 21-Day Shakti Leadership Challenge. Basically, you take one of these qualities on, either as a 21-day or 21-week enterprise, and you take each quality and you practice it until you master it. You know? So in Buddhism, for example, the master will give you four higher emotions to practice: Karuna, Mudita, Metta and Upekkha. You spend years as a novice monk practicing Karuna, compassion, practicing Mudita, joyful empathy, practicing Metta, loving kindness, and practicing Upekkha, equanimity. These are called four higher emotions.

Instead of trying to get over our jealousy and get over our anger and get over our judgment and get over cruelty, *we take on higher emotions. Instead of trying to fight those negative emotions, what if we actually flip it and just cultivate the healthy opposites of those? And then very naturally this energy becomes that. These are called the four Brahmavihara, the four abodes that we are invited to reside in. Vihara is residence, Brahma is the divine, so the divine residence or abode. These are the four divine abodes for us.*

*The first is when you see someone sad, may there be a joyful, spontaneous arising of compassion in you. When you see someone happy, may there be a joyful arising empathy, a joyful empathy in you instead of jealousy. When you see others, instead of being threatened by them or being in judgment of them, may there be a joyful sense of loving kindness or friendship. Meet people in friendship. And in any situation, may there be a calm equanimity, an equality to all things. Good news, bad news, let there just be a meeting of it from a place of equanimity and equality. So if we just work on these four positive human emotions, we will naturally no longer experience or feel the negative opposites.*

*So these 12 qualities can work in the same way. If we naturally start practicing these 12 qualities, we will not have to experience eros, logos, mythos and thanathos in the sense that I mean when I write the words using the lower cases; we will experience them as their conscious expressions, what I am pointing to when I use upper-case letters to write them. They then become the bases of our further evolution.*

*The four, there's something about the number four, which means the square. The square is the base for creation, for materialization, for manifestation. And currently our* base is a fallen base because they are unconscious drives. Whereas we can flip them by practicing these twelve qualities. We can raise up these four bases into consciousness and then they become conscious bases for our growth humans. They will fuel us in a conscious way rather than drag us down in an unconscious way.

**In the diagram you showed me, what is there in the middle?**

It's unity. It's Adi Shakti, the supreme Shakti, unity consciousness. In that is contained the Sat Chit Ananda. At that point logos, eros, everything becomes one. Logos is Eros and Eros is Logos. It's all one. It's the nondual Self. Or you can call it the integral self that has expressed its fullness. That's why this yoga is called Integral Yoga. Sri Aurobindo called it Integral Yoga back in the early twentieth century. It's sometimes called Purna Yoga, which means the yoga of wholeness and completion.

Jeff Hearn

# Seven Challenges for Sexualities, Intimacy and Non-Sexualities at Work: What (and What Not) to Do?

\*\*\*

**Jeff Hearn** has been working on gender, sexuality and violence in and around workplaces since the late 1970s. He is currently Professor Emeritus, and Research Director, GODESS (Gender, Organisation, Diversity, Equality & Social sustainability) Institute, Management & Organisation, Hanken School of Economics, Finland; Professor of Sociology, University of Hudders-

298

field, UK; Senior Professor, Gender Studies, Örebro University, Sweden; co-managing editor, Routledge Advances in Feminist Studies and Intersectionality book series; and co-editor, NORMA: The International Journal for Masculinity Studies. Recent books include: Men of the World: Genders, Globalizations, Transnational Times, Sage, 2015; Men's Stories for a Change: Ageing Men Remember, (Older Men's Memory Work Group), Common Ground, 2016; Revenge Pornography: Gender, Sexuality and Motivations, with Matthew Hall, Routledge, 2017; Engaging Youth in Activism, Research and Pedagogical Praxis: Transnational and Intersectional Perspectives on Gender, Sex, and Race, co-ed. with Tamara Shefer, Kopano Ratele, Floretta Boonzaier, Routledge, 2018; Unsustainable Institutions of Men: Transnational Dispersed Centres, Gender Power, Contradictions, co-ed. with Ernesto Vasquez del Aguila, Marina Hughson, Routledge, 2019; Does Knowledge have a Gender? co-ed. with Sofia Strid, Dag Balkmar, Louise Morley, Örebro UP, 2020; and Age at Work: Ambiguous Boundaries of Organizations, Organizing and Ageing, with Wendy Parkin, Sage, 2021.

\*\*\*

Workplaces are typically highly gendered – often dramatically so, in terms of organisational hierarchies of authority, divisions of labour, and many other features. Yet, at first sight, many organisations might appear to convey an air of gender-neutrality, even sexlessness, and may present, or might like to present, an image of themselves as sites of genderless and sexless professionalism. The office or the factory can seem at times dull passionless places. But ... then again workplaces are not just deeply gendered, but are also places of sexuality, intimacy (and distance), and ambiguous mixes with non-sexuality – often also along with all kinds of antagonisms and violations. So, what is going on with sexuality, intimacy and what can be called non-sexualities at work?

In the complex situations of the world of work, finding ways for people to work together across gender and other divisions and differences is not so easy. This is not just about going through the motions of working together but working together in creative, innovative and indeed enjoyable ways. Likewise, another question is: to what extent it is necessary or even advisable to make visible and discussable the gender, sexual and intimate dynamics at work?

Workers, professionals and managers can be caught in a cleft stick. Naming these dynamics, making them conscious, can sometimes be hazardous, embarrassing, shameful or simply violating, but not naming, and being in denial, can also be difficult or worse. This predicament can be especially confusing, and even highly irritating, for those who, for whatever reason, are dominating or are inclined to authoritarian, autocratic ways of working and leading, and are thus used to simply asserting and not listening. Also, in a different way, this conundrum can be especially difficult for those who are subjugated at work, are highly stressed, have severe unresolved personal issues, and who react to criticism defensively (or worse). And perhaps to say the obvious, sometimes these workplace issues can be exacerbated by conflicts or excessive (often gendered) demands from home, family or personal life.

Employed work and workplaces can also so easily be truly alienating, so that what happens there can be at odds with peo-

300

ple's own preferences, priorities, political values and purposes. As such people may bring only a small part of themselves to the 'workstation': that is alienation. To get beyond that state may often involve facing some sensitive issues, such as those around sexuality, intimacy, non-sexuality, and indeed antipathy, with what might be thought of as literacy around those issues, and with physical and emotional security and safety in the workplace.

So, what kinds of challenges face dealing with sexuality, intimacy, and ambiguous mixes of what might be called non-sexualities at work? Here, I first outline three basic issues in workplaces and organisations that raise immediate and practical attention: sexual and intimate relationships, sexual harassment and bullying, and ambiguities around sexuality, intimacy and non-sexualities. However, these three issues are in turn complicated by four contemporary processes: digitalisation, multiplication of gender and sexual identities, the #MeToo movement, and COVID-19.

# 1. The workplace as a place for meeting people, for crushes, romance and sex: what to do?

For a start, workplaces, including places of study and education, are obvious places to meet people, socialise, and sometimes find close, intimate and sexual relationships and partners. Many studies have found that workplaces are places were people meet potential partners. Proximity, as well as social similarity, for example, by age, class, interests, education, values, and repeated meeting (so-called 'mere exposure'), can tend to make for greater likelihood of close and potentially intimate and sexual relationships.

Indeed, there is a long series of studies on the extent of sexual relations – in the broadest sense of the term – amongst those working together in workplaces. Some occupations and sectors, especially those that demand special or extended commitment, such as the police, medicine, even the military, can be especially prone to such coupling.

There have been a range of studies on sexual relations amongst work colleagues for many decades now. An early study was Robert Quinn's 1977 study, 'Coping with Cupid', in which the creative methodology of third-party reports was used to map out how most of such relations involve a man in a higher organisational position than the woman, and how it is the woman who is more often adversely affected in career terms.

Moreover, these relations are not some obscure, minority pursuit. According to a 2020 US study of nearly 700 workers conducted by the Society for Human Resource Management (SHRM) and the University of Chicago's AmeriSpeak Panel,

- 54 percent have had a crush on a co-worker;
- 27 percent have had a workplace romance;
- 27 percent who dated someone from work dated their boss or a higher up, while 20 percent dated a subordinate or someone lower in their organisation;
- 25 percent have had a "work wife" or "work husband," and more than half admit feeling romantic feelings for this person;
- 41 percent have been asked on a date by a co-worker while 23 percent have asked a co-worker on a date. (SHRM, 2020)

Since at least the late 1980s and early 1990s, there has been growing awareness in some organisations at least of the chal-

lenges around what were then sometimes called "consensual relations" – meaning in practice sexual and intimate relations or occasionally also family or other close ties that were less than well-
known. But generally, this debate concerned: should or how co-
workers date, have sex, be in a shorter or longer intimate relationship, and if so with what degree of knowledge of colleagues
and managers?

To be more concrete, when I started working in universities
in the mid-1970s, sexual relations between staff and student
were not so uncommon, and yet not even formally declared or
registered. There are plenty of novels about all this. Looking back
there were unethical situations that were turned a "blind eye" to.
By the late 1980s, this had changed, at least in the UK university
where I worked. Following pressure from various quarters, including the trade union at local and national levels, I remember
when, as head of a medium-sized university department, a new
managerial edict was issued specifying that members of staff
should declare "consensual relations" with students to their superior and should not be involved in assessment or marking of
those students. With these new guidelines on staff code of con-
duct introduced and circulated, the next day one of the staff, and
in fact a rather new member of staff, came to see me to record
that they had begun in a relationship with an undergraduate.
Putting to one side any ethical considerations, this news was, to
put it mildly, inconvenient at a departmental level – as I had to
carefully negotiate both how to deal with the student's own assessment, the teaching of the student group concerned as a
whole, and also the member of staff's situation, especially as they
were on probationary tenure, which meant that they could not
easily have their workload rearranged without their initiative or

consent. Untangling in an ethical and appropriate educational way what was, in some respects, a reasonably straightforward situation took a lot of time and effort, and diplomatic skills.

Nowadays, these questions are not so novel. But there are very different rules and guidelines around sexual relations among work colleagues – ranging from discouragement, if not outright banning, to recording to even facilitating spousal hiring. In terms of business,

> *Some companies have even required employees involved in consensual, romantic relationships to sign a "love contract" which, according to Susan Heathfield of the human resources website Balanced Careers, is "a required document signed by the two employees in a consensual dating relationship that declares that the relationship is by consent". The contract may include guidelines for behavior and benefits the employer because it "makes arbitration the only grievance process available to the participants in the office romance. They eliminate the possibility of a later sexual harassment lawsuit when the relationship ends."* (Marks, 2020)

## 2. The workplace as a place for sexual harassment and sexual violence: what to do?

Sadly, workplaces can also be places of gender and sexual harassment, as well as other kinds of harassments, bullying, violence and violations, whether gender- or sexuality-based or constructed in terms of, for example, age or race. Moreover, what can

304

be construed at one time or by one party as a consensual sexual relationship may later be reconstrued as not, but rather as a pressurised, uncomfortable or non-consensual relationship, even as sexual harassment or assault.

The whole question of sexual harassment is of course far from new. More, it is just that it was not always named as such. There are, for examples, many examples chronicled from the earlier centuries (MacKinnon, 1979; Lambertz, 1985; Bratton, 1987). Mary Bulzarik (1978: 25) has reported on how the victims/survivors of sexual harassment in the nineteenth century were in all occupational areas:

> ... *railway cashiers, union organizers, garment workers, whitegoods workers, home workers, doctors, dressmakers, shopgirls, laundry workers, models, office workers, cotton mill workers, cannery workers ... broom factory workers, assistant foremen [sic], stenographers and typists, soap factory workers, hop-pickers, shoe shine girls, barmaids, legal secretaries, actresses, sales demonstrators, art students, and would-be workers at employment interviews.*

More to the contemporary point, research and policy development have become well, if unevenly, developed, since its naming in the 1970s. It sometimes seems as if sexual harassment keeps being "re-discovered" – especially in and by the mainstream media. For example, 35 years ago in 1987, the Finnish Ministry of Health and Social Affairs published a survey and bibliography detailing 341 publications and no less than ten *bibliographies* on sexual harassment (Högbacka et al., 1987). The same year, Liz Stanley and Sue Wise published *Georgie Porgie: Sexual Harassment in Everyday Life*, in which they argued against the *"percentage of women who have experienced sexual harassment"* approach to sexual harassment, as all women have experienced it.

Since the 1980s, this whole question of sexual harassment has been taken up and confronted in organisations through a wealth of research studies, policy developments and legal reforms and interventions – albeit in highly uneven ways, across countries, and across work sectors. Yet it is clear that sexual harassment does not go away, and moreover awareness of sexual harassment ebbs and flows amongst those responsible for preventing and acting against it. And apart from the obvious gender/sexual injustice and the violations of personal and bodily integrity, how indeed can workers and managers work in their best way, if safe working environments are not created? How can workplaces be places of social justice and appropriate intimacy without exploitation and harassment? This challenge needs direct intervention, as summed up with the 7 Ps:

- measuring and monitoring Prevalence
- Prevention
- Protection of (potential) victim/survivors
- Punishment of perpetrators
- Provision of services for (potential) victim/survivors, as well as bystanders, colleagues and perpetrators
- Partnership with relevant expertise, organisations and stakeholders, and
- coherent Policy development for the whole organisation and its members (UniSAFE, 2021).

These kinds of interventions are simply a baseline in any workplace and organisation for stopping and not tolerating sexual harassment. Of course, they do not in themselves "abolish" sexual harassment, either immediately or in the longer term. Organisations need good basic policies and practices to deal with harassment, bullying and violence in and around the workplace. They also need allocated resources, available expertise, and quick responsive action.

In addition, fundamental prerequisites for the maintaining non-harassing and non-bullying workplaces are the enactment and enhancement of ways of managing, organising and carrying out everyday work that are democratic, non-hierarchical and non-autocratic, but still clear and structured, and certainly not *laissez-faire*. There is now rather a lot of research which shows that it is not only autocratic management that facilitates bullying and harassment, but – importantly – also *laissez-faire* management, where there is avoidance and a reluctance to act, or simply an inability or reluctance to even meet with staff at all (see, for example, Skogstad et al. 2007; Ågotnes et al., 2018). It is somewhat of a paradox how laissez-faire management and leadership can actually make for greater bullying, harassment and violation. However, there are still more challenges to be faced.

# 3. The workplace as a place for ambiguities of sexuality, intimacy and non-sexualities: what to do?

It is perhaps now not so surprising that work and workplaces are often ambiguous and uncertain when it comes to sexualities and intimacy. Intimacy and sexuality at work are much more than a question of either sexual relationships or sexual violation. In 1987, Wendy Parkin and I published the book, 'Sex' at 'Work': The Power and Paradox of Organisation Sexuality (Hearn and Parkin, 1987), which looked at those issues at work and in organisations more generally. We were keen to recognise the interplay of power and sexuality at work, along with the complexity and ambiguity of sexuality and sexual meanings there. To speak of this, we used the term, 'organisation sexuality' (rather than organisational sexuality) – to refer to the simultaneous operation of sexuality and organisations, and sexual and organisational dynamics, without prioritising one over the other. [92]

These ambiguities can be understood at rather general social and societal processes. For example, sexuality and sexualisation, even if constructed paradoxically as desexualisation, are part of many workplaces and other organisations. But these ambiguities are also much more immediate.[93] Have you ever had an acquaintanceship, perhaps a friendship with a work colleague, that is impossible to categorize, as not sexual and not non-sexual? Having talked to various people about this, I gather this is not such a rare occurrence. Many years ago, I started trying to 'conceptualise' this in-between world; categories that came to mind included: 'friends that don't fit'; 'soulmates without sex', 'lovers without lust', 'cool companions', 'intimate acquaintances', 'couples that are not' ... you can make up your own terms, in both senses. On a slightly different tack, in a recent interview, the therapist, Esther Perel, spoke of 'eros' and 'healthy eros', not in strictly sexual terms, but rather more broadly and loosely in referring to "a feeling of curiosity, aliveness, exploration – the happenstance, the chance encounter." (Conroy, 2021).

---

92  The book was revised and updated in 1995 in the light of the growing amount of new empirical studies of both heterosexuality and non-normative sexualities, and vigorous theoretical debate in that period.
93  The following three paragraphs draw in part on Hearn, 2018.

All this might sound similar to what Lilian Faderman (1981) and others have called 'romantic friendship' or 'passionate friendship' (also see Deitcher, 2001), but I think that may be fixing it too much as about romance and friendship. The term 'passionate colleagueship' sounds a bit tortuous but is perhaps closer. It is of course tempting to say that this is all about sublimated, repressed or latent sexuality (how to avoid Freud?), and it might well be so in some instances, but that seems too reductive or simply inaccurate. Rather, I am thinking here of the blurred boundary between what has to be called sexualities, with all the desire, orientation, arousal, fantasy, and practices involved, and what I will call 'non-sexualities'.

The line between sexuality, intimacy and non-sexualities is not always clearcut. To put this another way, what are the exact boundaries around sexuality? And how does this work at work? Also, the word 'boundary' isn't quite right; perhaps the word 'zone' is better, so I shall refer to this as a zone of uncertainty – which can apply, albeit with different languages, dynamics and implications, in personal practice, sexuality politics and policy, and theorising on sexualities, and indeed at work. This zone of uncertainty is usually unnamed, including an ambiguous zone or zones within and around workplaces and other organisations.

Such passionate colleagueship can be bound up with the very business of work, and may have very little, if anything, to do with social relations outside work. Academia and research work more generally can be another interesting example here. Such workplaces are often characterised by strong age-, ethnic- and gender-differentiation, both vertically and horizontally. In many cases, there are relatively fixed layers of older, professorial and more senior staff, predominantly men, together with shifting, temporary populations of women and men members, students and less established staff. Furthermore, some academic institutions and social sites, such as some university departments and some conferences, involve *both* formality and informality, thus bringing social and interpersonal ambiguities. These in turn may include the presence of hierarchical aged, gender, social, sexual and intense emotional dynamics. In sum, academe houses both strong pressures and opportunities to conform, and at least in some traditions the occasion to subvert that conformity. Navigating and negotiating of workplace ambiguities in appropriate and non-oppressive ways can be a challenge for both managers and employees, especially in certain sectors and occupational fields.

# 4. The workplace as a place of gender and sexual diversity: what to do?

At the very least, it is clear that many organisations have, or include within them, cultures of norms, discourses and ideologies around intimacy and sexuality. These are often dominantly heterosexual and often heterosexist, and typically binary, that is, gender binaristic. Such characteristics are limiting, or worse. They can fail to recognise and take account of differential sexualities and gender identities, as often summed up in the neologism, LGBTIQA+ (lesbian, gay, bisexual, transgender, intersex, queer, agender, and further) or one of its similar or associated alternatives. On the one hand, the shorthand of LGBTIQA+ is a manifestation and consolidation of the long-term politics that are likely to oppose heterosexism; on the other, it is a somewhat cumbersome amalgamation, and often a loose coalition, of a diverse set of identities, with different formations and positionings.

Raewyn Connell (2019: 57) has recently written directly on some of these complication and critiques, specifically:

"... the convergence, in the United States, of post-structuralist thought and sexual politics ... produced queer studies and, a recent offshoot, trans studies. This is easily misinterpreted, since so much of the practical work of the movements takes the shape of identity politics, for instance, mobilizations around a shared self-image, being or experience. That infuriating and incoherent acronym LGBT (lesbian, gay, bisexual and transgender), invented as a euphemism in US homosexual politics, makes the point even without the additional transsexual, transgender, intersex, queer, querying (TTIQQ). For what are T, L and G here except the names of identity groups, assembled in a tactical alliance that has become strangely reified?

Therefore, it is worth recalling that the subtitle of Gender Trouble (Butler, 1990) was Feminism and the Subversion of Identity. Poor Judith Butler has been reminding people of that 'subversion' ever since."

But further to this, the multiplication of gender and sexual identities, including multiple non-binary identities, is astounding. Various third sexes and third genders are rather commonplace (Herdt, 1993), but now, there are gender and sexual identities, including multiple non-binary identities, in their hundreds, at least. Tumblr lists over 140 different sexualities (allthegendersallthe-sexualities.tumblr, 2021) including "alterous": that is, "neither being (entirely/completely) platonic nor romantic, an attraction best described as wanting emotional closeness without necessarily being (at all or entirely) platonic and/or romantic, used in place of -romantic or -platonic." In recent years, nonbinary wiki has included various lists, with an earlier list of 170 nonbinary identities now reduced to about 80 (List of uncommon nonbinary identities, 2021). The list of gender and sexual identities, including nonbinary and agender identities, keeps growing.

The multiplication of gender identities and sexualities also necessarily means there has to be greater concern with diversity in gender and sexual rights, and gender and sexual justice (Hearn et al., 2018), both across society and in and around workplaces. For example, in Europe, Article 35 of the EU Charter of Fundamental Rights states that individuals are entitled to healthcare, and a high level of human health protection. In 2015, the Council of Europe also adopted a historical resolution (Resolution 2048) on transpersons' human rights, including requirements to undergo sterilisation and to facilitate processes with medical gatekeepers in order to gain legal recognition (also see The Yogyakarta Principles plus 10 (YP+10), Yogyakarta Principles, 2017).

Multiple gender and sexual identifications raise both broad and profound questions for understanding, and indeed managing as colleagues and managers, gender relations, and at the same time very specific issues, such as the use or not of gendered pronouns. It is perhaps, first, important to remember that gendered pronouns only exist in some languages, far from all. In Finnish,

312

'hän' is used for all persons. The language use is gendered in other ways. Where gendered pronouns are used, one question becomes: should one ask people what pronoun they prefer – this is certainly an issue in education and training situations. Another very practical issue in organisations concerns the so-called toilet debate. In the two workplaces I mostly frequent, single booth toilets are the model across the workplace; in the third that I go to occasionally, there is still strict and very old fashioned 'collective' facilities for women/females and men/males. This is a concrete issue to be addressed.

That said, there are many different ways of interpreting these complex moves around multiple gender and sexual identities at a societal or cross-societal level – the framing of politics around identity (identity politics and the 'identiti-cation' of politics), various forms of individualism, the self as project, social fragmentations (and the loss of grand narratives), multiplication of intersectionalities, neoliberalism(s), late modernity through consumption, and of course the internet – and it is to that last listed phenomenon we now turn.

## 5. Does digitalisation change everything?

And so, on top of this, there is now of course the internet, the online worlds of all sorts, as well as numerous and transforming digital devices, as with the Internet of Things. One consequent major change that has occurred in sexuality and work, is the huge growth of online socialising, online dating, online search for sexual partners, and online sex, along with the expansion of social media more broadly. All of these can occur when at work, whether in the physical workplace, or not. Depending on access to different digital devices, socialising, intimacy and sex (at least its prospect) online can figure, within the ordinary working day, or night, and/or interrupt, disrupt ruin or enhance ordinary day-to-day work. A business meeting may be transformed by such an actual or potential online message or meet-up.

Some of the many impacts of ICTs on sexuality, sexual-social interaction and sexual violence, even in the 1990s, were documented in my 2001 collaboration with Wendy Parkin, *Gender, Sexuality and Violence in Organizations* (Hearn and Parkin, 2001), when these things seemed quite novel. Since then, proliferating information and communication technologies have facilitated all manner of new and diverse virtual/ITF/IRL intimate and sexual practices. Grindr, Tinder (and their many derivatives), sexting and the rest are normalized; talk of machinic sex robots is almost mainstream. Digitalisation can also bring online gender and harassment, bullying and violence in new online forms, as with so-called 'revenge porn' and other digital sexual violations, along with sexualisation of public space. Without assuming any fixed determinism, technologisation, ICTs and virtualisation have contradictory effects, with greater support for gender and sexual minorities and yet greater attacks on gender and sexual citizenship (Hearn, 2006).

It is worth commenting here on some significant age and generation dimensions. Younger generations of workers have grown up with the online world as totally normal, blending and crossing over to real life and offline worlds, so that the very terms, online and offline, can become out of synch with reality, even redundant. Writing on Japan, Abigail Haworth (2013) has stressed the prevalence of "easy or instant gratification, in the form of ca-

314

sual sex, short-term trysts and the usual technological suspects: online porn, virtual-reality "girlfriends", anime cartoons. Or else they're [young people] opting out altogether and replacing love and sex with other urban pastimes", suggesting that future Japanese relationships will be largely technology-driven; likewise, humans doing "robot-style dating" may themselves become metaphorical "sex robots" (Kilberd, 2017). Close intersections of sexuality, non-sexuality and ICTs likely expand further the zone of uncertainty between sexuality and non-sexuality.

In terms of the implications for workplaces, it can be very difficult, perhaps almost impossible, to control the impact of ICTs on working life. For example, digital intimate partner violence (DIPV) can take place both within and outside working time, and then affect the victim/survivor(s) in the workplace, as well as colleagues, bystanders, subordinates and managers. The responsibility of employers and managers in such situations remains a contested and urgent ethical and political question, not to mention how to deal with in-house perpetrators of digital violation and DIPV – who of course themselves may also be supervisors or managers with associated relevant responsibilities to address such issues. Managerial, supervisory and policy vigilance and policy/practice development are clearly needed in workplaces to take account of socio-technological change in this arena, with, for example, the development of easy access to deep fakes technologies, and the Internet of Things.

# 6. Does #MeToo change everything?

Another major relevant development linked to digitalisation is the rise of the #MeToo movement, with its own complex ripples

and consequences, taking different forms and impacts across occupations, organisations, careers, and workplaces across the
world (see Chandra and Erlingdóttir, 2021, for accounts of
#MeToo from different parts of the world, and major synthesis-
ing commentaries). #MeToo has shown the importance of the internet in working against sexual violence, of collective action,
and in some case at least of rethinking the past. #MeToo has also
shown the need to problematise what has sometimes been constructed and construed as "normal" behaviour. In March 2018,
the UK Guardian newspaper began the advice series 'Dating
after #MeToo: welcome to our newest advice column' (Edelstein,
2018), which ran at least until mid-May that year. #MeToo, in all
its variegated guises, has also led onto various discussions and
debates, online or off, about such questions as: are touch (of different kinds), hugging (of different kinds), and flirting (of different kinds) ever acceptable at work. These are questions for
workplace culture, practice, policy, and responsibilities.

As noted, different generations may be more or less familiar
– or more or less (un)comfortable – with these shifts and the ne-
gotiations around them. Younger generations are growing up
with #MeToo – and also #GirlsToo – unlike older generations.
Many younger people may be more 'savvy' than others when living daily in this online environment. Both #MeToo and greater
pornographisation of public/cyberspace are part of normal life
for many, especially younger generations, along with the blurring
of offline/online. Dealing with the combination of wall-to-wall
social media, internet-based abuse, widespread sexting, and
sometimes ambiguous 'hanging out' and 'dating' can be very demanding for many, especially girls, young women and LGBTIQA+

---

94  For further discussion, see Hearn, 2021.

people, and it can lead to major harms and suffering for some (Ringrose et al., 2012, 2013; Hall and Hearn, 2017).

Addressing such circumstances calls for creative interventions in and around work and workplaces. Just to give one example: in Finland, *Yksittäistapaus* [Isolated case] is a collectively created collection of short films, a feature film entitled *Force of Habit*, and a linked campaign, *"that reveal the hidden way power is exercised on women in both private life and in society."* The project was begun late spring 2016, before #MeToo, by the film production company Tuffi Films and a group of fifteen film industry professionals, artists, researchers and social influencers to make short films "to give a physical form for "that thing", the incidents that were regarded as a one-off but that were, in reality, caused by power structures and our unconscious operating models" (Yksittaistapaus, n.d.). Such initiatives provide different kinds of resources for engaging with sexuality and intimacy in the #MeToo era, and for changing and challenging what are still often embedded and taken-for-granted gender power structures.[94]

# 7. And now does COVID-19 change everything?

And then more recently, there is the COVID-19 pandemic. This has brought many further and continuing challenges. It has also tended to reinforce and deepen some of the challenges already described. With the pandemic, many parts of the world have seen shifts to high levels of remote working and working from home – so that the workplace, and other organisations, become dispersed and, in a sense, ambiguous parts of the domestic sphere, with further multiple consequences.

94 *For further discussion, see Hearn, 2021.*

With COVID-19, many organisational boundaries have changed in nature: some are reinforced, others blurred, especially through reformulated work-family relations. One's own doorstep may become a firm boundary. Work-family (or work-household) relations have changed through remote working from home, individualisation (or familialisation) of sociality, limitations on movement, and shifting definitions of work, care and organisations, with increased burdens on many women and those doing most carework, and the immense harms experienced from increased violence and the difficulties in escaping abusive situations.

Further important questions include: the physical and social dispersion of work in relation to gender and digitalisation; uneven and changing (over time) gender effects of digitalisation on employment structures; the embedded pervasiveness of 'the transnational' and transnational socio-economic processes, including ICTs, and not just for transnational workers or those who migrate, as many, perhaps most, workplaces are in some sense transnational, even if just through the use of IT systems, as well as complex transnational business trading and ownership patterns, not least in the field of care; the everyday impacts of both the positive and negative aspects of greater digitalisation – for example, social and political networking, image- and text-based online abuse and violation, and their effects on the world of work and employment; new forms, and sometimes problems, of cyber-management; the closer intertwining of work and home/family/household, which have had negative effects for some women, including increases in intimate partner violence; changing and non-local forms of power for men and masculinities online; and, probably increasingly, the blurring of the on- and offline in hybrid forms of sociality.[95]

---

95 For further discussion, see Hearn and Parkin, 2021; von Alemann et al. 2020.

In terms of the form, substance and contradictions of sociality, increased individualism and less close bodily contact may go along with greater sense of communitas and new solidarities. Categorisations of/in interaction, friendship, intimacy, neighbourliness, sexuality, marriage, family, organising, politics, social divisions, the very senses of the social and sociality, may be less clear-cut. Privatised individualism and family-orientation, public communitas, the state, and transnational corporations can all strangely be reinforced. Linked to this is the widespread embedded normalisation of digital life. The pandemic can be a means and process towards greater technologisation, automation and dispensability of the human. Online/offline blurring is not just the preserve of the younger, but now known well across generations.

In short, workplaces are changed through dispersion of organisational places, locations and spaces, and the home itself can become a site of knowledge-intensive organising. *The very questions of what is work and not work, and what is a workplace, are now not so easy to answer for very many people.*

## What next, wider complexities?

In these changing and multi-layered situations and challenges, sexuality, intimacy, emotions and non-sexualities at work become more complex. In 2008, writing on the future of sexuality, I noted six interconnecting key themes: the expansion of LGBTIQA+ movements and politics, the persistence of (sexual) violence, population ageing in at least some parts of the world, environmental change, problematisation of sex and biology, and ICTs and virtualisation – these six trends still seem important and together are likely to produce significant changes for sexualities, intimacy and non-sexualities at work. This includes challenging even what *sexuality is or is assumed to be* (Hearn, 2008, 2014). Such social changes also affect what may at first may seem rather fixed and given experiences. And thus, both work and sexuality are in process of problematisation.

In this short article, I have outlined three pervasive issues that need attention in workplaces and organisations: sexual and intimate relationships, sexual harassment and bullying, and ambiguities around sexuality, intimacy and non-sexualities. All of these three raise challenges in terms of what is to be done, ethically, politically, organisationally. In addition, these challenges are overlain by four relatively recent and contemporary processes: digitalisation, multiplication of gender and sexual identities, the #MeToo movement, and COVID-19. These three basic issues and four contemporary processes are heavily interconnected, for example, in how digitalisation pervades work and workplaces, including sexual and intimate relationships, online and online/offline harassment, gender and sexual identities, and the contradictions, ambiguities and paradoxes arising.

If we stand back a moment and consider these questions in more macro-historical terms –interestingly, and somewhat paradoxically, sexualisation of public space is accompanied by reports of declines in sexual activity and desire. Reduction in (with-other, in-the-flesh [ITF]) sexual activity has been reported from many parts of the world.[96] At the same time, in many parts of the world, increased time seems to be spent on looks, "looking good" and self-grooming, especially for social media, especially by girls and young women, but also boys and young men, ... and older people too. Looks and lookism are now key social currency, as part of the increased power of the visual.

---

[96] Such reports have emanated from, for example, Finland (Kontula, 2009), Japan (Haworth, 2013) and USA (Twenge et al., 2017). US Centers for Disease Control and Prevention data indicates significant decreases in teenage sexual activity since 1988, with reported rates down 22 percent among males and 14 percent among females (Leonard, 2015). According to the Japan Family Planning Association, '45% of women aged 16-24 "were not interested in or despised sexual contact". More than a quarter of men felt the same way.' (Haworth, 2013).

320

In these ambiguous, contradictory and paradoxical situations, questions of how co-workers should behave, with what level of intimacy (or distance), become more commonplace, even everyday and very ordinary, rather than dramatic or simply embarrassing. Recognising feelings and emotions, and finding effective ways to manage, express and include these in a working situation, above all appropriately, may be becoming a more normalised business? Dealing with such issues, ambiguities and at times intense antipathies needs what can be called a certain metaphorical literacy, an openness to talk on what may seem difficult things, without freaking out or acting out, and with the ensuring of physical and emotional security and safety in the workplace. The possibilities to express attraction, reluctance and perhaps even repulsion to other people, so that feelings are not hurt, bodily integrity is not violated, and further constructive collaboration is created, maintained, or promoted, might even become a more mundane question in at least some workplaces.

## References

Ågotnes, K.W., Einarsen, S.V., Hetland, J. and Skogstad, A. (2018) The moderating effect of laissez-faire leadership on the relationship between co-worker conflicts and new cases of workplace bullying: a true prospective design. Human Resource Management Journal, 28(4), 555–568.

allthegendersallthesexualities.tumblr (2021) Gender and sexuality. https://allthegendersallthesexualities.tumblr.com/glossary (Accessed 10 April 2021).

Bratton, Eleanor K. (1987) The eye of the beholder: An interdisciplinary examination of law and social research on sexual harassment. New Mexico Law Review, 17(Winter), 91–114.

Bulzarik, Mary (1978) Sexual harassment at the workplace: Historical notes. Radical America, 12(4), 25–43.

Butler, Judith (1990) Gender Trouble: Feminism and the Subversion of Identity. New York: Routledge.

Chandra, Giti and Erlingdóttir, Irma (eds.) (2021) The Routledge Handbook of the Politics of the #MeToo Movement, London: Routledge.

Connell, Raewyn (2019) New maps of struggle for gender justice: Rethinking feminist research on organizations and work. Gender, Work and Organization 26(1), 54–63.

Conroy, J. Oliver (2021) Esther Perel on life after Covid: 'People will want to reconnect with eros'. The Guardian, 6 April. https://www.theguardian.com/lifeandstyle/2021/apr/06/esther-perel-interview-pandemic-relationships-work-life-balance)

Edelstein, Jean Hannah (2018) Dating after #MeToo: welcome to our newest advice column. The Guardian, 29 March. https://www.theguardian.com/lifeandstyle/2018/mar/29/dating-after-metoo-advice-column

Faderman, Lilian (1981) Surpassing the Love of Men: Romantic Friendship and Love between Women from the Renaissance to the Present. New York: Morrow.

Haworth, Abigail (2013) Why have young people in Japan stopped having sex? The Observer, 20 October. https://www.theguardian.com/world/2013/oct/20/young-people-japan-stopped-having-sex

Hall, Matthew and Hearn, Jeff (2017) Revenge Pornography: Gender, Sexuality, and Motivations. London: Routledge.

Hearn, Jeff (2006) The implications of information and communication technologies for sexualities and sexualised violences: Contradictions of sexual citizenships. Political Geography, 25(8), 944–963.

Hearn, Jeff (2008) 'Sexualities future, present, past ... Towards transsectionalities', Sexualities: Studies in Culture and Society, 11(1), 37–46.

Hearn, Jeff (2014) 'Sexualities, organizations and organization sexualities: future scenarios and the impact of socio-technologies (A transnational perspective from the global "North")', Organization: The Critical Journal of Organization, Theory and Society, 21(3), 400–420.

Hearn, Jeff (2018) 'Where are the boundaries of sexuality? Hovering in a zone of uncertainty between sexualities and non-sexualities', Sexualities: Studies in Culture and Society, 21(8), 1368–1373.

Hearn, Jeff (2021) #MeToo as a variegated phenomenon against men's violences and abuse: Implications for men and masculinities. In: Giti Chandra and Irma Erlingsdóttir (eds.) The Routledge Handbook of the Politics of the #MeToo Movement, London: Routledge, 65–84.

Hearn Jeff, Aboim, Sofia and Shefer, Tamara (2018) Sexualities, social justice and sexual justice. In: Craig G (ed.) The Global Handbook on Social Justice. Cheltenham: Edward Elgar, 228–240.

Hearn, Jeff and Parkin, Wendy (1987/1995) 'Sex' at 'Work': The Power and Paradox of Organisation Sexuality. New York: St. Martin's Press.

Hearn, Jeff and Parkin, Wendy (2001) Gender, Sexuality and Violence in Organizations. London: Sage.

Hearn, Jeff and Parkin, Wendy (2021) Age at Work: Ambiguous Boundaries of Organizations. Organizing and Ageing. London: Sage.

Herdt, Gilbert (ed.) (1993) Third Sex, Third Gender. New York: Zone.

Högbacka, Riitta, Kandolin, Irja, Haavio-Mannila, Elina and Kauppinen-Toropainen, Kaisa (1987) Sexual Harassment. Helsinki: Ministry of Social Affairs and Health. Equality Publications. Series E: Abstracts 1/1987.

Kilberd, Roisin (2017) Tinder Gold takes us nearer the app's grim endpoint: Robot-style dating. The Guardian, 7 September. https://www.theguardian.com/commentisfree/2017/sep/06/tinder-gold-app-robot-swipe

Kontula, Osmo (2009) Between Sexuality and Desire: The Evolution of Sex in Finland. Helsinki: Family Federation of Finland.

Lambertz, Jan (1985) Sexual harassment in the nineteenth century English cotton industry. History Workshop, 19(Spring), 29–61.

Leonard, Kimberly (2015) Teens today have less sex than their parents did. US News. 22 July. www.usnews.com/news/blogs/data-mine/2015/07/22/cdc-report-shows-declines-in-teen-sexual-activity-pregnancies

List of uncommon nonbinary identities (2021) https://nonbinary.miraheze.org/wiki/List_of_uncommon_nonbinary_identities (Accessed 10 April 2021).

MacKinnon, Catharine A. (1979) The Sexual Harassment of Working Women. New Haven, Conn: Yale University Press.

Marks, Gene (2020) Employers can't forbid romance in the workplace – but they can protect workers. The Guardian, 20 February. https://www.theguardian.com/business/2020/feb/20/workplace-romances-metoo-rules-protection

Quinn, Robert E. (1977) Coping with Cupid: The formation, impact, and management of romantic relationships in organizations. Administrative Science Quarterly, 22(1), 30–45.

Ringrose, Jessica, Gill, Rosalind, Livingstone, Sonja and Harvey, Laura (2012) A Qualitative
Study of Children, Young people and 'Sexting'. London: NSPCC.

Ringrose, Jessica, Harvey, Laura, Gill, Rosalind and Livingstone, Sonja (2013) 'Teen girls,
Sexual double standards and 'sexting': gendered value in digital image exchange', Feminist
Theory, 14(3), 305–323.

Skogstad, A., Einarsen, S., Torsheim, T., Aasland, M. and Hetland, H. (2007) The
destructiveness of laissez-faire leadership behavior. Journal of Occupational Health
Psychology, 12(1), 80–92.

Society for Human Resource Management (SHRM) (2020) Crushing on your co-worker? You're not alone. 12 February. https://www.shrm.org/about-shrm/press-room/press-releases/pages/new-survey-on-workplace-romance-2020.aspx

Stanley, Liz and Wise, Sue (1987) Georgie Porgie: Sexual Harassment in Everyday Life. London: Pandora.

Twenge, Jean M., Sherman, Ryne A. and Wells, Brooke E. (2017) Declines in sexual frequency among American adults, 1989–2014. Archives of Sexual Behavior DOI: doi.org/10.1007/s10508-017-0953-1

UniSAFE (2021) Gender-based violence and institutional responses: Building a knowledge base and operational tools to make universities and research organisations safe. https://cordis.europa.eu/project/id/101006261

von Alemann, Annette, Gruhlich, Julia, Horwath, Ilona, and Weber, Lena (2020) International perspectives about COVID-19, digital labour and gender work pattern: A collective interview. Gender and Research / Gender a výzkum, special issue on 'Economy 4.0 – The digitalization of labor from a gender perspective', 21(2), 86–102. https://www.genderonline.cz/pdfs/gav/2020/02/03.pdf

Yksittaistapaus (n.d.) https://www.yksittaistapaus.fi/en/about-the-campaign-2/

Yogyakarta Principles (2017) Principles on the application of international human rights law in relation to sexual orientation and gender identity. http://www.yogyakartaprinciples.org/

# Endnote

..........................................

This book is an unfinished piece of work.
I would love to see a bigger variety of perspectives
in a future edition.

You can meditate on the next white page and find
out if you want to contribute an essay, interview, or
some ideas, or if you know somebody who might be
interested to collaborate.

We could need more men in it!

Contact via e-mail

eros@vibrantcollaboration.com

More info about Vibrant Collaboration
you will find on the website

http://vibrantcollaboration.com